The **Sounds** of

Korean

This introduction to the sounds of Korean is designed for English-speaking students with no prior knowledge of the language, and includes online sound files, which demonstrate the sounds and pronunciation described. It will be an invaluable resource for students of Korean wanting to understand the basis of the current state of Korean phonetics and phonology, as well as for those studying Korean linguistics.

- Provides a complete and authoritative description and explanation of the current state of Korean phonetics and phonology
- Gives clear comparisons with English, and provides practical advice on pronunciation
- Provides a wealth of authentic Korean examples
- Each chapter contains exercises and *Did you know?* sections to help students put their knowledge into practice.

JIYOUNG SHIN is a Professor in the Department of Korean Language and Literature at Korea University, Seoul. She has published widely in Korean phonetics/phonology and is the author of *Understanding Speech Sounds* (2000), *The Sound Pattern of Korean* (2003, with Jaeeun Cha) and *Articulatory and Phonological Disorders* (2007, with Sujin Kim).

JIEUN KIAER is Young Bin Min-Korea Foundation University Lecturer in Korean Language and Linguistics in the Oriental Institute of the University of Oxford. Her current research is on the pragmatic aspects of syntactic architecture and the role of prosody in syntax.

JAEEUN CHA is an Associate Professor in the Department of Korean Language and Literature at Kyonggi University. She specialises in Korean phonology and the history of the Korean language and is the author of *Middle Korean Phonology* (1999) and *The Sound Pattern of Korean* (2003, with Jiyoung Shin).

The **Sounds** of

Korean

Jiyoung Shin
Jieun Kiaer
Jaeeun Cha

CAMBRIDGE
UNIVERSITY PRESS

University Printing House, Cambridge CB2 8BS, United Kingdom

One Liberty Plaza, 20th Floor, New York, NY 10006, USA

477 Williamstown Road, Port Melbourne, VIC 3207, Australia

314-321, 3rd Floor, Plot 3, Splendor Forum, Jasola District Centre, New Delhi - 110025, India

79 Anson Road, #06-04/06, Singapore 079906

Cambridge University Press is part of the University of Cambridge.

It furthers the University's mission by disseminating knowledge in the pursuit of education, learning and research at the highest international levels of excellence.

www.cambridge.org
Information on this title: www.cambridge.org/9781107672680

© Jiyoung Shin, Jieun Kiaer and Jaeeun Cha 2013

First published 2013

A catalogue record for this publication is available from the British Library

Library of Congress Cataloging in Publication data
Sin, Chi-yong, 1966 Sept.-
The sounds of Korean / Jiyoung Shin, Jieun Kiaer, and Jaeeun Cha.
    p.   cm.
Includes bibliographical references and index.
ISBN 978-1-107-03005-3 (hardcopy)
1. Korean language – Phonology.   2. Korean language – Phonetics.   3. Korean language – Study and teaching – English speakers.   I. Kiaer, Jieun.   II. Ch'a, Chae-un.   III. Title.
PL915.S5525   2013
495.7′83421 – dc23   2012017770

ISBN 978-1-107-03005-3 Hardback
ISBN 978-1-107-67268-0 Paperback

This book is published with the generous support of the International Center for Korean Studies, Korea University's Research Institute of Korean Studies. The International Center for Korean Studies was established in 2003 to support scholarship and exploration of Korea in the humanities and social sciences and to promote new research in Korean Studies to a wide international audience.

Additional resources for this publication at www.cambridge.org/shin

Contents

Figures

Tables

Preface

In learning a foreign language, it is essential to familiarise oneself with the sound properties of the language such as the inventory of sounds and phonological processes. Native speakers will acquire these naturally, but learners of the second language must learn them formally. This book aims to provide an introduction to the phonetics and phonology of Korean for those who study the Korean language and/or linguistics. More specifically, the target audience of this book consists both of academics in Korean Linguistics (or in Korean Studies or in linguistics) and of learners of Korean. Among the learners of Korean, this book is targeted particularly at learners of Korean who are familiar with English. Hence, comparison with English is also provided whenever necessary.

This book is rare in terms of being well balanced for these two audience groups. We believe that it will become the first comprehensive book to provide a complete and authoritative description and explanation of the current state of Korean phonetics and phonology.

Previous knowledge of the Korean language or linguistics will be beneficial to readers. We have provided the Korean alphabet with the revised Korean government romanisation or the IPA (International Phonetic Alphabet) transcription. We have adopted IPA (International Phonetic Alphabet) description at the phonemic level for each word. Knowing the Korean alphabet will be a great help in following this book.

The website (www.cambridge.org/shin) will of course be a very useful/ practical guide to the sound of Korean. Ample examples from the real use of contemporary spoken Korean form the key feature of this book – making it accessible to all those who are interested in the Korean language.

Each chapter contains two kinds of exercises – firstly, those which help the learner get used to practical pronunciation (i.e., experiment yourself/performance exercises); and secondly, exercises which encourage learners to evaluate what they have learned about the sounds of Korean (i.e., content exercises). Not only this, each chapter has a very intriguing 'Did you know?' question, so that the learner can easily be exposed to how the Korean language is used on a day-to-day basis. In this book, we focus on Standard Seoul Korean pronunciation. Yet, whenever necessary, we have also included the synchronic and diachronic realisation of the sounds. The majority of Korean grammars and textbooks only provide a 'normative' or 'written' grammar, ignoring how the language is truly 'spoken'. Our book focuses on Seoul Korean speakers' 'real' pronunciation unless stated otherwise, but whenever comparison is needed, we also provide information regarding differences between dialects.

Finally, we would like to thank our husbands – Dr DoneSik Yoo, Dr Ian Kiaer and Dr Naehyun Kwon – for their full support in the process of writing this book. We are also grateful to Sookyoung Kwak, Marshall Craig, Deborah Smith and Matthew Hunter for their various editorial help. We thank our copy-editor Anna Oxbury for her wonderful work, and Helen Barton for her patience and encouragement throughout the project.

Notational conventions

.   syllable boundary
| minor break boundary (phonological phrase boundary)
‖   major break boundary (intonational phrase boundary)
( )   eojeol 'word phrase' unit
-   bound morpheme
+   morpheme boundary
#   word boundary
ω   phonological word boundary

Consonants

Korean alphabet	IPA	Korean alphabet	IPA	Korean alphabet	IPA
ㄱ	k	ㅇ	ŋ	ㄲ	k*
ㄴ	n	ㅈ	tɕ	ㄸ	t*
ㄷ	t	ㅊ	tɕʰ	ㅃ	p*
ㄹ	l	ㅋ	kʰ	ㅆ	s*
ㅁ	m	ㅌ	tʰ	ㅉ	tɕ*
ㅂ	p	ㅍ	pʰ		
ㅅ	s	ㅎ	h		

Vowels

Korean alphabet	IPA	Korean alphabet	IPA	Korean alphabet	IPA
ㅏ	ɑ	ㅜ	u	ㅚ/ㅞ/ㅙ	wɛ
ㅑ	jɑ	ㅠ	ju	ㅟ	wi
ㅓ	ʌ	ㅡ	ɯ	ㅘ	wɑ
ㅕ	jʌ	ㅣ	i	ㅝ	wʌ
ㅗ	o	ㅔ/ㅐ	ɛ	ㅢ	ɯi
ㅛ	jo	ㅖ/ㅒ	jɛ		

Except in special cases, all phonetic notation in this book uses broad transcription at the phonemic level.

We follow in this book the Revised ROK Romanisation Convention.

1 Characteristics of the Korean language

In this chapter, we will provide an overview of the Korean language and briefly discuss its main characteristics. In 1.1, we will discuss the origin, history and distribution of the Korean language; in 1.2, the Korean alphabet and its romanisation will be discussed; 1.3 focuses on the characteristics of the Korean lexicon; in 1.4, the structural characteristics of Korean will be explored; and in 1.5, the socio-pragmatic characteristics of Korean will be discussed.

1.1 Origin, history and distribution

1.1.1 The Korean language in East Asian history

It is impossible to think about the history of Korea without considering the history of Northeast Asia. In the same vein, the history of the Korean language cannot be considered without reference to the influence of Korea's neighbours; namely, China, Japan and Mongolia. Figure 1.1 shows how the Korean language has evolved from Old Korean into Contemporary Korean within the bigger picture of East Asian history. The classification is based on K.-M. Lee (1998).

As seen in Figure 1.1, social and political changes at home and abroad became the crucial factor in shaping the Korean language. For instance: the unification of the Three Kingdoms (676) resulted in the Silla language, the first unified language on the Korean peninsula; later on, the establishment of the Koryo dynasty (918) gave rise to the central dialect of Korean, which became the basis of modern Korean; the Imjin War (1592–8) marks the division between late Middle Korean and Modern Korean; and lastly, the Korean War (1950–3) yielded the language division between North and South Korea.

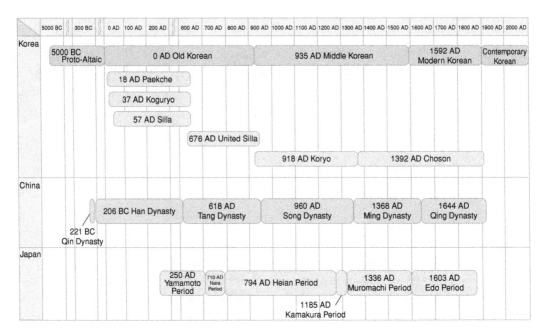

Figure 1.1   The Korean language in the East Asian history

1.1.2   Where is the Korean language from?

The origin of the Korean language is still not clearly known. Although there were some predecessors, it was the Finnish linguist Ramstedt (1873–1959) who first proposed the genetic affinity between Korean and Altaic languages such as Manchu, Mongolian, Tungus and Turkish, through a systematic comparison. These languages share grammatical properties with Korean such as agglutinative morphology; that is, grammatical relations such as a subject or an object are mainly realised by attaching (or 'gluing') particles to nominal expressions. Nevertheless, it is hard to prove this genetic affinity with Altaic languages due to the lack of reliable evidence.

1.1.3   Korean vs. Chinese and Korean vs. Japanese: are they related, and if so, how?

Korea and Japan, under the umbrella of the Chinese cultural sphere, have not only shared socio-cultural heritages, but also a shared linguistic heritage. This is represented in the lexicons of the Korean and Japanese languages. As we will see in 1.3, roughly 57 per cent of the Korean vocabulary is Sino-Korean and derived from Chinese. Yet structurally, the two languages are completely unrelated.

Chinese has a strict subject–verb–object word order and does not have grammatical particles like those found in Korean. Korean and Japanese, however, share a great deal of structural similarity. For instance, Japanese and Korean share an almost identical particle system. Nevertheless, it is still debatable whether Korean and Japanese belong to the same language family. Vovin (2008) recently argued that there is no genetic relation between the two languages. Once again, however, a lack of reliable evidence makes it difficult to prove any linguistic affinity.

1.1.4 Korean as a global language: is the Korean language for the Korean peninsula only?

Korean is no longer simply the language of the Korean peninsula, nor simply the language of Terra Incognita. This is due to the increase of the Korean 'diaspora', now consisting of roughly 7 million people. They include both descendants of early emigrants from the Korean peninsula, as well as more recent emigrants. Most of them live in China (2.34 million), the United States (2.1 million) and Japan (0.9 million). As a result, Korean is increasingly more widely spoken. With 79 million people speaking it across the globe (48.6 million in South Korea, 23.8 million in North Korea, 7 million overseas according to Statistics Korea), Korean is now the seventeenth most widely used amongst all the world languages (Ethnologue, 2008, www.ethnologue.com/web/asp). Figure 1.2 shows the distribution of the Korean language outside Korea as of 2010.

Education in the Korean language overseas has also been expanded over the last few decades. For instance, the number of students in the USA choosing Korean as their SAT (Scholastic Aptitude Test) foreign language has been steadily on the rise in recent years. In 2007, the Korean Embassy in the USA reported that Korean was the fourth most popular foreign language chosen by SAT students.

Economic development, cultural exchange and trade also provide motives for foreigners to learn Korean. From the late 1990s, there has been a rapid increase in the influx of foreign labour into Korea, particularly from South Asia, as well as an increase in international marriages between Korean men and South Asian women. According to a recent survey by Statistics Korea, the number of students (of primary to high-school level) with foreign mothers was about 18,778 in 2009. Korean pop culture, or *Hallyu*, has also played an important role in raising interest in the Korean language and culture, particularly in China, Japan and Southeast Asia.

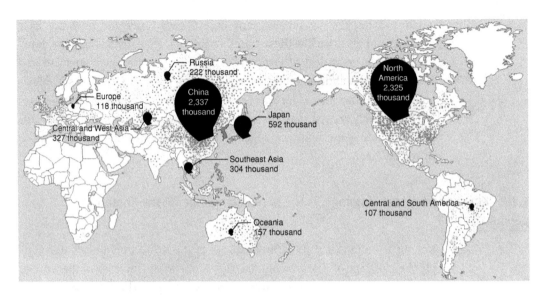

Figure 1.2   Distribution of the Korean language outside Korea

1.2 Korean alphabet and romanisation

1.2.1 Hangeul: the Korean alphabet

Hangeul 한글, invented in 1443, is the unique alphabet used to write the Korean language. Hangeul 한글 is a phonemic alphabet; in other words, there is one-to-one correspondence between a phoneme and a letter.

Consonants and vowels are given in alphabetic order in (1). There are twenty-four basic letters and sixteen complex letters. Among the twenty-four basic letters, fourteen are consonants and ten are vowels.

(1)   Korean alphabet
    a. Basic letters for consonants (14)
       ㄱ, ㄴ, ㄷ, ㄹ, ㅁ, ㅂ, ㅅ, ㅇ, ㅈ, ㅊ, ㅋ, ㅌ, ㅍ, ㅎ
    b. Basic letters for vowels (10)
       ㅏ, ㅑ, ㅓ, ㅕ, ㅗ, ㅛ, ㅜ, ㅠ, ㅡ, ㅣ
    c. Complex letters for consonants (5)
       ㄲ, ㄸ, ㅃ, ㅆ, ㅉ
    d. Complex letters for vowels (11)
       ㅐ, ㅒ, ㅔ, ㅖ, ㅘ, ㅙ, ㅚ, ㅝ, ㅞ, ㅟ, ㅢ

Systematic correspondence is observed between letters. For instance, an addition of a stroke makes a lax sound into an aspirated sound (e.g., ㅂ → ㅍ, ㄷ → ㅌ, ㄱ → ㅋ), whilst consonant doubling results in the tensing of sounds

Table 1.1 Comparison of three romanisation methods

Word	M-R	Revised ROK	Yale	Meaning
평가	p'yŏngga	pyeongga	phyengka	valuation, rating
진리	chilli	jilli	cinli	truth, fact
햇볕	haetpyŏt	haetbyeot	hayspyet	sunlight
첫사랑	chŏtsarang	cheotsarang	chessalang	a first love
협회	hyŏphoe	hyeopheo	hyephoy	a society, association, league
학회	hakhoe	hakheo	hakhoy	an institute, academy
비빔밥	pibimpap	bibimbap	pipimpap	common Korean dish (rice topped with vegetables, usually with an egg and mincemeat)
더욱	tŏuk	deouk	tewuk	still more
여덟	yŏdŏl	yeodeol	yetelp	eight
핥다	halta	halda	halthta	lick
모든	modŭn	modeun	motun	all, whole, every, each
재미	chaemi	jaemi	caymi	interest
여기	yŏgi	yeogi	yeki	here; a hobby
서울	Sŏul	Seoul	Sewul	Seoul (Korea's capital)
세기	segi	segi	seyki	a century
빨리	ppalli	ppalli	ppalli	fast, rapidly, quickly
자주	chaju	jaju	cacwu	often, repeatedly
곶감	kotkam	gotgam	kockam	dry persimmons

(e.g., ㅂ → ㅃ, ㄷ → ㄸ, ㄱ →ㄲ). Lastly, the sounds that are pronounced in the same place of articulation show visual similarity (e.g. (ㅂ ㅃ ㅍ), (ㄷ ㄸ ㅌ), (ㄱ ㄲ ㅋ), (ㅅ ㅆ, ㅈ ㅉ ㅊ)).

In 1933, the Korean Language Council (*Joseoneohakhoe* 조선어학회) decided that words should be spelled as they sound, but should also conform to grammatical principles. They also decided that there should be a space between each word in the sentence and the particles attached to the previous word. These two rules became the basis of orthography in Contemporary Korean. This means that although the noun 사람 *saram* 'person' plus a subject particle -이 -*i* is pronounced 사라미 [sa.ɾa.mi], the written form remains 사람이, respecting the morphological combination of noun plus particle. This is in contrast to Middle Korean orthography, where Korean is written as it is pronounced.

1.2.2   Romanisation: how many styles and how different is each option?

There are three ways to romanise the Korean language: the McCune-Reischauer (M-R) system, the Revised Republic of Korean (ROK) system, and the Yale system. Inside Korea, the Revised ROK system is invariably used. (See www. korean.go.kr/09_new/dic/rule/rule_roman_0101.jsp for the Revised ROK Romanisation system.) Outside Korea, the McCune-Reischauer system and Yale system are mainly used. Whilst the McCune-Reischauer system respects the actual pronunciation of Korean, the Yale system follows the original morphological form. The former system is used by most Koreanologists and Korean studies authorities including the Library of Congress. The latter system is mainly used by linguists. The following table shows how the three systems romanise each sample word.

1.3   Lexicon

1.3.1   What is the proportional ratio between Sino-Korean and pure Korean words?

In terms of vocabulary, the Korean language has been heavily influenced by the Chinese language. (This is also true for Japanese.) Most conceptual or professional terms are Sino-Korean. The more basic terms, however, tend to be pure Korean. According to the *Standard Korean Dictionary* edited by the National Institute of Korean Language (NIKL, 2000), and containing some 440,000 words, the ratio of (i) pure Korean (PK) words; (ii) Sino-Korean (SK) words; (iii) other foreign loanwords is 25.28 : 57.12 : 17.6.

1.3.2   Increase of English loanwords

The proportion of loanwords is closely related to a nation's socio-cultural and political situation. As western influence grows rapidly in South Korea, the number of English loanwords has risen dramatically in the last fifty years. The number of loanwords became one of the main causes of discrepancy between the North and South Korean languages. Whilst the South has adopted English loanwords, the North has replaced them with PK words wherever possible.

1.3.3   New words in the twenty-first century

A language's lexicon vividly reflects the socio-cultural change of a particular society. This is also the case in the Korean lexicon. Korea University's *Korean Language Dictionary*, published in 2009, contains words such as those presented in (2)–(4). The words in (2) are information technology-related terms that have appeared in the last ten years. The vocabulary in (3) reflects the socio-cultural aspects of present-day Korean society. For instance, *gireogiappa* 기러기아빠 'Wild Goose Father' in (3) means a father who sends his wife and children abroad to further the children's early foreign-language education, whilst he himself remains in Korea to earn money to send to the family. As shown in (4), some terms are English in origin, but are only used in Korea.

(2) 악플 *ak-peul* 'internet bullying', 넷맹 *net-maeng* 'internet-illiterate', 스팸메일 *spam-mail* 'e-mail spam or junk email', 악성코드 *akseong-kodeu* 'malignant-code', 프로게이머 *pro-gamer* 'professional gamer'

(3) 기러기아빠*gireogiappa* 'wild goose father', 꽃미남 *kkonminam* 'pretty-boy', 생얼 *saengeol* 'makeup-free face', 비호감 *bihogam* 'muddied reputation'

(4) 원샷 *one-shot* 'bottoms up!', 스킨십 *skin-ship* 'physical contact', 커닝 *cunning* 'cheating'

How many blues and blacks?

Colour terms are well developed in Korean. Consider (5)–(6). All words in (5) refer to the colour blue and (6) refer to the colour black.

(5) Blue
새파랗다, 파랗다, 파르스름하다, 파릇파릇하다, 퍼렇다, 푸르다, 푸르뎅뎅하다, 푸르스름하다, 푸르죽죽하다, 푸릇푸릇하다, 시퍼렇다

(6) Black
가맣다, 거멓다, 거무스레하다, 거무스름하다, 거무죽죽하다, 거무튀튀하다, 검다, 검붉다, 검퍼렇다, 까맣다, 까무잡잡하다, 새카맣다, 새까맣다, 시커멓다, 시꺼멓다

1.3.4 Motion- and sound-symbolic words

Mimetic words (i.e., motion-symbolic words) and onomatopoeic words (sound-symbolic words) are also well developed in Korean. According to NIKL, the Korean language contains some 2,900 motion- or sound-symbolic words. Consider (7) and (8).

(7) 지나가 침을 꿀꺽 삼켰다. (sound-symbolic)
Jina-SUBJ spit-OBJ *kkulkkeok* swallowed.
'Jina swallowed with a gulp.'

Table 1.2 Lexical differences between South and North Korea

English loanwords			Sino-Korean vocabulary		
South (EL)	North (PK)	English gloss	South (SK)	North (PK)	English gloss
노크	손기척	knock	관절	뼈마디	joint (bone)
레코드	소리판	record	교목	키나무	a tall tree
스프레이	솔솔이	spray	능력	일본새	ability
시럽	단물	syrup	멸균	균깡그리죽이기	sterilisation (pasteurisation)
젤리	단묵	jelly	살균	균죽이기	sterilisation
카스텔라	설기과자	sponge cake	월동	겨울나이	wintering
커튼	창문보	curtain	인력	끌힘	labour force
코너킥	모서리뿔	corner kick	추수	가을걷이	harvest
훅	맞단추, 겉단추	hook	홍수	큰물	deluge, flood

(8) 지나가 나긋나긋 미소를 지었다. (motion-symbolic)
Jina-SUBJ *nageunnageut* (tenderly) smile-OBJ made.
'Jina smiled tenderly.'

1.3.5 Can South Koreans and North Koreans understand each other?

The answer to this question is yes. However, it is not easy for South and North Koreans to understand each other one hundred per cent. This is due to the difference in vocabulary. As mentioned above, whilst the South has adopted English loanwords (EL) as they are, the North has invented corresponding PK words instead. In the North, not only EL, but also many SK words were replaced with PK words as shown in Table 1.2.

1.4 Structural properties of Korean

1.4.1 How are words and sentences composed?

The smallest meaning-bearing unit in Korean is called a morpheme. Morphemes are divided into *free* and *bound morphemes* according to whether the morpheme can be used independently of any other host category or not. At the same time, a morpheme is classified according to whether it has *lexical* meaning, or whether it only represents *grammatical* meaning. For instance, the verbal suffix -었- cannot be used on its own (i.e., it is a bound morpheme),

Table 1.3 Examples of compound and derivational words

	Simple words	Derived words		Compound words
		Prefix	Suffix	
Pure Korean	손 'hand'	맨- + 손 → 맨손 'bare hands'	가위 + -질 → 가위질 'scissoring'	밤 + 나무→ 밤나무 'chestnut tree'
	사랑 'love'	첫- + 사랑 → 첫사랑 'first love'	멋 + -쟁이 → 멋쟁이 'dandy'	사랑 + 싸움 → 사랑싸움 'love quarrel'
Sino-Korean	강(江) 'river'	대(大)- + 선배(先輩) → 대선배 'great senior'	교육(敎育) + -계(界) → 교육계 'the world of education'	초등(初等) + 학교(學校) → 초등학교 'primary school'
	산(山) 'mountain'	미(未)- + 완성(完成) → 미완성 'incompletion'	가정(家庭) + -용-(用) → 가정용 'home use'	정치(政治) + 조직(組織)→ 정치조직 'political structure'

but it contributes to the meaning of the past tense (i.e., it is a grammatical morpheme). Verbal stems contribute to the meaning of a word (i.e., they are lexical morphemes), but cannot be used on their own (i.e., they are bound morphemes).

The smallest free or independent grammatical unit is a word. Korean words can have one of the following structures:

(9)   Types of words
      a. simple word: root (e.g., 나무 'tree')
      b. derived word: prefix + root (e.g., 첫-+ 사랑 'first-love')
      c. root + suffix (e.g., 가위 +-질 'scissoring')
      d. compound word: root + root (e.g., 밤 + 나무 'chestnut tree')

Table 1.3 shows examples of compound and derivational words.

The next grammatical unit after a word is the *eojeol* 어절 'word-phrase'. Word phrases are separated by a space in Korean orthography, and each is composed of a lexical morpheme (e.g., a noun) and a grammatical morpheme (e.g., a particle). Simply speaking, a word phrase is a basic grammatical unit that can function as a subject or object within a sentence. Note that in (10) the word 지나 itself does not have any grammatical role, but with the case particle – 가 attached, it becomes the subject.

(10) 지나-가 아침-에 우유-를 마셨어요.
      Jina-SUBJ morning-at milk-OBJ drank
      'Jina drank milk in the morning.'

A nominal expression with a particle attached forms one word phrase, and a verb plus verbal suffixes also forms one word phrase, regardless of the number of suffixes attached. In Korean orthography, each word phrase is individually spaced. Consider (11). L stands for lexical morpheme, F stands for free morpheme, G stands for grammatical morpheme and B stands for bound morpheme. Therefore (11) consists of three word phrases and seven morphemes.

(11) Word phrase {지나-가} {밥-을} {먹-는-다} 'Jina is having a meal.'
              Subject   Object   Verb
      Morpheme   지나-가   밥-을   먹-는-다
              L/F-G/B   L/F-G/B L/B-G/B G/B

It is still an unsettled issue whether to regard a particle as an independent word or not. In South Korean grammar it is considered an independent word, but in North Korean grammar it is not. However, we will not dwell on this issue in this book.

Word phrases whose host categories are nouns take particles, whereas word phrases whose host categories are verbs take inflectional suffixes. We will return shortly to discussion of particles and suffixes. Word phrases form a longer phrase such as a noun phrase or verb phrase, and these longer phrases then constitute a clause and finally a sentence.

1.4.2   Is the word order rigid or free?

The word order in Korean is freer than in English, the only general rule being that the verb tends to come at the end of a sentence. Yet there are cases where the word order is more rigid; for instance, a modifying expression will always precede the noun being modified. Consider (12). * denotes an ungrammatical sentence.

(12) a. 유나-가 새 구두-를 신었다.
      Yuna-SUBJ new shoes-OBJ put-on
      'Yuna put on new shoes.'
   b. *유나-가 구두 새-을 신었다.
      Yuna-SUBJ shoes new-OBJ put-on
      (modifiee precedes modifying expression)

1.4.3   If it is not through word order, how are grammatical roles and relations expressed?

Grammatical functions are realised by 'attaching' or 'gluing' particles to the content words. For instance, regardless of the location of 지나-가, the agent or subject of the sentence is the same; that is, 지나 in (13) is clearly the subject because of the subject particle -가.

(13) a. 지나-가 아침-에 우유-를 마셨어요.
     Jina-SUBJ morning-at milk-OBJ drank
     'Jina drank milk in the morning.'

   b. 우유-를 지나-가 아침-에 마셨어요.
     milk-OBJ Jina-SUBJ morning-at drank
     'Jina drank milk in the morning.'

   c. 아침-에 우유-를 지나-가 마셨어요.
     Morning-at milk-OBJ Jina-SUBJ drank
     'Jina drank milk in the morning.'

This grammatical characteristic is shared by the so-called Altaic languages such as Mongolian, Turkish, Tungus and Manchurian. In the following section, we will briefly discuss the inventory of particles (for nominal expressions) and inflectional suffixes (for verbal expressions).

Particles: What are they and how are they used?

Particles that are attached to nouns can be classified into two groups: (i) case particles; (ii) additional particles. There are no words in English that directly correspond to the subject/object particles found in Korean. Prepositional/adverbial particles, however, can be easily translated into *in/on/at* or *to/from/ towards* in English. Additional particles in Korean either add some additional meaning to the host noun or connect two nouns. A list of the most frequently used particles according to B.-M. Kang and H.-G. Kim (2009)'s Sejong Corpus search is given below:

(14) a. Case particles
   (i)   Subject/object particles: -이가, -께서, -을/를
   (ii) Prepositional/adverbial particles: -에게, -한테, -의, -에,
         -(으)로, -에서, -처럼, -보다, -로서
   b. Additional particles
   (i)   Additional meaning particles: -은/-는, -도, -만
   (ii) Connective particles: -와/과, -(이)나, -하고, -랑

A word phrase whose stem is a verb can have a series of inflectional suffixes. (Inflectional suffixes are also referred to as endings in this book.) These inflectional suffixes can be classified as follows:

(15) Classification of inflectional suffixes (endings)
    I. Pre-final
    II. Final
        A. Sentence-final
        B. Non-sentence final
            (i)   Conjunctive
            (ii) Function-converting
                a. Nominalising
                b. Adnominalising

In the following section, we will focus on pre-final and sentence-final endings.

1.4.4 How is the speaker's attitude expressed in Korean?

In English, the speaker's attitude is expressed through auxiliary verbs such as *would, could, may, might, should* etc. at the early stage of a sentence, as in (16). In Korean, the speaker's attitude is expressed by a pre-final ending or an auxiliary verb that is attached by a connective to a main verb, as in (17).

(16) a. Would you give me that book?
     b. You should come to the class.

(17) a. 생일파티-에　　와-주세요.
        Birthday party -at come-please
        'Please, come to the birthday party.'
     b. 책 좀 주시-겠-어요?
        book please give -FUT /VOL -Q
        'Will you give me the book, please?'

(18) shows the different kinds of pre-final sentence ending suffixes and their primary functions. These suffixes come right after the verb stem but before the sentence-final ending.

(18) a. Honorification suffixes: -시-
        E.g. 오다 (to come) 오시다 (to come; subject honorification)
     b. Temporal/Aspectual suffixes: -었-/-았- (past tense),
        -았었-/-었었- (past perfect)
        E.g. 먹다 (to eat) 먹었다 (to eat; past tense)
     c. Modal suffixes: –겠- (volition)
        E.g. 막다 (to block) 막겠다 (to block; volition)

Where more than one suffix is required, there is a specific order determining which suffix goes where in relation to the other suffixes. Hence, the example in (19) is ungrammatical.

(19) *오-더-겠-시-니 (instead of 오-시-겠-더-니)

1.4.5 How is the mood of a sentence realised?

Sentence-final endings decide the mood of a sentence (e.g., declarative, imperative, question interrogative, etc.). (20) is a list of frequently used sentence-final endings according to B.-M. Kang and H.-G. Kim (2009)'s Sejong Corpus search. Even where sentence endings are morphologically identical, different moods can be realised by changing one's intonation. A rising tone implies a question, whereas a falling tone normally implies a statement. In Chapter 7, we will discuss the role of prosody in realising mood.

(20) a. Declarative: -다, -ㄴ/는다, -ㅂ/습니다, -어/아요, -어/아,
       -야, -지, -지요, -에요, -오
    b. Exclamatory: -구나, -어/아라, -어/아요, -군, -군요, -ㄴ/는데
    c. Interrogative: -아/어요, -어/아, -야, -지, -ㄴ/는가, -ㄹ/을까, -지요
    d. Imperative: -어/아라, -ㅂ시오, -요
    e. Propositive: -자, -어/아요, -ㅂ/읍시다

1.5 Socio-pragmatic characteristics of Korean

Unlike English, in Korean it is impossible to 'finish' a sentence without knowing who is speaking. For instance, (21) shows a conversation between a boy and his neighbour, who is much older than him. Shifting the verb endings between the two parties would make the conversation sound rather odd. Although Korean society is becoming less hierarchical, misusing honorification can still insult the listener. Therefore (22) sounds inappropriate.

(21) Old man (in the neighbourhood): 밥 먹었니? 'Have you eaten?'
     Boy: 아뇨, 안 먹었어요. 'Not yet.'

(22) Boy: 밥 먹었니? 'Have you eaten?'
     Old man (in the neighbourhood): ???

There are three kinds of honorification in Korean: subject, hearer and object honorification. Subject honorification is realised by the use of the pre-final ending -시- as in (23).

Figure 1.3   Map of Korean dialects

(23) Subject honorification
       손님들-이 집-에 가-시-었-다.
       Guests-SUBJ home-at go-HON-PAST-DECL
       'Guests went home.'

   Hearer honorification is now the most commonly used and is realised by different endings. (24a) shows high respect of the speaker towards the hearer, while (24b) reveals the hearer being lower than the speaker.

(24) Hearer honorification
       a. 부디 열심히 공부하-십시오.
          'Please diligently study.'
       b. 부디 열심히 공부하-여라.
          'Please diligently study.'

Object honorification is rarely used; only its trace can be found in the use of case particles such as -께, or in certain words as in (25).

(25) Object honorification

a. Adverbial particle: -께 (← – 에게)

b. Noun: 진지 (← 밥) 'meal', 댁 (← 집) 'house'

c. Verb: 뵙다 (← 보다) 'to see', 드시다 (← 먹다) 'to eat', 여쭙다 (← 묻다) 'to ask', 드리다 (← 주다) 'to give'

d. 지나-가 할아버지-께 편지-를 드리-었-다.
    Jina-SUBJ grandfather-to letter-OBJ give(HON)-PAST-DECL
    'Jina gave a letter to her grandfather.'

Factors such as age, power and familiarity determine whether honorification is required, and what degree of honorification is appropriate.

1.6   Dialectal variation

We saw earlier that North and South Korean speakers can understand each other, although there is some difference between their vocabularies. How about the speakers within the South or within the North? Can people from Seoul understand people from Jeju or Pusan without difficulty? The answer is no. This is mostly due to the difference in prosody between dialects. Consider the dialectal map of Korea in Figure 1.3.

As shown above, the sounds of Korean have many dialectal variants. This book, however, will concentrate on the Standard Seoul Korean dialect. In Chapter 7, we will discuss the prosodic difference between dialects further. Now, let's start our journey into the world of Korean sounds.

2 Production of sounds

Some of you may not be familiar with Korean and may never have even heard the Korean language spoken. Fortunately for you, the vocal organs used to pronounce both Korean and English are almost the same. Moreover, the process of sound production is known to be universal and does not differ from one language to another. We believe that understanding the general process of sound production will help greatly the reader's understanding of the sounds of Korean and make you feel more familiar with the sounds of the Korean language. Hence, in this chapter, we will discuss the vocal organs that are used in speech production in 2.1, the major cavities in 2.2, the processes of speech production in 2.3 and ways of classifying speech sounds in 2.4.

2.1 Vocal organs

2.1.1 Overview

In this section, we will examine the various vocal organs involved in the production of speech. Figure 2.1 lists the vocal organs involved in speech production.

2.1.2 Larynx

The larynx is a common name for part of the vocal organs which extends vertically from the inferior border of the cricoid cartilage to the hyoid bone. The larynx is made up of five important cartilages: the thyroid cartilage, the cricoid cartilage, the epiglottis and the paired arytenoid cartilages.

Figure 2.2 shows the larynx as viewed from above. The vocal folds are composed of ligaments, muscles and mucous membrane. One end of the vocal folds is connected to the arytenoid cartilage, and the other end to the thyroid cartilage. The vocal folds are opened and closed through the adduction and

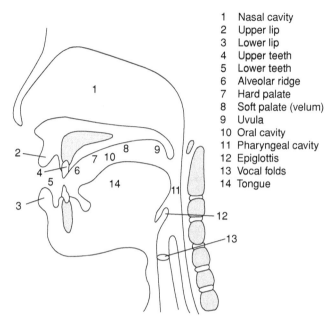

1 Nasal cavity
2 Upper lip
3 Lower lip
4 Upper teeth
5 Lower teeth
6 Alveolar ridge
7 Hard palate
8 Soft palate (velum)
9 Uvula
10 Oral cavity
11 Pharyngeal cavity
12 Epiglottis
13 Vocal folds
14 Tongue

Figure 2.1   The vocal organs

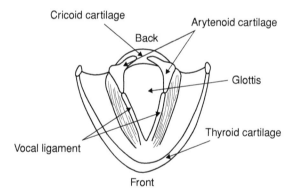

Figure 2.2   View of the larynx from above

abduction of the arytenoid cartilage. The gap produced by the abduction of the vocal folds is called the glottis. The vocal folds are the principal vocal organs involved in the process of phonation.

2.1.3 Tongue

In the production of sound, the next most active organ after the vocal folds is probably the tongue. In order to understand the production of sound, it

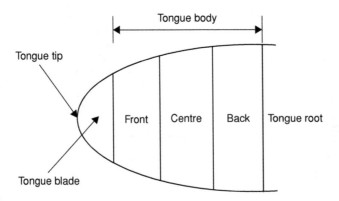

Figure 2.3   Subdivisions of the tongue

is important to know the names of the various parts of the tongue. These are shown in Figure 2.3.

The foremost part of the tongue is called the tongue tip, and the part above it, which lies beneath the alveolar ridge when the tongue is in a relaxed state, is called the tongue blade, and measures about 10–15 millimetres. The rest of the tongue is known as the tongue body, and can be further divided into three parts, front, central and back, or sometimes into just two parts, front and back. If the body of the tongue is divided into two parts, the front of the tongue refers to the part which makes contact with the hard palate during articulation, and the back of the tongue refers to the part which makes contact with the velum during articulation. Beyond the back of the tongue is the tongue root, which forms the front wall of the pharynx.

2.1.4 Palate

Figure 2.4 shows the various parts of the palate. As is shown, the palate is divided into four areas: the protruding area behind the upper front teeth, known as the alveolar ridge; the part supported by bone, known as the hard palate; the part which is not supported by bone, known as the soft palate or velum; and finally, the end part of the velum, known as the uvula.

2.2 Major cavities

As shown in Figure 2.5, the upper part of the vocal folds is divided into three sections around the tongue, the pharyngeal wall and the palate, referred to as the pharyngeal cavity, oral cavity and nasal cavity. Air from the vocal folds is modified in this upper space as it passes through. The particular sound the air

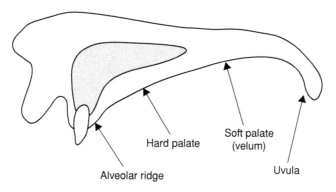

Figure 2.4   Subdivisions of the roof of the mouth

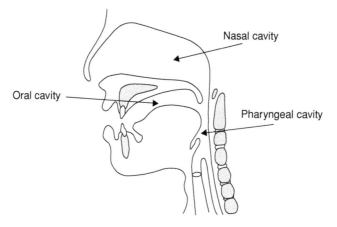

Figure 2.5   The three major cavities involved in speech production

makes when it is emitted as depends on the cavity in which it resonates as it leaves the larynx. Sound production is mostly done in the pharyngeal, oral and nasal cavities. The varying movements of the vocal organs transform the space inside these cavities, giving the air leaving the vocal folds a very different sound from the uniform sound as which it began.

When we inhale, we usually breathe in and out of our noses with our mouths closed. Generally, when we exhale, air is released from our lungs and leaves through the nose. But we can exhale through our mouths as well as through our noses. Figure 2.6 shows the passage of airflow through the nasal and oral cavities when we exhale.

In contrast to when we breathe, when we speak we use our mouths rather than our noses, and air from the lungs only passes through the mouth. In order to prevent air from entering the nasal cavity, the levator veli palatini, located at the back of the velum, contracts. When this muscle contracts, the

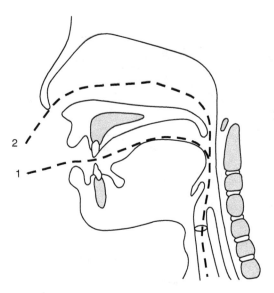

Figure 2.6   Two passages of airflow from the glottis

palate rises and lies flush with the pharyngeal wall. Thus, as the nasal passage is blocked, the air leaves through the oral cavity on its way out.

In speech, sounds that are produced with the nasal passage obstructed are called oral sounds, and sounds produced with the nasal passage open are called nasal sounds. Most speech sounds are oral sounds, and may be assumed such unless otherwise specified. In addition, as most pronounced sounds are oral – nasals are the exception – the velum is raised flat against the pharynx most of the time. However, the velum is in this position during breathing.

2.3 Processes of speech production

Generally speaking, speech sounds are produced as air is exhaled from the lungs through the vocal folds and the vocal tract.

This process can be divided into three main stages. First, the supply of air needed for sound formation; second, modulation of that air supply; and finally, transformation of the regulated air. The linguistic terms for these stages are *initiation*, *phonation* and *articulation*, respectively (Catford, 1988). In the following, we will discuss each stage in detail.

2.3.1 Initiation

Let's take a closer look at initiation, the first stage. Initiation is the stage in which air is supplied for sound production. We can classify initiation processes by *initiator*, the place from which air is supplied, and also by direction

Table 2.1 Patterns of initiation

Airstream	Initiator	Direction	Names of stop consonants
Pulmonic egressive	Lungs	Outwards	Stops
Glottalic egressive	Vocal folds	Outwards	Ejectives
Glottalic ingressive	Vocal folds	Inwards	Implosives
Velaric ingressive	Velum (tongue)	Inwards	Clicks

of airflow. The initiators of most sounds known to exist are the lungs, and the direction of airflow is outward. We call sounds which are initiated from the lungs *pulmonic* sounds. Sounds with an outward airflow are called *egressive* sounds. In other words, egressive sounds are sounds that require exhalation in order to produce them. All of the sounds in the Korean language are *pulmonic egressive* sounds, sounds that are produced by air exhaled from the lungs. Not only the sounds of Korean, but also the sounds of English, Japanese, Chinese, French and German are all pulmonic egressive sounds. In fact, as noted above, most sounds known to exist are pulmonic egressive sounds.

However, not all speech sounds are pulmonic egressive sounds. Though rare, the vocal folds and the velum can also be the initiators of some speech sounds, and the direction of airflow can also be from the outside in rather than from the inside out. Thus, theoretically, there are six possible patterns of initiation, according to type of initiator and direction of airstream, through which speech sounds can be produced: (i) pulmonic egressives; (ii) pulmonic ingressives; (iii) glottalic egressives; (iv) glottalic ingressives; (v) velaric egressives; and (vi) velaric ingressives. However, in reality, only (i) pulmonic egressives, (ii) glottalic egressives, (iii) glottalic ingressives and (iv) velaric ingressives are observed in actual speech sound production. For instance, *ejectives* are glottalic egressive sounds, *implosives* glottalic ingressives, and *clicks* velaric ingressives. Pulmonic ingressives and velaric egressives are not observed in the speech production of any of the world's known languages. Patterns of initiation are listed in Table 2.1.

DID YOU KNOW…?

Two kinds of ingressives

When something surprising happens, or when you feel sympathy for somebody, what kinds of sound do you make? Let's have a closer look at those sounds.

Sounds made when something surprising happens

When something unexpected happens, what sound do you make? Try it now. Did you inhale or exhale to produce the sound? Native Korean speakers breathe in to produce this sound. In this case, initiation takes place in the lungs, and the direction of airflow is ingressive. This sound is a pulmonic ingressive sound. Pulmonic ingressives are easy to make and familiar to us. Interestingly, however, no pulmonic ingressive speech sounds are known to exist. Why might this be? To answer this question, try saying the words, "I am reading a book entitled *The Sounds of Korean*" while breathing in – that is, with pulmonic ingressive sounds. You may well be out of breath before finishing the sentence. Pulmonic ingressives are far too inefficient and unnatural to be used as speech sounds. This is likely to be the reason why no pulmonic ingressive speech sounds exist.

Sounds made to express sympathy or disapproval

This time, make the "tut" sound that you would make when you feel sympathy for someone or to express disapproval. Try to think about the direction of airflow. You will discover that air rushes into your mouth as the sound is being produced. You may be able to feel the direction of the airflow more slowly by making a clicking noise. Next, click while holding your nose. When you click, you will notice that you are not breathing, although your mouth is open. You know that you cannot breathe while you are holding your nose, but you may wonder why you are not breathing through your mouth. This is because although the tip of the tongue is resting on the bottom of the mouth, the body of the tongue is obstructing the soft palate. When this clicking sound is produced, the body of the tongue touches the soft palate. At the same time, the blade of the tongue touches the alveolar ridge, and thus air is trapped in the space in between. This is the air used to produce the sound.

Ultimately, according to its process of initiation, this clicking sound is a velaric ingressive, since the velum supplies the air, and the direction of airflow is ingressive. Clicking sounds are easy to produce, but rarely found as speech sounds, except in some African languages.

What is the difference between these two ingressive sounds?

Although the sounds we produce when we are surprised or feel sympathy are both ingressive, there are important distinctions between the two.

First, as previously mentioned, when you produce a surprised sound, you can hold your nose and still breathe naturally. However, you cannot breathe if you hold your nose while making a clicking noise with your tongue. The reason for this is that the mouth is blocked in two places, only one of which is released during the production of sound. Furthermore, even after the sound is made, one end of the oral cavity remains obstructed, thus preventing air from escaping.

Second, reproducing the sound you make when surprised will require you to consciously inhale air. However, when producing clicking sounds, you inhale naturally without needing to consciously inhale. The reason why clicking your tongue does not require you to consciously inhale air is because this particular airstream mechanism naturally generates inward airflow. When you click with your tongue, the back and front parts of the tongue cause an obstruction inside the mouth, trapping air between them. Before the click sound is produced, the tongue pulls down this middle area that traps air, expanding the space a little. When this space is expanded, the pressure inside it drops, and the front part of the tongue is released. Air rushes in because the pressure inside is lower than the pressure within the oral cavity.

2.3.2 Phonation

After air is provided through initiation, it passes through the vocal folds and is modulated. This process is called *phonation*.

The vocal folds control the air exhaled from the lungs by adduction and abduction. That is to say, the vocal folds function as a valve which controls airflow. For instance, when the vocal folds are closed, air cannot be released, but when the vocal folds are open, air can flow freely. The vocal folds can be opened and closed repeatedly. In everyday life, when we strain our vocal folds are closed, when we breathe they are opened, and when we cry or shout they vibrate.

We produce speech sounds by opening and closing our vocal folds. Some sounds are produced by a rapid and repeated opening and closing of the vocal folds. When the vocal folds rapidly open and close repeatedly, they vibrate. On the basis of their phonation, speech sounds can be divided into *voiced sounds* and *voiceless sounds*. Voiced sounds are accompanied by vibrations in the vocal folds, and voiceless sounds are not. A summary of voiced and voiceless sounds appears in Figure 2.7.

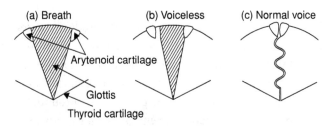

Figure 2.7   Schematic view of laryngeal configurations

When voiceless sounds are produced, the vocal folds either separate, causing the glottis to open, or come together, causing the glottis to close. When voiced sounds are produced, the vocal folds vibrate either completely or only partially.

DID YOU KNOW...?

Making vibrations in the vocal folds

Three conditions are required in order to produce vibrations in the vocal folds. When all three conditions are fulfilled, the vocal folds vibrate naturally. If any one of these conditions is not met, vibration is unlikely to occur. First, the vocal folds must be as close together as possible. Second, the vocal folds must be relaxed. Third, subglottal air pressure must be sufficiently greater than supraglottal air pressure.

Vowel sounds are produced with the mouth open, so subglottal air pressure is more likely to be greater than supraglottal air pressure. Therefore, all vowels are voiced sounds.

However, it is easy for supraglottal air pressure to increase during the phonation of consonantal sounds such as *stops* or *fricatives*. This is because these sounds are produced either with both the oral and nasal cavities obstructed (i.e., stops), or with the nasal tract obstructed and the oral cavity severely narrowed (i.e., fricatives). Therefore, in these cases, additional effort is needed in order to keep the subglottal air pressure sufficiently higher than the supraglottal air pressure.

This is why it is common for stops and fricatives to be classified as voiceless. However, some stops and fricatives can also be produced as voiced sounds. Sounds that do not cause vibrations in the vocal folds are called voiceless sounds, and sounds that are accompanied by vibrations are called voiced sounds.

DID YOU KNOW...?

How to quieten your voice

You have bumped into a friend in one of the aisles in the library. You naturally lower your voice to greet your friend so as not to disturb other students. "Hi, long time no see. How are you?" Now, bring out your acting skills and talk as you would if you found yourself in such a situation. Is your phonation not different to what it would normally be? You will find that your voice is breathier than normal. This is because instead of the vocal folds vibrating in their entirety, only the front part is now vibrating, leaving the part further back open, in order to produce quieter sounds. This kind of phonation is called *breathy voice*.

This time, imagine you are whispering to your friend something top secret, and say, "This is top secret. Please don't tell anyone." What about this time? Are you still using a breathy voice? Because breathy sounds are produced by vibrating vocal folds, you can feel vibrations in your throat. What about when you are whispering to your friend? This time, the vocal folds do not vibrate, and you will not be able to feel any vibrations in your throat.

In fact, these two phonation types are not effective methods of phonation. To begin with, the tone is quiet, and you need to breathe more often than normal in order to continue speaking in this way. Of course, these sounds are inevitably quieter than normal voiced sounds, as the vocal folds are vibrating only partially (breathy sounds) or are not vibrating at all (voiceless sounds). Furthermore, as the vocal folds are entirely or partially open, more air will escape compared to when you produce normal voiced sounds, and it will thus be harder to speak for longer using one breath. Though these phonations are inefficient, we still resort to them when we need to speak quietly or have a bad throat. This will help us to understand why, cross-linguistically, the voiced period of an utterance is much longer than the voiceless period. Voiced phonation is much more effective in producing louder sounds as it is accompanied by vibration. Also, air is released bit by bit, because the vocal folds are rapidly opening and closing, and so more sounds can be pronounced over a single breath.

2.3.3 Articulation

As the air that is supplied through initiation enters the stage of phonation, it is modified and transformed as it passes through the vocal tract. The vocal tract refers to the oral and nasal tracts through which air from the vocal folds passes before being released. These cavities can take on many shapes to produce different kind of speech sounds. This process, called articulation, can produce two different types of sound: consonant sounds, which are produced by obstruction in the central part of the oral cavity, and vowel sounds, which are produced without such obstruction.

2.4   Classification

2.4.1   Sonorants vs. obstruents

Speech sounds can be divided into two main categories: sonorants and obstruents. When sonorants are produced, airflow is unhindered as it passes through the vocal tract. When obstruents are produced, however, airflow leaving the vocal tract is obstructed. As a result, obstruents are accompanied by noise caused by disturbance in the airflow, whereas sonorants are not. There are two general ways in which airflow is obstructed. The first is by constriction of the passageway through which air passes to create sound through turbulent airflow. The second is a complete obstruction and then reopening of the air passage to produce a momentary noise. Fricatives are of the former kind, and stops are of the latter kind. Both of these sounds are accompanied by noise, but the duration of that noise is different for each.

DID YOU KNOW...?

Sonorants and obstruents vs. consonants and vowels

Sonorants and obstruents are distinguished on the basis of whether or not they are accompanied by noise, whereas consonants and vowels are distinguished on the basis of whether or not the central part of the oral cavity is obstructed. As noted above, consonantal sounds are produced with obstruction of the oral cavity, and vowel sounds are produced without any such obstruction. This obstruction is not made differently from the way in which obstruents are created; both cause narrowing of the airway. Why, then, are obstruents and consonants categorised separately? Why are all vowels sonorants and all obstruents consonants? Furthermore, why are some sonorants consonants?

The answer lies in their very definitions. Although the nasal cavity is obstructed in the pronunciation of vowels, the central part of the oral cavity remains open. Thus, there is no obstruction in the midsagittal region of the vocal tract. Furthermore, vowels are produced without any concomitant noise; hence they are sonorant. On the other hand, consonants can be either sonorant or obstruent. Fricatives, stops and affricates are obstruents, but nasal sounds and approximants are sonorants.

Fricatives, stops and affricates are all sounds produced with the nasal cavity blocked off and by an obstruction to the centre of the oral cavity. As the airflow meets this obstruction, noise is created. On the one hand, nasal sounds and approximants are grouped as consonants because they are produced by a far narrower central part of the oral cavity than required when producing vowels, but they are classified as sonorants as they are not accompanied by noise. First of all, like stops, nasal sounds are produced with complete obstruction of the oral cavity. However, unlike in the case of stops, air is allowed to escape through an unobstructed nasal cavity. Furthermore, approximants block air passing into the nasal cavity and constrict the central part of the vocal tract far more than is the case in the production of vowels, but this constriction is not accompanied by noise, as the passageway is not narrow enough to produce turbulence.

2.4.2 Consonants

As mentioned before, consonants are sounds produced by obstruction along the centre line of the oral cavity during articulation. The various types of consonants may differ in several ways depending on: (i) the place of obstruction within the oral cavity; (ii) the particular kind of obstruction of airflow; and (iii) the state of the vocal folds. These three variables are linguistically known as place of articulation, manner of articulation and phonation type or voice type respectively.

2.4.2.1 Place of articulation

Consonants may be classed as bilabial, labiodental, dental, alveolar, palato-alveolar (or postalveolar), alveolo-palatal (or prepalatal), retroflex, palatal, velar, uvular, pharyngeal or glottal according to their place of articulation.

Places of articulation get their names from the lower and upper articulators involved in the articulation process. For example, when the lower lip is the lower articulator and the upper lip is the upper articulator, this is referred to as labiolabial. When the lower articulator is the lower lip and

Table 2.2 Summary of places of articulation

Place of articulation	Lower articulator	Upper articulator
Bilabial	Lower lip	Upper lip
Labiodental	Lower lip	Upper teeth
Dental	Tongue (tip or blade)	Upper teeth
Alveolar	Tongue (tip or blade)	Alveolar ridge
Palato-alveolar (postalveolar)	Tongue (tip or blade)	Rear of alveolar ridge
Alveolo-palatal (prepalatal)	Tongue (tip or blade)	Front of hard palate
Retroflex	Tongue (tip)	Hard palate
Palatal	Tongue (body: back)	Hard palate
Velar	Tongue (body: back)	Soft palate (velum)
Uvular	Tongue (body: back)	Uvula
Pharyngeal	Tongue (Root)	Pharyngeal wall
Glottal	Vocal fold[*]	Vocal fold

[*]In the case of the glottal sounds, the vocal folds play the role of articulator. Therefore, unlike for other places of articulation, the concept of upper and lower articulators is not applicable here. Instead, just the two vocal folds are involved in articulation.

the upper articulator is the upper teeth, this is referred to as labiodental. As labiolabial sounds are articulated with both lips, they are commonly referred to as bilabial sounds. When the lower articulator is the tongue, the name of a place of articulation is determined by its upper articulator. Thus, dental sounds are produced when the lower articulator is the tongue and the upper articulator is the teeth, and alveolar sounds are produced when the lower articulator is the tongue and the upper articulator is the alveolar ridge. An overview of the places of articulation with their various articulators is given in Table 2.2.

2.4.2.2 Manner of articulation

Consonants are also classed according to the manner of their articulation: stops/plosives, nasals, trills, taps/flaps, fricatives, lateral fricatives, approximants, lateral approximants and affricates, among others. These sounds are divided on the basis of whether or not they are produced with complete obstruction of the oral cavity. Whereas stops/plosives, nasals, trills and taps/flaps are produced by completely blocking off the oral cavity, fricatives and approximants are produced by allowing some air to escape through the oral cavity. Sounds produced by total obstruction of the oral cavity are known as sounds

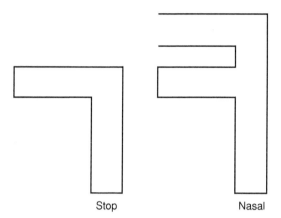

Stop   Nasal

Figure 2.8   Schematic view of the vocal tract for stops and nasals

with complete oral closure, and sounds produced without total obstruction are known as sounds without complete oral closure.

(1)   Types of consonants according to the extent of oral closure
  • Oral cavity blocked: stops/plosives, nasals, trills, taps/flaps
  • Oral cavity open: fricatives, approximants

Among sounds with complete oral closure, nasal sounds differ considerably from stops, trills and taps/flaps in that the velum is not raised and thus allows air to escape into the nasal cavity. Consequently, sounds with complete oral closure may be further divided on the basis of whether the nasal cavity is open or closed. That is, nasals, which are produced with the oral cavity closed but the nasal cavity open are classed as one group, and stops, trills and taps/flaps, which are produced with both the oral and nasal cavities closed, form another. The differences in the articulation of stops and nasal sounds are shown in Figure 2.8.

(2)   Sounds with complete oral closure divided according to the state of the nasal cavity
  • Closed nasal cavity: stops, trills, taps/flaps
  • Open nasal cavity: nasal sounds

Stops, trills and taps/flaps can be further divided into two categories depending on the number of times the oral cavity is blocked. The first category contains stops and taps/flaps, where closure occurs once, and the second contains trills, where closure occurs more than twice. How, then, are we to distinguish stops and taps/flaps from each other? The difference lies in the duration of their respective closure. The closure that occurs in the production

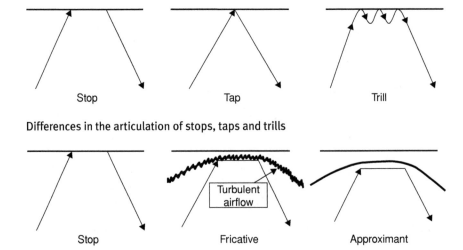

Figure 2.9   Differences in the articulation of stops, taps and trills

Figure 2.10   Differences in the articulation of stops, fricatives and approximants

of stops lasts relatively longer than the obstruction that occurs in the production of taps/flaps. Figure 2.9 shows the differences between stops, taps/flaps and trills.

(3)   Consonantal sounds produced by a complete closure of the oral and nasal cavities
  • Number of closure: once (stops, taps/flaps), more than twice (trills)
  • Duration of closure: long (stops), short (taps/flaps, trills)

At the moment of emission, fricatives and approximants are both produced without complete closure of the oral tract, but they differ in whether or not they are accompanied by noise. A fricative is a sound produced by turbulent airflow caused by a narrowed airway. By contrast, an approximant is a sound created with a wider airway, and hence no turbulent airflow.

Fricatives and approximants can be further distinguished according to whether air escapes through the middle of the oral cavity or down the sides. These are called median fricatives and median approximants, and lateral fricatives and lateral approximants respectively. As fricatives and approximants are usually produced by constriction in the central part of the airway, they are referred to simply as fricatives and approximants. However, the word 'lateral' must be attached to the names of those sounds that are produced by air escaping around the sides of the mouth when the centre is blocked, i.e. lateral fricative, lateral approximant. The differences between stops, fricatives and approximants are shown in Figure 2.10 and the difference between median and lateral articulations is shown in Figure 2.11.

Figure 2.11   Difference between median and lateral articulations

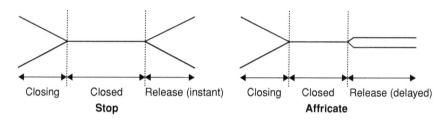

Figure 2.12   Schematic view of the differences between the articulation of stops and affricates

(4)   Types of consonants produced with an open oral cavity
- Sounds produced with(out) noise produced by turbulence: with noise (fricative), without noise (approximant)
- Sounds produced with(out) using the lateral passage: lateral (lateral fricative, lateral approximant), non-lateral (median fricative, median approximant)

Affricates are produced by successive complete and incomplete oral closure. Thus, like stops, affricates are initially articulated with complete oral closure, but, like fricatives, are disrupted by turbulent air created by narrowing of the airway. Figure 2.12 shows the differences in the articulation of stops and affricates. As shown in the diagram, whereas stop sounds are created by closure and sudden release, affricates are different as they are created by closure and delayed release (i.e., friction).

Table 2.3 summarises the manners of articulation examined so far.

2.4.2.3 Phonation (or voice) types

Consonants are classified not only by place and manner of articulation, but also by phonation (or voice) type. The two most general phonation types are voiced and voiceless sounds. As all vowels are voiced sounds, the division between voiced and voiceless is irrelevant to them. However, some consonantal sounds are produced by vibrations in the vocal folds and some are not. Moreover, some consonantal sounds share the same place and manner of articulation and can only be distinguished according to whether or not the vocal folds vibrate. Why is this?

Table 2.3 Summary of manners of articulation

Manner of articulation	Complete oral closure	Nasal closure	Closure only once	Longer closure	Friction noise	Lateral passage
Stop	o	o	o	o	–	–
Nasal	o	X	o	o	–	–
Trill	o	o	X	X	–	–
Tap	o	o	o	X	–	–
Fricative	X	o	–	–	o	X
Lateral fricative	X	o	–	–	o	o
Approximant	X	o	–	–	–	X
Lateral approximant	X	o	–	–	–	o
Affricate	o X	o o	o –	o –	– o	– X

° = yes, X = no, – – = not applicable.

In order to answer this question, we need first to understand some points about vibrations in the vocal folds. Three conditions must be met in order for the vocal folds to vibrate. Of course, if any one of these conditions is not met, vibration will not occur, and additional effort will be required to cause vibrations. The conditions are as follows: first, the proximity between the vocal folds must be as close as possible; second, the vocal folds must be relaxed; third, air pressure from below the vocal folds (subglottal air pressure) must be sufficiently greater than air pressure from above the vocal folds (supraglottal air pressure).

Of these three conditions, the first two are controlled by the vocal folds, and the last condition depends on the airstream mechanism and is related to configuration of the vocal tract. In other words, when the vocal tract is constricted excessively, air is delayed in escaping from the vocal folds and the supraglottal pressure increases. As a result, the subglottal pressure is less likely to be sufficiently greater than the supraglottal pressure. On the other hand, when there is no such constriction and the airstream passage is wide, supraglottal pressure is more likely to be sufficiently lower than subglottal pressure. Because of the aerodynamic factors noted above, vowels and sonorant consonants are by their nature voiced sounds, and obstruents are by their nature voiceless. This helps to explain why some languages have only voiceless obstruents, but no languages have only voiced obstruents.

Apart from vibrations in the vocal folds, phonation types are also distinguished by the presence of aspiration and the amount of tension in the vocal folds. Sounds produced by glottal friction are called aspirates, and sounds

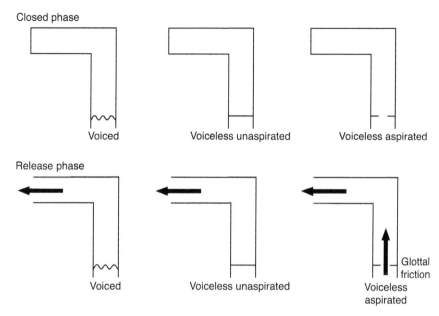

Figure 2.13   Phonation types of stops during closure and release phases

produced with tension in the vocal folds are called tense sounds. Aspiration is created when sounds are articulated with the vocal folds apart, and as air passing through the narrow gap between them becomes turbulent. Tension is created by complete tension of articulators such as the vocal folds. Sounds are classed as 'aspirated' or 'unaspirated' depending on whether or not they are produced with aspiration, and as 'fortis' or 'lenis' depending on whether or not they are accompanied by tension in the vocal folds.

Consonants can be basically divided, on the basis of voicing and aspiration, into the following: voiced aspirated, voiceless aspirated, voiced unaspirated and voiceless unaspirated. Voiced sounds require the vocal folds to be close enough together to allow them to vibrate. Therefore aspirates, which are produced with the vocal folds parted, are naturally voiceless. Furthermore, voiced sounds are unaspirated, for the same reason. This is the reason why voiced unaspirated sounds are rarely found in any language. Figure 2.13 shows the closed and release phases of three kinds of phonological stop sounds: voiced, voiceless unaspirated and voiceless aspirated stops.

Although sounds are generally divided on the basis of voicing and aspiration, the Korean language cannot be subdivided in such a way.[1] This is because although it contains stops and affricates that share the same place and manner of articulation, these are all phonemically voiceless. Therefore, because the three types of stops and affricates in Korean are all voiceless, they cannot be distinguished by the presence of voicing, as shown in (5), Korean bilabial stops categorised by the presence of voicing.

(5)　Korean bilabial stops with(out) voicing

p (ㅂ)　　　　p* (ㅃ)　　　pʰ (ㅍ)
(voiceless)　(voiceless)　(voiceless)

On the other hand, they may be distinguished by the presence of aspiration, as shown in (6). As aspiration only provides two distinct categories of sound, it is insufficient for distinguishing the three types of Korean stops and affricates from one another.

(6)　Korean bilabial stops with(out) aspiration

p (ㅂ)　　　　　　　　p* (ㅃ)　　　　　　　　pʰ (ㅍ)
(voiceless unaspirated)　(voiceless unaspirated)　(voiceless aspirated)

Therefore another class feature is needed here to distinguish between phonation types. This new class feature is tension. Sounds that are tense are called fortis, and sounds that are not are called lenis. Sounds that are tense tend to be strong sounds with lengthy articulation. With aspiration and tense as class features, we are now able to distinguish between the types of stops and affricates in the Korean language. (7) shows bilabial stops categorised according to the three phonation types of stops and affricates.

(7)　Korean bilabial stops with(out) tension

p (ㅂ)　　　　　　　　p* (ㅃ)　　　　　　　　pʰ (ㅍ)
(voiceless unaspirated　(voiceless unaspirated　(voiceless aspirated
lenis)　　　　　　　　fortis)　　　　　　　　fortis)

In Korean, the voiceless unaspirated lenis is referred to as lax, the voiceless unaspirated fortis as tense, and the voiceless aspirated fortis as aspirated. Korean linguists commonly refer to these three kinds of phonation types as lax, tense and aspirated. However, some scholars may use the terms 'plain' or 'lenis' instead of lax, and 'reinforced' or 'fortis' instead of tense. For example, Peter Ladefoged calls the three Korean phonation types unaspirated, fortis and aspirated (www.phonetics.ucla.edu/appendix/languages/korean/korean.html).

DID YOU KNOW...?

Notating Korean tense sounds

Many Korean language scholars denote that a consonant is tense by placing an apostrophe after it, for example, p', t', k'. However, the IPA uses the apostrophe to denote ejectives. This, of course, does not mean that both these usages denote the same thing. During its initiation, a Korean tense sound is an ordinary pulmonic egressive, but ejectives are glottalic egressives during initiation.

Of course, it is misleading that the sign used to denote an ejective should coincide with the sign used to denote Korean tense sounds. In order to get around this problem, Korean tense sounds are often denoted using a capital letter P, T, K or an asterisk p*, t*, k*, although this differs from scholar to scholar. Ladefoged's method of using an asterisk to signify tense sounds and using ^h to signify aspiration has proved useful, and will be adopted in this book.

Although Ladefoged's method will be used to signify tense sounds here, please bear in mind that terminologies other than Ladefoged's have been used. This is because using the terms lax and tense is more appropriate than Ladefoged's unaspirated and fortis for demonstrating the phonological features or differences in the phonation types of the three variants of Korean consonants.

2.4.3 Vowels

Vowels are sounds that are emitted through the oral cavity without any obstruction during articulation. For this reason, vowel sounds cannot be grouped according to the place or manner of obstruction as can consonants. Furthermore, as previously mentioned, the production of vowel sounds fulfils all the conditions necessary for the vocal cords to vibrate, and thus all vowels are voiced sounds. Hence it is not meaningful to distinguish vowels on the basis of phonation type.

Vowels are produced by changes in the form of the pharyngeal and oral cavities, caused by movements of the tongue and lips. Therefore, vowels are categorised according to the elements that comprise such changes. The tongue and lips are the articulators that alter the form of the two cavities. Vowels can be categorised using the following class features: tongue height, tongue backness and roundedness of the lips.

2.4.3.1 Height

Tongue height can be divided into four levels: high, mid-high, mid-low and low. Tongue height is proportional to the openness of the mouth; hence high vowels are referred to as close vowels, and low vowels are referred to as open

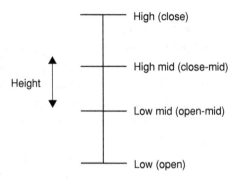

Figure 2.14   Tongue height

vowels. Therefore, high, mid-high, mid-low, and low vowels are also referred to as close, close-mid (half-close), open-mid (half-open), and open vowels respectively (see Figure 2.14). When only three levels of tongue height are specified, the mid-high or close-mid, or sometimes the mid-low or open-mid position does not feature as part of the categorisation. Instead, a mid vowel is added between the high vowel and low vowel, thus leaving us with three levels: high, mid and low.

The reason why tongue height affects vowel quality is because the form of the vocal tract changes according to tongue height. Even if all other conditions remained unchanged, the form of the oral and pharyngeal cavities when the tongue was high would be different from when the tongue was low, and such a difference would cause a difference in resonance frequency, which in turn would produce a vowel sound with a different quality.

2.4.3.2 Backness

Vowels are often distinguished according to tongue backness, the part of the vocal tract that is most constricted during their articulation, as shown in Figure 2.15, using the following designations: front vowel; central vowel; and back vowel. The form of the vocal tract also changes according to which parts of the tongue and palate are used during the articulation of a vowel. If we consider the vocal tract simply as a single 'tube', then stricture at any point along that tube will divide it into two parts, front and back. If the constriction takes place in the front, the front part will be shorter and the back part be longer; if the constriction takes place at the back, that is, at the base of the tongue, the front part will be longer and the back part shorter. Variations in the length of this 'tube' will produce different vowel qualities caused by different resonance frequencies.

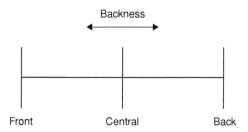

Figure 2.15   Tongue backness

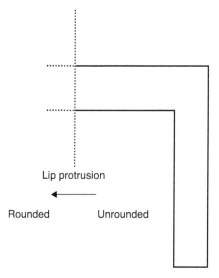

Figure 2.16   Roundedness

2.4.3.3 Roundedness (protrusion of the lips)

The shape of the lips in vowel articulation is either termed 'rounded' or 'unrounded' depending on whether or not the lips protrude outwards. Again, if we consider the vocal tract as simply a single 'tube', protruding the lips will affect the length of the whole tract, as shown in Figure 2.16. When the lips protrude, the vocal tract is longer than normal. This change produces differing vowel qualities caused by a change in the resonance frequency.

2.5 Summary

The production of sounds is divided into three main stages: initiation, phonation and articulation. Initiation involves supply of airflow, phonation involves modulation of that airflow and articulation involves transformation of the airflow. Initiation, the stage in which air is supplied, may be classified according to the initiator of the sound (lungs, vocal folds or velum), and whether the sound is ingressive or egressive. Among six possible combinations, four exist in spoken language: pulmonic egressive, glottalic ingressive (ejectives), glottalic ingressive (implosives) and velaric ingressive (clicks). Phonation, the stage in which air is modulated, may be divided into two main types, voiced and voiceless, depending on whether or not the sound is accompanied by vibration of the vocal folds. However, phonation also encompasses aspirated and unaspirated, and tense and lax sounds. During articulation, the stage at which air is transformed into sound, consonants are produced by obstruction along the centre line of the oral cavity, and vowels are produced without any such obstruction. Consonantal sounds are distinguished according to the place and manner of their articulation and their phonation type, while vowels are distinguished by tongue height, tongue backness and roundedness of the lips.

EXERCISES

1 State whether the following sounds are easy to produce with(out) voicing, and explain why.
   a. Stops
   b. Fricatives
   c. Nasal sounds
   d. Vowels
   e. Aspirates

2 What kind of sounds would the following forms of the vocal tract produce?

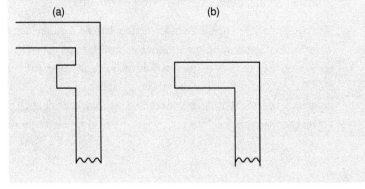

3 Identify the various parts of the vocal organs on the diagram as indicated.

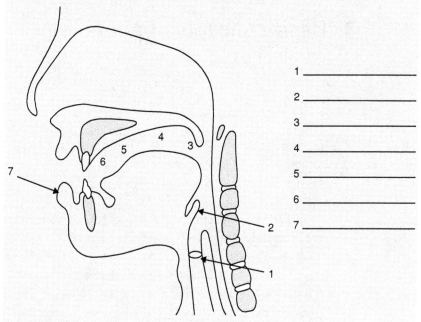

1 _____

2 _____

3 _____

4 _____

5 _____

6 _____

7 _____

4 Explain the similarities and differences of stops and taps/flaps.

5 Explain the differences between the articulation of fricatives and that of affricates.

3 Basic concepts of phonology

In the previous chapter we discussed the general aspects of sound production, and learned that there are three steps in the production of sound: (i) initiation, (ii) phonation and (iii) articulation. Whereas the purpose of the last chapter was to help readers familiarise themselves with the physical basis of sound production, this chapter will focus on the abstract reality of sounds, and will introduce the background to phonology. Once speech sounds are produced by a speaker, they are transferred to a listener as a sequence of acoustic signals. These acoustic signals will then be understood by the listener according to his/her knowledge of the relevant language. Even if the listener has perfect hearing, without knowledge of the language being spoken, he/she will find it difficult to segment sounds or to distinguish between different sounds. Hence, in acquiring the sound system of our mother tongue we learn not only an inventory of sounds, but also how to determine which sound distinctions are significant and which not. Understanding the phonological basis of a sound system is also crucial for second language speakers. Together with Chapter 2, this chapter will provide a useful background for understanding the sounds of Korean.

DID YOU KNOW...?

Do we actually listen with our ears? Why do Korean pigs say '꿀꿀 /kʼulkʼul/' and English pigs 'oink'?

Why is it that Korean people think that pigs say 꿀꿀 /kʼulkʼul/, but English people think that they say 'oink'? Is it because onomatopoeic sounds are different in every language? Do English dogs 'bow-wow', and Korean dogs 멍멍 /mʌŋmʌŋ/, because the two make different noises? Do foreign languages exist for animals as well?

Let's think about the sound of a computer mouse click. Following the same logic, the reason Koreans hear 딸깍 /t* ɑlk*ɑk/ and English people hear 'click' when using a mouse would be that the two make different noises. However, the mouse noise is the same; it is just that Korean and English speakers hear it differently. Almost all onomatopoeic sounds differ from language to language, not just animal sounds or mouse-clicking.

Onomatopoeic words break up a sequence of continuous sounds into discrete segments. 꿀꿀 /k*ulk*ul/ and 'oink' are the result of the conversion of the continuous, indiscrete sound made by a pig into linguistically discrete segments. In other words, although onomatopoeia are expressions of natural sounds, they cannot but be influenced by the sounds of a particular language. Therefore, while the sound a pig makes is neither Korean nor English, the onomatopoeias 꿀꿀 /k*ulk*ul/ and 'oink' are formed from the sounds of those languages.

3.1 Speech sounds, phones and phonemes

Imagine a boy and a girl, saying 안녕하세요 /ɑnnjʌŋhɑsɛjo/ 'hello' to each other. Although they have said the same word, is what they have said to each other truly the same? Are their speech sounds the same? Perhaps not, as they may have different voices and different accents. But, at the same time, it would be difficult to argue that their speech sounds are different. The reason why the above question is difficult to answer is that the term 'speech sounds' can mean two different things. So far we have used the term 'speech sounds' to refer to sound as both a physical and an abstract entity. But, strictly speaking, these terms need to be further classified.

Sound as a physical entity is called a 'phone', whereas sound as an abstract and psychological entity is called a 'phoneme'. Often, a phone is written inside square brackets [ ], whereas a phoneme is written between slashes / /. This is the convention adopted in this book.

The study of phones is called 'phonetics' and the study of phonemes is called 'phonology'. Hence, there is a fundamental difference between the foci of the two disciplines. In phonetics, a phone is understood as a physical, continuous, time-limited and quantifiable unit. It is continuous because it is difficult to distinguish the beginning and end of a sound; it is quantifiable because the various physical properties of a phone can be measured; it is time-limited because the length of a phone can be measured and is significant. On the other hand, in phonology, a phoneme is understood as a psychological, discrete and unquantifiable unit which has no time constraints. It is discrete because it is a psychological entity, and has no time constraints because the physical length of a phoneme is of no significance.

DID YOU KNOW...?

Speech Sounds are like Baron Ashura!

You may have heard of Baron Ashura, a Japanese manga animation character. Baron Ashura is a villain from a Japanese made-for-TV anime film called 'Mazinkaiser Z'. However, for the benefit of those who have not seen 'Mazinkaiser Z' (quite possibly many of you), it may be necessary to explain who the Baron is before you can understand why he is being likened to the speech sound. Baron Ashura works for an evil boss, Dr Hell, who dreams of ruling the world. The Baron is actually an artificial creation, which Dr Hell made by combining mummies from Mycenae. As a result, the Baron is half woman, and half man. The image in the figure is the face of the Baron from the animation. As you can see, his right half is female, and his left half is male.

Is Baron Ashura a woman, or a man? You could quite rightly say, 'the Baron is a man', or 'the Baron is a woman', depending on which part of the face you are looking at. You could also rightly say, 'he seems to be both a man and a woman', if you were looking at the whole face. The speech sound, like Baron Ashura, also has two 'faces'. Depending on which part of its 'face' you are looking at, the greetings 안녕하세요 /annjʌŋhasejo/ spoken by a male and a female student, as discussed in the example from the previous section, can be said to sound both alike and different. Baron Ashura has only one name, but speech sound has a name for each of its faces: phone and phoneme.

3.2 Phonemes and allophones

A phoneme is often defined as the smallest sound unit which can alter the meaning of a word. A single phoneme may have different phonetic forms according to the phonetic environment in which it occurs. The term 'phoneme' describes an abstract reality of the core properties which those different phonetic forms share.[1] Try to pronounce the following English words:

(1)   pin   spin   nip

After that, put your hand in front of your mouth and repeat. Do you notice any difference in the pronunciation of the three words?

Although the three words in (1) all have /p/ as a phoneme, their phonetic realisations are different. At first, when you pronounce the /p/ in 'pin', you should be able to feel your breath strongly on your hand. However, you should not be able to feel any breath when you pronounce the /p/ in 'spin'. When pronouncing the /p/ in 'pin' and 'spin', your lips should open after you put them together. However, when you pronounce the /p/ in 'nip', your lips remain closed.[2] In other words, the /p/ in 'pin' is aspirated, while the other two are unaspirated, and the /p/ in 'nip' is not released after the closure of lips, whereas the other two are. The phonetic realisations of /p/ in the words listed in (1) are shown in (2).

(2)   pin [pʰɪn]   spin [spɪn]   nip [nɪp˺]

A superscript h refers to aspiration; hence '[pʰ]' denotes an aspirated 'p'. A '˺' placed to the top-right of 'p' denotes that the stop sound 'p' is unreleased.

Native speakers of English are often unable to tell the difference between these three sounds because they systematically occur in certain positions, as shown in (3). Though these three sounds share a common abstract and psychological identity, they are still regarded as variants of the same phoneme, known as 'allophones'.

(3)   phoneme

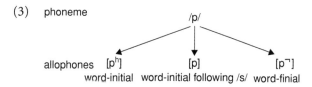

However, if the words listed in (3) are heard by native speakers of Korean, they will invariably say that the /p/ sounds in 'pin' and 'spin' are different. Moreover, they would denote the /p/ in 'pin' and the /p/ in 'spin' in written form with the Hangeul ㅍ and ㅃ respectively.

The reason why speakers of English and Korean perceive the same sounds differently is because the two languages have different inventories of phonemes. In other words, whether or not a consonant is aspirated can alter the meaning of a word in Korean, hence aspiration as a sound feature is significant for Korean speakers; however, this is not the case for English speakers. In order to determine which sound properties are significant in a language, we need to be able to distinguish the phonemes of that language. Guidelines for distinguishing phonemes are discussed below.

3.3 Criteria for phoneme identification

Suppose that we were asked to transcribe a sequence of speech sounds without any knowledge of the language in question and then to distinguish the allophones and phonemes within that sequence.[3] How might we do this? In this section we will discuss criteria that can be used to distinguish phonemes and allophones.

3.3.1 Minimal pairs

Minimal pairs are pairs of words which differ in only one phonological element and have distinct meanings. That is to say, apart from this one differing phonological element, such word pairs are phonetically identical, including having the same number of segments. For instance, 'meal' [mil] and 'kneel' [nil] form a minimal pair, but 'meal' [mil] and 'eel' [il] do not because they have a different number of segments; 'meal' [mil] has three segments and 'eel' [il] has two. On the other hand, 'meal' [mil] and 'mood' [mud] do not form a minimal pair because although they have the same number of segments, they differ in more than one segment.

As shown by the minimal pair 'meal' and 'kneel', the phonetic difference between [m] and [n] has an effect on meaning in English. The same phonetic difference is also meaningful in Korean, as shown by the minimal pair 말 [mɑl] 'horse' and 날 [nɑl] 'day'.

Setting up minimal pairs is the key to determining whether or not a speech sound is a phoneme in any given language.

3.3.2 Complementary distribution, phonetic similarity and free variation

Looking at the distribution of speech sounds also provides insights useful for establishing an inventory of phonemes. If two speech sounds show complementary distribution, that is, they are mutually exclusive (when A appears B does not and vice versa), it is highly unlikely that each sound acts independently as a phoneme.

If A and B do not appear in the same phonetic environments, it will be impossible to find any minimal pairs for them. Therefore, if A and B are variants of the same phoneme, and therefore show complementary distribution, it should be impossible for them to form minimal pairs.

Most speech sounds that show complementary distribution are allophones of a single phoneme. Although each allophone is phonetically different, since they systematically occur in different environments, they are abstracted into one phoneme. The three phonetic realisations of /p/ in English serve as one example of this phenomenon. Each sound shows complementary distribution: [pʰ] systematically appears in word-initial position; [p] in consonant clusters after /s/; and [p̚] in word-final position. Hence each becomes an allophone of the phoneme /p/.

If this is the case, then can we say that all sounds that show complementary distribution are allophones of one phoneme? Let's use the two criteria examined above, i.e. minimal pairs and complementary distribution, to see whether the sounds [h] and [ŋ] in English and Korean are two distinct phonemes, or allophones of one phoneme.

In both Korean and English, [h] can be found in syllable-initial position, as in 하나 [hɑnɑ] and *high* [haɪ], but not in syllable-final positions. Conversely, [ŋ] can be found in syllable-final position, as in 왕 [wɑŋ] and *king* [kɪŋ], but not in syllable-initial position. [h] and [ŋ] therefore show complementary distribution. However, no minimal pairs are available for these speech sounds in either language. In this case, can we say that the two sounds are allophones of one phoneme? The answer is no, because there is no phonetic similarity between the two sounds. Phonetic similarity is the basis for grouping allophones and phonemes. Note that the three phonetic realisations of /p/ share a great deal of phonetic similarity. [pʰ] in word-initial position is a voiceless aspirated bilabial stop, [p] in a consonant cluster after /s/ is a voiceless unaspirated bilabial stop and [p̚] in word-final position is an unreleased voiceless bilabial stop. Phonetically speaking, all these sounds are voiceless bilabial stops. However, [h] and [ŋ] do not share any phonetic similarity. First of all, their respective places of articulation are different; [h] is glottal, whereas [ŋ] is velar. Moreover, they have different phonation types; [h] is voiceless, but [ŋ] is voiced. The manner of articulation differs too, as [h] is fricative, but [ŋ] is nasal.

Another important concept to consider is free variation. Free variation refers to the phenomenon of two (or more) sounds or forms appearing in the same environment, without resulting in a change in meaning. If two sounds are realised in the same environment, but do not result in any change of meaning, then the phonetic difference between the two sounds is not significant for native speakers of the language, and they cannot be regarded as two independent phonemes. For instance, in Korean, no distinction is made between /r/ and /l/. Hence, the English words *rice* and *lice* sound the same to a native speaker of Korean.[4] In English, /r/ and /l/, which have minimal pairs such as *rice* and *lice*, are phonemes. In Korean, whether /r/ is pronounced as [ɹ] or [l] its abstract form is /l/. [ɹ] and [l] in word-initial position can therefore be regarded as free variants in Korean.

Another example can be found in released and unreleased stops in English. As discussed earlier, the /p/ in *nip* is pronounced [p̚], where /p/ is unreleased. However, the /p/ in *nip* could also be pronounced [p], where /p/ is released, without any change in meaning from the usual [p̚]. Hence, sounds which show free variation can be regarded as a single phoneme.

DID YOU KNOW...?

Superman and Clark Kent

We can understand principles of complementary distribution in phonemes and phonetic similarities more easily using the analogy of Superman and Clark Kent, or the analogy of a couple who cannot both attend a social function because they have a newborn baby at home.

First, let us look at the case of Superman and Clark. Clark disappears when Superman arrives on the scene, and when Clark comes back, Superman is gone. I can see that Superman is present only in emergency situations, while Clark is present in all other non-emergency situations. Thus, Superman and Clark show complementary distribution.

Second, let us look at the case of the couple with a newborn baby. I see both of them individually at social gatherings, but I have never seen the two of them together at a gathering. When Mrs K is present, Mr K is not, and vice versa. I can see that Mrs K attends gatherings which involve children and that Mr K attends all other social functions. One can therefore say that their attendance of meetings also shows complementary distribution.

Both Superman and Clark Kent, and Mr and Mrs K show complementary distribution, according to my observations. But why is it that I suspect that Superman and Clark might be the same person, but I think that Mr and Mrs K are two different people?

This is due to similarities in the physical attributes of the first pair. Superman and Clark have the same height, the same build, and even the same facial features. However, Mr and Mrs K do not look alike at all. Mr K is 185 centimetres tall with broad shoulders, but Mrs K is 155 centimetres tall and very skinny. Their facial features are also extremely different. Thus we might suspect that Superman and Clark are two different images of the same person, but we would never think the same for Mr and Mrs K.

It is the same with sounds. Just because sounds show complementary distribution does not mean that they are allophones of the same phoneme. There must be phonetic similarities in addition to complementary distribution in order to conclude that two sounds are allophones. Because the voiceless glottal fricative /h/ and the voiced velar nasal /ŋ/ in both Korean and English show complementary distribution, but share no phonemic similarities, they are two different phonemes rather than allophones of the same phoneme. This corresponds to the analogy of Mr and Mrs K, who are just so physically different that even though they show a complementary distribution of sorts, they must be seen as two distinct individuals. Going off topic slightly, we may find it difficult to understand how Lois Lane doesn't realise that Superman and Clark are the same person. Perhaps, the best way to distinguish who is who would be to ask both of them to turn up at the same place at the same time. Essentially, this is the logic behind the principle of complementary distribution.

3.4 Position of sounds

3.4.1 Sounds within a syllable: onset, nucleus and coda

A syllable, like a phoneme, is an abstract unit. Phonemes do not exist independently, but are grouped together with other phonemes according to a set of principles. The unit which is formed by a sequence of phonemes is termed a prosodic unit. A syllable is the smallest prosodic unit formed by phonemes.[5] A syllable has at least one phoneme and an internal structure with three elements: onset, nucleus and coda, as shown in (4). Of these, the nucleus is the most important part, being absolutely necessary for the formation of a syllable.

(4)

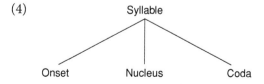

In Korean, only vowels can act as the nucleus of a syllable, whereas consonants can only be the onset or coda of a syllable. Only one consonant is allowed in either the onset or coda of a Korean syllable.

This is not the case in English. As demonstrated by the words *listen* [lɪsn̩] and *shuttle* [ʃʌtl̩], both vowels and consonants can be used as the nucleus of a syllable.[6] Consonant clusters can also appear in the syllable-initial or syllable-final position, as in the case of *strip* [strɪp] and *texts* [teksts]. A maximum of three consonants can appear in syllable-initial position and four in syllable-final position. The concepts of onset, nucleus and coda are universal to all languages, but the ways in which these come together to form syllable structures vary from language to language.[7]

3.4.2 Sounds in word-initial, word-medial and word-final position

The phonetic realisation of sounds is influenced by where they occur in a word. A consonant in word-initial position is always an onset, and a consonant in word-final position is always a coda. However, a consonant in word-medial position can be either an onset or a coda depending on the environment in which it occurs. A word-medial consonant can also appear either after another consonant or between vowels. For instance, [m] and [p] in *sympathy* both occur in word-medial position, but [m] is a coda, whereas [p] is an onset. The [p] in *sympathy* [sɪ́mpəθɪ] comes after another consonant [m], but the same word-medial [p] also appears in the word *topic* [tɔ́pɪk] between vowels.

In Korean, a coda sounds the same regardless of its position in a word. However, onsets are realised differently according to their position in a word. Hence, in comparison to word-medial and word-final onsets, word-medial and word-final codas are rarely discussed in Korean linguistics. In this book, 'word-initial' is taken to mean a word-initial onset and 'word-medial' is taken to mean a word-medial onset. However, 'word-final' refers here only to a word-final coda. With regard to the word-initial onset, we have mostly discussed only those cases where it occurs between vowels – i.e. in 'intervocalic position' – although, phonetically speaking, a word-medial onset occurring after a consonant is not vastly different from a word-medial onset that occurs between vowels.

3.5 Underlying form, surface form and phonological rules

The underlying form (UF) or underlying representation (UR) of a morpheme refers to its phonemic information. This is encoded in the mental lexicon of native speakers. On the other hand, surface form (SF) or surface representation

(SR) of a morpheme refers to its phonetic form – what is actually heard when the morpheme is spoken. In generative phonology, SF is achieved by applying a phonological rule (PR) to UF. This process is called derivation.

(5)

$$\text{UF} \xrightarrow{\quad\quad\text{PR}\quad\quad} \text{SF}$$

To understand the notion of UF, let's consider how the morpheme {꽃k*otɕ^h} 'flower' is realised.

(6) a. 꽃이 핀다. [k*otɕ^{h}i| p^{h}inta]
     b. 꽃만 딴다. [k*onman| t*anta]
     c. 꽃! [k*ot]

{k*otɕ^h} can have three different phonetic realisations; [k*otɕ^h], [k*on], [k*ot]. Though they sound different, they all mean the same thing, 'flower'. In this case, for simplicity's sake, it is better to consider one of these forms as the underlying form, and the others as being derived from that form via different phonological rules. In this way, by positing the concept of underlying form, we achieve simpler and more convincing explanations of phonological phenomena. Useful criteria for defining underlying form include predictability, economy and plausibility.

Let's see how predictability is used in determining underlying forms. First of all, in positing that /k*otɕ^h/ is the underlying form of {k*otɕ^h} we predict that /k*otɕ^h/ becomes [k*ot] at the end of a syllable, but [k*on] in front of a nasal. To validate this underlying form, we need to find examples of /tɕ^h/ becoming [t] in syllable-final position, as in [k*ot], but [n] in front of nasals, as in [k*onman].

On the other hand, if /k*on/ is chosen as the underlying form for {k*otɕ^h}, we must predict that the abstract sound /k*on/ becomes [k*ot] at the end of a syllable, but becomes [k*otɕ^h] between vowels.

Likewise, for /k*ot/ to be the underlying form for {k*otɕ^h}, we have to predict that /t/ in /k*ot/ becomes nasalised in front of a nasal, but becomes [tɕ^h] between vowels. Again, for this prediction to be true, we need to find examples where /t/ becomes [n] in front of a nasal but [tɕ^h] between vowels in Korean.

To evaluate the second and third predictions, consider the word {kɑn} 'liver'. /kɑn/ is realised as [kɑn] in syllable-final position, but as [kɑn] in intervocalic position. This proves that the second prediction is wrong. Consider another example {kot-} 'straight'. The underlying form of [kot], /kot-/ is realised as [kotɑ] or [kotɯni] between vowels. Hence, the third prediction, that /t/ becomes [tɕ^h] in intervocalic position, is also wrong.

Finally, let's evaluate the first prediction. The underlying form of {natɕʰ} 'face' is /natɕʰ/. As in the case of /kˀotɕʰ/, /natɕʰ/ is realised as [nat] at the end of a syllable, and as [nan] in front of a nasal. Therefore, the first prediction, that /tɕʰ/ becomes [t] in syllable-final position, but becomes [n] in front of a nasal, is valid.

Next, let's look at economy. This is related to the number of phonological rules and the efficiency of grammar. Since underlying form is an abstract concept, the underlying form for {kˀotɕʰ} could therefore be either /kˀon/ or even /kˀo&/, which contains the very abstract phoneme /&/. Nevertheless, if we take /kˀon/ as the underlying form, then in order to derive [kˀotɕʰ] from /kˀon/, we need a rule whereby /n/ changes into [tɕʰ] between vowels. However, when we first selected /kˀotɕʰ/ as the underlying form, no such rule was required. In other words, if we select /kˀon/ as the underlying form we require one rule more than we did for /kˀotɕʰ/ as the underlying form, hence it can be said to be less economic. Moreover, this rule does not state that any /n/ appearing between vowels will turn into [tɕʰ], just the /n/ in {kˀotɕʰ}, 'flower'. Therefore, when /kˀon/ is the underlying form of the morpheme {kˀotɕʰ}, there is a further problem, in that the application of this rule is subject to special conditions. Furthermore, if the abstract form /kˀo&/ is set as the underlying form for {kˀotɕʰ} 'flower', even more rules are required to link this underlying form to its various surface representations. Needless to say, this is far less economic.

Finally, let us consider plausibility. The rules by which 'plausibility' is derived or, one might say, the methods by which it is resolved, are natural parts of human language. In other words, plausibility is linked to what is natural in a language. In the example above, if /kˀon/ is taken as the underlying form for {kˀotɕʰ} 'flower', a rule is required whereby /n/ becomes [tɕʰ] between vowels. However, for the nasal /n/, which is a sonorant consonant, to change into a voiceless aspirated obstruent such as [tɕʰ] between voiced sounds is always an unnatural process in phonetics. Therefore, it is difficult to consider this rule plausible.

Underlying forms are determined by taking the above points, among others, into consideration, and in order to avoid excessive abstraction, an underlying form is usually chosen from one of its surface forms. In cases like the one above, where an abstract underlying form must be determined in the absence of a suitable surface form, an alternative rule for deriving the underlying form is necessary.

3.6 Phonological features

So far, we have assumed that a phoneme is the smallest unit of speech sounds. However, a phoneme can be analysed further. In Chapter 2, we discussed how speech sounds can be classified as either consonants or vowels. Consonants can be further classified according to place of articulation, manner of articulation and phonation type. Vowels on the other hand can be classified according to the height of the tongue (high or low), the backness of the tongue (e.g. back or front) and roundedness of the lips (e.g. rounded or unrounded).

With the advent of feature theory in phonology, the phoneme has come to be understood as a set of phonological features whose value can be represented either as positive (+) or negative (−). Phonological features are also called distinctive features. In this section, we will discuss the necessity of postulating phonological features and major class features. Features for consonants and features for vowels will be discussed in Chapters 4 and 5 respectively.

FURTHER STUDY

Chomsky and Halle (1968, abbreviated hereafter as SPE) criticised Jakobson, Fant and Halle (1952, abbreviated hereafter as JFH) for focusing only on acoustic features. They then proposed to look at the articulatory features of sounds. Though at times the feature system has been criticised, it nevertheless forms the basis of discussions and analyses in phonology. We will follow the basic feature systems proposed in SPE, though we will only focus on what is relevant to discussions of Korean phonology. Although the feature system in SPE applies universally to all languages, it contains certain features that are unnecessary in establishing a system for Korean. In addition, we have replaced some of the features from SPE in order to provide a better explanation of Korean phonology. These newly introduced features include [+/−tense] and [+/−aspirated]. In SPE, phonological features are divided into the following four major categories: major class features, cavity features, manner of articulation features and source features. This book, however, does not follow SPE's categorisation method. Instead, phonological features are divided into (i) major class features, (ii) features for consonants and (iii) features for vowels. Features for consonants are further divided into the necessary features for manner of articulation, place of articulation and phonation types.

3.6.1 Why are phonological features needed?

Consider the Korean examples in (7).

(7)   국물 /kuk + mul/ → [kuŋmul]   k → ŋ/ _ m[8]   'the liquid part
                                                                          of a dish'

밥물 /pɑp + mul/ → [pɑmmul]   p → m/ _ m   'water for
                                                                                       boiling rice'
첫머리 /tɕʰʌs + mʌli/ → [tɕʰʌnmʌli] s → m/ _ m   'the beginning'
속내의 /sok + nɛ- + -ɯi/ → [soŋnɛi] k → ŋ/ _ n   'inner wear'
톱날 /tʰop + nɑl/ → [tʰomnɑl]   p → m/ _ n   'a saw tooth'
첫눈 /tɕʰʌs + nun/ → [tɕʰʌnnun]   s → n/ _ n   'a first look'
(+ = morpheme boundary)

In (7), we can see that the phonemes that undergo change, /k/, /p/, and /s/, the resulting phonemes, /ŋ/, /m/, and /n/, and the phonemes /m/ and /n/ that appear in the environment where change occurs all seem to have phonological similarity.[9] Yet, this similarity is difficult to define. Furthermore, it is difficult to define a clear reason as to why this sequence of obstruents is nasalised. However, by considering their phonological features, we discover a clue to this question. In (7), the input consonants are all obstruents and all of them are followed by nasals. Now this problem can be explained by stating that obstruents became nasalised when followed by nasal consonants. By positing features, it is possible not only to explain such phenomena but also to make predictions using relevant data. In the following section, we will discuss major class features.

3.6.2 Major class features

Phonemes can be classified into consonants, vowels and glides according to their phonetic and functional characteristics. Consonants can be further divided into obstruents and sonorants. A feature may be classed as one of two values, either positive (+) or negative (−). Therefore, in order to define the three categories above, that is, consonant, vowel and glide, at least two features are needed. They are [consonantal] and [syllabic]. Definitions of these features are given in (8).

(8)   Major class feature (I)
       a. [+/−consonantal]:
          [+consonantal] sounds produced with radical obstruction of the
          midsaggital region of the vocal tract.
       b. [+/−syllabic]:
          [+syllabic] sounds are able to form a syllable peak, and can therefore
          stand alone as a syllable.

According to the definition given in (8), the airflow of a sound with the value [+consonantal] is obstructed while passing through the central part of the oral cavity, unlike a sound with the value [−consonantal]. Hence, consonants are [+consonantal], whereas vowels and glides are [−consonantal].

Table 3.1 Major class features I

	Consonant	Vowel	Glide
[consonantal]	+	−	−
[syllabic]	−	+	−

In order to have the value [+syllabic], a sound must be able to constitute a syllable on its own. Vowels can have the value [+syllabic], whereas consonants and glides can only have the value [−syllabic]. Based on this observation, we can classify consonants, vowels and glides in the manner shown in Table 3.1.

In order to distinguish obstruents from sonorant consonants, another feature, [sonorant], is required. A sonorant can be defined as shown in (9).

(9)   Major class feature (II)
      a. [+/−sonorant]:
          [+sonorant] sounds are produced with a vocal tract cavity
          configuration in which spontaneous voicing is possible.

In the above definition, "a vocal tract cavity configuration in which spontaneous voicing is possible" refers to a vocal tract configuration which satisfies the aerodynamic conditions necessary for voicing. In other words, sonorants can be understood as a group of sounds which have the necessary conditions for voiced sounds to be produced with spontaneous voicing as the channels that they pass through are enlarged, causing air pressure in the vocal tract to drop. Therefore, all sonorant consonants have the value [+sonorant], as do all glide vowels.

As shown in Table 3.2, phonemes can be classified into the major classes: obstruent, sonorant, consonant, vowel and glide, according to the three major class features [consonant], [syllabic] and [sonorant]. In this way it is possible to clarify the similarities and differences between the major categories of sounds.

Table 3.2 Major class features II

	Consonant		Vowel	Glide
	Obstruent	Sonorant consonant		
[consonantal]	+	+	−	−
[syllabic]	−	−	+	−
[sonorant]	−	+	+	+

3.7 Summary

In this chapter, we have discussed how to identify the most basic units of sounds (Sections 3.1–3.3) and their structural properties (Section 3.4). The same segment sequences can be interpreted differently by speakers of different languages due to the phonological differences between languages. We have also discussed the basics of major phonological concepts. First, in 3.1 we saw that there are two types of speech sounds, namely phones and phonemes. Whereas phonemes represent the psychological aspects of a sound, phones represent sounds as physical entities. Not all phones correspond to phonemes, and the inventory of phonemes differs in each language. For instance, in English, the phoneme /p/ is realised as [pʰ], [p] or [p̚] according to the phonetic environment in which it appears. Though each phonetic realisation is different, English native speakers are unable to distinguish between them. Hence, these sounds are allophones of one phoneme, /p/. In 3.3, we discussed criteria for identifying phonemes. Setting up minimal pairs, with two words whose meaning differs through only one sound in the same position in each word being different, plays a key role in establishing the phoneme inventory of a language. If two sounds show complementary distribution, then no minimal pairs are available for them; hence they cannot be allophones of one phoneme. However, phonetic similarity between sounds is essential in identifying the relationships between phoneme and allophones. Two (or more) sounds can appear in the same environment without resulting in a change in meaning, as in the case of [ɹ] and [l] in Korean. They are regarded as free variants of the phoneme /l/. For a better explanation of phonological processes, however, we need to think about the sound properties which constitute each phoneme. These are called phonological features or distinctive features. We discussed major class features in 3.6. Features for consonants and vowels are discussed in Chapters 4 and 5 respectively.

EXERCISES

1   Please state whether or not the following pairs of words form minimal pairs in English and explain why.
a. **p**in, s**p**in
b. **l**ice, **r**ice
c. **m**ince, **n**ice
d. **n**ice, **m**ice

2   Explain the difference between a phone and a phoneme with examples.

3   Can length or accent also be regarded as phonemes? Explain why or why not.
4   Explain the benefits of using features in phonological explanation. Provide examples.
5   What is a "phonological (distinctive) feature"?
6   Define the features [sonorant] and [syllabic] with examples.

4 Consonants

In Chapters 2 and 3, general aspects of sound systems were discussed. In Chapter 4, consonants in Korean will be discussed, and in particular, what consonants exist in Korean and what their phonetic and phonological characteristics are. With this aim, in 4.1, the inventory of Korean consonants will be discussed; in 4.2, the phonetic and phonological characteristics of obstruents; and in 4.3, the phonetic and phonological characteristics of sonorants. In 4.4, we will discuss phonological features needed to discuss consonants in Korean, and in 4.5 we conclude.

4.1 Consonant chart

Table 4.1 shows the consonants of Korean classified according to the place (across the top of the table) and manner (down the left side of the table) of their articulation. The nineteen consonants of Korean can be classified as either (i) bilabial, (ii) alveolar, (iii) alveolo-palatal, (iv) velar or (v) glottal according to the place of their articulation. They can also be classified as (i) stop, (ii) fricative, (iii) affricate, (iv) nasal or (v) liquid (lateral approximant) according to the manner of their articulation.[1] Furthermore, each consonant class has two or three sub-classifications. For instance, stop sounds have lax, tense or aspirated sounds, and fricative sounds can be classified as either lax or tense.

DID YOU KNOW...?

Dialectal differences in the list of consonants

There are few differences in the inventory of consonants between regional dialects. In certain dialects the phonetic realisation of consonants is different, but the actual list of consonants is usually the same as that of Standard Korean. However, in certain regional dialects of *Gyeongsang* 경상 province, no contrast between /s/:/sˀ/ ㅅ:ㅆ is observed. Thus, to the speakers of these regional dialects, there is no audible difference between /sal/ 살 'flesh' and /sˀal/ 쌀 'rice'.

Table 4.1 Consonants

	Bilabial	Alveolar	Alveolo-palatal	Velar	Glottal
Stop (plosive)					
Lax	p (ㅂ)	t (ㄷ)		k (ㄱ)	
Tense	pˀ (ㅃ)	tˀ (ㄸ)		kˀ (ㄲ)	
Aspirated	pʰ (ㅍ)	tʰ (ㅌ)		kʰ (ㅋ)	
Fricative					
Lax		s (ㅅ)			h (ㅎ)
Tense		sˀ (ㅆ)			
Affricate					
Lax			tɕ (ㅈ)		
Tense			tɕˀ (ㅉ)		
Aspirated			tɕʰ (ㅊ)		
Nasal	m (ㅁ)	n (ㄴ)		ŋ (ㅇ)	
Liquid (lateral approximant)		l (ㄹ)			

4.2 Obstruents

An obstruent is a sound made as airflow is obstructed by narrowing of the vocal tract. Korean has a rich inventory of these sounds; fifteen of its nineteen consonants are obstruents. The main characteristic of Korean obstruents is that they are, without exception, voiceless. The phonetic and phonological characteristics of Korean obstruents will be discussed individually below.

4.2.1 Stops

As shown in Table 4.2, Korean stop consonants, that is, bilabial, alveolar and velar sounds, all have lax, tense and aspirated types. First of all, let's discuss the

Table 4.2 Stops

	Bilabial	Alveolar	Alveolo-palatal	Velar	Glottal
Lax	p (ㅂ)	t (ㄷ)		k (ㄱ)	
Tense	p* (ㅃ)	t*(ㄸ)		k* (ㄲ)	
Aspirated	pʰ (ㅍ)	tʰ (ㅌ)		kʰ (ㅋ)	

places of articulation for Korean stop sounds. Bilabial sounds are produced using the lips. Alveolar sounds are pronounced with the tip of the tongue (or the tip and the blade) touching the teeth and alveolar ridge. Velar sounds are pronounced with the body of the tongue touching the velum. As the tongue is not involved in their articulation, bilabial sounds are not influenced by surrounding vowels. However, alveolar and, to a greater extent, velar sounds are affected by surrounding vowels.

Let's look at some verifiable minimal sets for Korean stop sounds.

(1)   Minimal sets

/p/ : /p*/ : /pʰ/   불 /pul/ 'fire' : 뿔 /p*ul/ 'horn' : 풀/pʰul/ 'grass'
반 /pɑn/ 'class' : 빤 /p*ɑn/ 'to suck (adnominal)' : 판 /pʰɑn/ 'board'
배 /pɛ/ 'ship' : 빼 /p*ɛ/ 'to extract (imperative)' : 패 /pʰɛ/ 'tag'
비다 /pitɑ/ 'be empty' : 삐다 /p*itɑ/ 'to sprain' : 피다 /pʰitɑ/ 'to bloom'

/t/ : /t*/ : /tʰ/   달 /tɑl/ 'moon' : 딸 /t*ɑl/ 'daughter' : 탈 /tʰɑl/ 'mask'
다 /tɑ/ 'all' : 따 /t*ɑ/ 'to pick (imperative)' : 타 /tʰɑ/ 'to ride (imperative)'
단 /tɑn/ 'column' : 딴 /t*ɑn/ 'to pick (adnominal)' : 탄 /tʰɑn/ 'to ride (adnominal)'
대 /tɛ/ 'bamboo' : 때 /t*ɛ/ 'dirt' : 태 /tʰɛ/ 'crack'
덜다 /tʌltɑ/ 'deduct' : 떨다 /t*ʌltɑ/ 'tremble' : 털다 /tʰʌltɑ/ 'shake off'

/k/ : /k*/ : /kʰ/   간 /kɑn/ 'liver' : 깐 /k*ɑn/ 'estimation' : 칸 /kʰɑn/ 'blank'
기 /ki/ 'energy' : 끼 /k*i/ 'talent' : 키 /kʰi/ 'one's height'
개다 /kɛtɑ/ 'to fold' : 깨다 /k*ɛtɑ/ 'to break' : 캐다 /kʰɛtɑ/ 'to dig'

In the case of velar consonants, where the body of the tongue is involved in articulation, the point at which airflow is blocked varies according to the following

Table 4.3 Voiceless alveolar stops in Korean and English

Korean		English	
/tʰɑ/ 타	'to ride (imperative)'	/tɑ/	'ta'
/tʰi/ 티	'a speck'	/ti/	'tea'

vowel. For instance, when /kɑ/ and /ki/ are pronounced by a native speaker, the /k/ in /ki/, which is followed by a front vowel, is pronounced more at the front than the /k/ in /kɑ/, which is followed by a back vowel. Phonetically speaking, the /k/ in /ki/ is actually closer to a palatal sound than to a velar sound. Velar sounds that appear in onset position are more influenced by the vowel that follows.

Alveolar sounds in Korean are articulated with the blade of the tongue (or the tip and the blade) touching the teeth and alveolar ridge, as airflow is blocked and then immediately released. Alveolar sounds in Korean are slightly different from English alveolar sounds, in that English alveolars are articulated further back than in Korean; Korean alveolar sounds are articulated with the blade or the tip of the tongue touching the teeth and alveolar ridge, whereas with English alveolars, the tongue only touches the alveolar ridge. For this reason, it sounds awkward when the Korean sounds /tʰɑ/ 타 and /tʰi/ 티 are pronounced like the English 'ta' and 'tea', or conversely if the English words *ta* and *tea* are pronounced as /tʰɑ/ 타 and /tʰi/ 티. (See Table 4.3).

Let's look at the three classifications of Korean stop sounds. In Chapter 2, we defined the three pronunciation forms for Korean stop consonants as lax, tense and aspirated, and characterised them as possessing the phonetic features voiceless unaspirated lenis, voiceless unaspirated fortis and voiceless aspirated fortis respectively. Lax sounds can appear in both onset and coda positions, and when realised as onsets they can appear either in word-initial or word-medial position. By contrast, tense and aspirated sounds may only appear in onset position, and cannot be realised in coda position.[2] Nevertheless, all of these sounds may be realised as word-initial and word-medial onsets.

DID YOU KNOW...?

Which Korean food do you like? 칼비 (rib) or 갈국수 (noodle)?

Harry is an Englishman who came to Korea to study the Korean language. He often met up with his Korean friend to practise speaking Korean, and one day, they talked about their favourite Korean dishes. When the Korean friend asked him what he liked best, Harry immediately replied "칼비" [kʰɑlpi]. Then, the Korean friend taught him that he had to pronounce it "갈비" [kɑlpi], not "칼비" [kʰɑlpi]. Soon after, the Englishman went to a Korean restaurant with his Korean friend. At the restaurant, his friend asked him what he would like to eat. This time, the Englishman replied very confidently, "갈국수" [kɑlkuksˀu]. Unfortunately for him, this time it should have been /kʰ/, not /k/.

4.2.1.1 Word-initial stops

Figure 4.1 shows a wide-band spectrogram and waveform of a native Korean speaker, of the standard Seoul dialect, a woman in her forties,[3] saying the syllables /tɑ/, /tˀɑ/ and /tʰɑ/. The spectrogram displays a two-dimensional plane from a three-dimensional image of changes in the intensity and frequency of the sound signal as time passes. The horizontal axis denotes time and the vertical axis denotes frequency. Intensity is represented using grey level mapping: when intensity is high in relation to time and frequency, the spectrogram will be darker, and when intensity is low in relation to time and frequency, it will be fainter. The waveform is a two-dimensional image which displays changes in the intensity of a sound signal over time. Time is displayed along the horizontal axis, and intensity is displayed along the vertical axis.

The letters (a), (b) and (c) denote /tɑ/, /tˀɑ/ and /tʰɑ/ respectively,[4] and the arrow shows the point of release for each. As can be seen in Figure 4.1, all three types of stop sound are released after closure. The momentary expulsion of air due to the release of the stop sound can be observed on the spectrogram as a vertical spike in the position indicated by the arrow. The white space which appears on the spectrogram before the vertical spike is a feature that appears when the level of sound energy is close to zero.

Let's look more closely at the three kinds of Korean stop consonant on the spectrogram and waveform. First of all, let's look at closure, that is, the point before the vertical spike created by the release of air. It can be seen that the three kinds of Korean stop consonant are all voiceless, that is, the stop sound is not accompanied by any vibration. If they were voiced sounds, then a periodic wave with small oscillations during the period of closure would be visible on the waveform, and on the spectrogram, an area of low frequency would be visible in the form of bars at regular intervals, known as voice bars, in the lower part of the diagram.

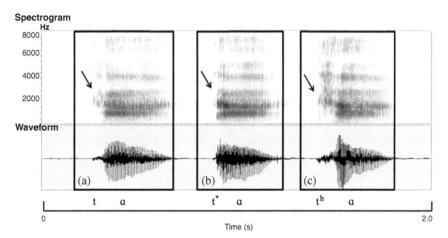

Figure 4.1   Spectrogram and waveform of lax, tense and aspirated alveolar stops in word-initial
position

Now let us turn our attention to the sound characteristics displayed by the three kinds of stop sounds after their release. The three show wide variance in phonation type after the vertical spike (which is common to all three). First of all, in the lax and aspirated sounds, a blurred mark can be seen on the right of the picture just after the vertical spike appears on the spectrogram, and an aperiodic wave can be seen on the waveform;[5] this is not the case for tense sounds, for which it would be difficult to discern either a blurred mark on the spectrogram or an aperiodic wave on the waveform.[6]

Similar features can be observed on the spectrograms and waveforms of the three kinds of stop sounds, and show that all stop sounds are accompanied by a degree of friction in the glottis after their release. That is to say, they are produced with a degree of aspiration. Based on this, we can see that although tense sounds in Korean are produced with almost no aspiration, lax and aspirated sounds in word-initial position are articulated with aspiration. It can also be seen that compared to lax sounds, aspirated sounds have a far greater degree of aspiration.

Lax sounds in Korean have been defined above as lenis voiceless unaspirated sounds. However, having observed their real phonetic forms, it can be seen that lax sounds are aspirated, not unaspirated in word-initial position. If this is the case, then why must Korean lax sounds be viewed as unaspirated sounds phonologically? In order to answer this question we must take a more comprehensive view of the characteristics of Korean stop sounds, including those realised not only in word-initial position but in other environments too.

TRY YOURSELF!

Ask a Korean friend to make the following sounds in sequence – /pɑ/, /p*ɑ/, /pʰɑ/ – and place your hand in front of your friend's mouth. Then notice the difference in the amount of airflow that can be felt on your palm. When she/he makes the /pɑ/ sound, which is lax, you should feel a slight flow of air on your palm, but when she/he makes the /p*ɑ/ sound, which is tense, you should hardly feel any airflow. When she/he makes the aspirated /pʰɑ/ sound, however, you should feel a strong current on your palm. The amount of airflow that can be felt on your palm therefore correlates to the degree of aspiration; whether it is lax, tense or aspirated.

If your native language is English, try to pronounce *pie* and *bye* with your palm in front of your mouth. When you make the *pie* sound, you ought to feel a strong rush of air as with aspirated sounds in Korean, but when you make the *bye* sound, you should feel almost nothing, as with tensed sounds in Korean.

DID YOU KNOW...?

Distinguishing the difference between three types of stops

As the story of 칼비 and 갈국수 shows, the three-way contrast in word-initial consonants is particularly difficult for learners of Korean to distinguish. Stop sounds in Korean in word-initial position are generally divided into two categories; those with aspiration, i.e. lax and aspirated stops, and those without aspiration, i.e. tense stops. In English, stops can be phonologically divided into voiced and voiceless stops. However, all stops are voiceless in word-initial position. The only difference observed among stops in word-initial position is therefore the presence/absence of aspiration, as in Korean. Hence, Korean and English native speakers can both easily distinguish unaspirated stops in word-initial position. Often, Koreans regard them as tense consonants, while English speakers regard them as voiced consonants.

However, it is not easy for English speakers to distinguish lax and aspirated stops in Korean, since both sounds are aspirated. The only difference between them lies in the degree of aspiration. Lax stops are aspirated but the degree of aspiration is very weak compared to that of aspirated stops. More importantly, the pitch of the vowel that follows a lax stop is very different to the pitch of the vowel that follows an aspirated stop. When you listen carefully to the pronunciation of [pʰɑ] and [pɑ] by Korean speakers, you will be able to tell that the [ɑ] that follows the aspirated stop is much higher in pitch than the [ɑ] that follows the lax stop. The diagram below shows the pitch difference in the pronunciations of [tɑlilɑsʌ] 'because (it is) a moon', where the first consonant is a lax stop (a) and [tʰɑlilɑsʌ] 'because (it is) a mask', where the first consonant is an aspirated stop (b).

a.   b.

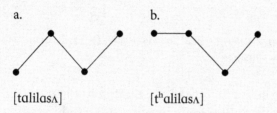

[tɑlilɑsʌ]   [tʰɑlilɑsʌ]

Pitch patterns in word-initial position are important in understanding the prosody of Korean. This will be discussed further in 7.5.

4.2.1.2 Word-medial (intervocalic) stops

Figure 4.2 shows the spectrogram and waveform of three alveolar stops pronounced between two /ɑ/ vowels. (a), (b) and (c) represent [ɑtɑ],[7] [ɑt*ɑ] and [ɑtʰɑ] respectively. One directional arrow indicates the time of the release and the other, double-ended arrow indicates the closure period.[8] All three alveolar stops show the release, but before and after the point of release they differ significantly.

Most significantly, the duration of closure differs; the tense stop displays the longest closure duration followed by the aspirated stop, while the lax stop has the shortest closure duration.[9]

The second noticeable difference is seen in the presence, or absence, of aspiration after the release. After the release of lax and tense sounds, the vocal folds begin to vibrate immediately for the following vowel, as can be observed.

However, in aspirated sounds, the point when the vocal folds begin to vibrate is relatively late due to the wide glottal opening. This results in longer VOT and strong glottal friction before the beginning of vibration of the vocal folds for the following vowel. In other words, in word-medial position, lax and

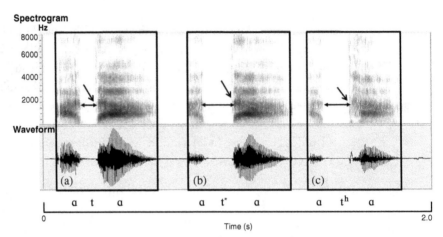

Figure 4.2   Spectrogram and waveform of lax, tense and aspirated alveolar stops in word-medial (intervocalic) position

tense sounds are articulated as unaspirated sounds, whereas only aspirated sounds are articulated with aspiration. It should be noted that the presence of aspiration in the lax sound here is different from when it appears as a word-initial onset. Lax sounds in word-initial position are realised phonetically as aspirates, whereas they are realised as unaspirated sounds in word-medial position. However, tense sounds and aspirates are pronounced the same in both word-initial and word-medial position, as unaspirated and aspirated sounds respectively.[10]

The third difference observed is whether or not there is any vibration of the vocal cords during the closure period. Figure 4.3, which is a magnification of (a) in Figure 4.2, shows that the vocal folds vibrate when a lax stop appears between vowels. The period of voicing for the lax sound can be seen on the spectrogram as a voice bar and on the waveform as a periodic wave, which occurs for the period of closure marked by a double-headed arrow. In other words, this means that unlike tense or aspirated stops, lax stops are voiced between vowels.

In addition, a difference can be seen in the length of the vowel that precedes the closure period, which varies according to the phonation type of the stop sound. As shown in Figure 4.2, the vowel preceding the lax stop is much longer than the vowels that precede the tense or aspirated stops.[11]

However, the most important thing to note is that lax stops in word-medial position are realised as voiced unaspirated sounds, which is different from word-initial position.[12] Unlike lax stops, tense and aspirated stops do not change from word-initial position, and are realised as voiceless unaspirated sounds and voiceless aspirated sounds respectively.

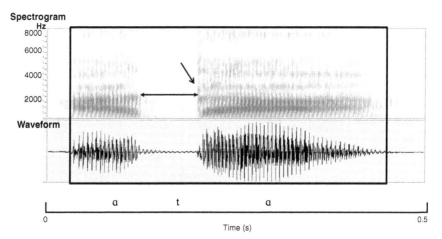

Figure 4.3   Spectrogram and waveform of the lax alveolar stop in word-medial (intervocalic) position

4.2.1.3 Word-final stops

Finally, we will discuss the characteristics of word-final stops. Because stop consonants in word-final position should not be released after closure, only lax stops can occur in word-final position. Figure 4.4 shows the spectrogram and waveform of a word-final lax stop. (a) indicates the duration of the vowel sound and (b) indicates the duration of the word-final lax stop.[13] No vertical spike indicates that the air has not been released after the closure. Hence, these sounds are realised as unreleased consonants.

4.2.1.4 Allophones and phonological identity of lax stops

So far, we have discussed how, unlike tense or aspirated stops, lax stops vary according to where they occur. That is, in word-initial position lax stops are aspirated, and in the word-medial position they are released as voiced un-aspirated sounds. Finally, in word-final position, they are released as voiceless unreleased stops. To demonstrate the various allophones of lax stops, we have provided a spectrogram and waveform of the word /kɑkɑk/.[14] In Figure 4.5, (a) indicates the word-initial /k/; (b) indicates the word-medial /k/ and (c) indicates the word-final /k/. The slanted arrow again indicates the point of release after closure.

Figure 4.5 clearly shows how the same phoneme /k/ can be realised differently according to the phonetic environment in which it occurs. Aspiration due to glottal friction can be seen in word-initial /k/ shown at (a). Conversely, word-medial, intervocalic /k/ at (b) has no such friction, but does show

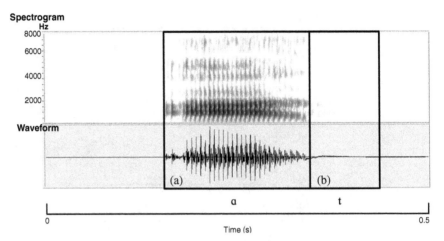

Figure 4.4   Spectrogram and waveform of the lax alveolar stop in word-final position

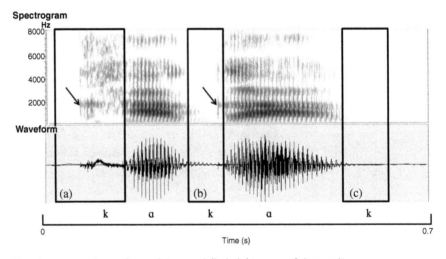

Figure 4.5   Spectrogram and waveform of the word /kɑkɑk/ 'corner of the road'

vibration of the vocal folds. In other words, it is a voiced unaspirated sound. In word-final position at (c), /k/ is realised as a voiceless unreleased sound. One question remains: if a lax stop is realised differently according to where it occurs, then why is the lax stop regarded phonologically as a voiceless unaspirated sound? To answer this question, we need to observe how native Korean speakers interpret and use lax stops phonologically.

First, let's see why native speakers of Korean regard lax stops not as aspirated, but as unaspirated sounds. In Korean, when a lax stop is preceded or followed by a glottal /h/ at a morphological boundary, it becomes aspirated through the process of phonological contraction. Examples are given in (2).

(2)   a. 놓고 /noh + ko/ → [nokʰo] 'to put (connective)'
     b. 법학 /pʌp + hak/ → [pʌpʰak] 'law'
       (+ = morpheme boundary)

The aspiration processes shown in (2) demonstrate that native speakers of Korean regard lax stops as unaspirated sounds. If we assumed that lax stops in Korean were aspirated sounds, then the examples in (2) would appear to show an aspirated sound becoming another aspirated sound when it meets a glottal /h/, which is itself an aspirated sound.[15] It is difficult to find a good reason to explain why an aspirated sound should change into another aspirated sound in this case, hence why lax stops are regarded as unaspirated sounds.

Furthermore, native speakers of Korean perceive lax stops as being voiceless. The phonological behaviour of lax stops is very different from that of voiced consonants such as nasals or liquids. If lax stops were voiced consonants, they would show some similarity with other voiced consonants. However there are no phonological processes in Korean that can be applied exclusively to voiced consonants and lax stops.

The process of Neutralisation, which will be discussed in 8.1.1, also supports the view that lax stops are voiceless. Due to Neutralisation, aspirated or tense consonants cannot appear in syllable-final position in Korean. Instead, those consonants are replaced with their lax counterparts as shown in (3).

(3)   a. 밖 /pak*/ → [pak] 'outside'
      c.f. /pak* + i/ → [pa.k*i] 'outside (subjective marker)'
     b. 부엌 /puʌkʰ/ → [pu.ʌk] 'kitchen'
      c.f. /puʌkʰ + i/ → [pu.ʌ.kʰi] 'kitchen (subjective marker)'
     c. 박 /pak/ → [pak] 'gourd'
      c.f. 박이 /pak + i/ → [pa.ki] 'gourd (subjective marker)'
      (. = syllable boundary)

In other words, the distinction between tense and aspirated sounds in syllable-final position is neutralised. If lax stops were voiced, this rule would suggest that voiceless unaspirated sounds and voiceless aspirated sounds both become voiced in syllable-final position. However, cross-linguistically, syllable-final position tends to be where voiced sounds become voiceless rather than the other way round. To say that Korean is an exception to this rule would not be a satisfactory explanation.

In terms of distribution, lax sounds are much more prevalent than tense or aspirated ones. As will be discussed further in Chapter 6, out of lax, aspirated and tensed consonants, lax sounds are used the most, constituting 68.6 per cent and 71.9 per cent of dictionary usage and spontaneous speech respectively.

The final thing to add is that Korean lax stops are not always realised as voiced sounds in word-medial position. In the above examples, we saw how Korean lax stops are realised as voiced sounds in intervocalic position; this is the case in all the examples in Figure 4.3 and Figure 4.5. However, by analysing the data of the actual utterances, it is possible to confirm whether or not lax stops appearing between two voiced sounds are necessarily realised as voiced sounds themselves. It has been observed that the rate at which voiced sounds are realised varies massively according to the speaker and the speed of the utterance (S.-A. Jun, 1995; J.-Y. Shin, 2000b). After J.-Y. Shin (2000b) observed the realisation angle of lax stops in various environments, she noted that the most regularly observed phenomenon in the phonetic realisation of lax sounds in Korean was not lax sounds in word-medial position realised as voiced sounds, but lax sounds realised with aspiration in word-initial position. Therefore, if sounds realised with aspiration in word-initial position are referred to as 'weak-aspirated' sounds, then the standard realisation of word-initial lax sounds may be termed 'weak aspiration'. The results of this research and the conclusion it has produced means many contemporary Korean phonologists find it difficult to view the process by which Korean lax sounds become word-medial voiced sounds as a phonological or allophonic process. Hence it is more appropriate to refer to the voicing of lax sounds in word-medial position as a phonetic implementation which varies according to the speaker, the speed of utterance and phonetic environment.

For the reasons stated above, it is better to regard lax consonants in Korean as voiceless. Neutralisation in syllable-final position also supports the view that lax sounds are the most unmarked. Frequency data also confirm this observation.

4.2.1.5 Major allophones of stops

Table 4.4 summarises the discussion of the major allophones of Korean stops thus far. In the table, the '˥' sign which appears above and the '˳' sign which appears above or below them are the signs for unreleased and unvoiced realisations of the phonetic sign respectively in IPA.

4.2.2 Fricatives

As can be seen in Table 4.5, the index of Korean fricatives is very simple indeed, especially considering the nine stops which exist in Korean. Fricatives in Korean are articulated in only two places: glottal and alveolar positions.[16] However, fricatives articulated at the alveolar ridge can be subdivided into lax or tense fricatives, whereas glottal fricatives have no such distinction.

Table 4.4 Major allophones of stops

Category	Phoneme	Major allophone	Environment
Lax	p	p	Word-initial
		b/b̥	Word-medial onset
		pˀ	Coda
	t	t	Word-initial
		d/d̥	Word-medial onset
		tˀ	Coda
	k	k	Word-initial
		g/g̊	Word-medial onset
		kˀ	Coda
Tense	p* t* k*	p* t* k*	Onset
Aspirated	pʰ tʰ kʰ	pʰ tʰ kʰ	Onset

Let's look at some minimal sets that can be used to determine the inventory of fricatives in Korean.

(4)   Minimal sets

/s/ : /s*/ : /h/   살 /sal/ 'flesh' : 쌀 /s*al/ 'rice': 할 /hal/ 'percentage'
설다 /sʌlta/ 'to be unfamiliar' : 썰다 /s*ʌlta/ 'to cut' :
헐다 /hʌlta/ 'to get old'
사리 /sali/ 'reason' : 싸리 /s*ali/ 'bush clover' : 하리
/hali/ 'low official'
소다 /sota/ 'soda' : 쏘다 /s*ota/ 'to shoot' : 호다 /hota
/ 'to sew together'
사다 /sata/ 'to buy' : 싸다 /s*ata/ 'to be cheap' : 하다
/hata / 'to do'
삭 /sak/ 'month' : 싹 /s*ak/ 'sprout' : 학 /hak/ 'crane'

Table 4.5 Fricatives

	Bilabial	Alveolar	Alveolo-palatal	Velar	Glottal
Lax		s (ㅅ)			h (ㅎ)
Tense		s* (ㅆ)			

삼 /sɑm/ 'flax' : 쌈 /sˀɑm/ 'rice wrapped leaves' : 함 /hɑm/ 'box'

삼지 /sɑmtɕi/ 'three fingers' : 쌈지 /sˀɑmtɕi/ tobacco pouch : 함지 /hɑmtɕi/ 'wooden bowl'

상 /sɑŋ/ 'table' : 쌍 /sˀɑŋ/ 'pair' : 항 /hɑŋ/ 'item'

생 /sɛŋ/ 'life' : 쌩 /sˀɛŋ/ 'ping' : 행 /hɛŋ/ 'line'

Let's examine the places of articulation for Korean fricatives. Alveolar fricatives are articulated in the narrow passageway between the tongue blade, and the back of the upper teeth and alveolar ridge. Glottal fricatives are articulated in the narrow passageway between the vocal folds. Korean alveolar fricatives are articulated in the same place as Korean alveolar stops. A good way to identify the location of a Korean alveolar fricative is to articulate it without enunciating the following vowel, and immediately afterwards to breathe in. When breathing in, the place that feels coolest is the place that was most constricted, and it was in that place that the sound was articulated. After the articulation of a Korean alveolar fricative, the back part of the upper teeth and the front part of the alveolar ridge will feel coolest.

However, an alveolar fricative's place of articulation differs when followed by the vowels /i/ or /j/ or the diphthong /wi/. Under the influence of these following vowels, the alveolar fricative shifts its place of articulation, becoming an alveolo-palatal fricative [ɕ, ɕˀ]. Korean alveolo-palatal fricatives are articulated slightly further back in the mouth than the English palato-alveolar fricatives /ʃ/ or /ʒ/, and the lips protrude slightly at the time of articulation. Protrusion of the lips is also characteristic during the articulation of palato-alveolar fricatives in English. Lip protrusion aside, let's take a closer look at the differences between Korean alveolo-palatal fricatives, that is, the allophonic variations of alveolar fricatives, and English palato-alveolar fricatives.

The biggest difference between the two can be seen for oneself, using the tip of the tongue. English palato-alveolar fricatives are usually articulated with the edge of the tongue touching only the lower gums. By contrast, in Korean, alveolo-palatal fricatives are articulated with the tip of the tongue touching the lower teeth as well as lower gums.

If we pronounce the two sounds without following vowels and then inhale, we can find the place of articulation more precisely. Pronounce Korean /s/ before /ɯ/, and English /ʃ/ and Korean /s/ before /i/, without following vowels, and then inhale each time. You will feel that the place where you can feel cool air shifts further backwards.

Finally, in English, the place of articulation of alveolar fricatives does not change under the influence of the vowel that follows them, whereas this type of allophonic variation is observed in Korean and Japanese. It is for this reason that Korean and Japanese native speakers often mispronounce the English word 'see', as they apply the allophonic rules of their native language to the pronunciation of the English word.

Glottal fricatives are articulated in the glottis; indeed, there is no other place within the oral cavity where they could be pronounced. The glottal fricative's place of articulation within the oral cavity is determined by the following vowel. To confirm this, try saying /hɑ/ and /hi/. At what point does the tongue assume the position necessary for pronouncing /ɑ/ and /i/? You will notice that when pronouncing the series /hɑ/ /hi/, the tongue is already in the correct position to pronounce the following vowel as you pronounce /h/. The same is the case in English.

Unlike other obstruents, alveolar fricatives do not possess three subdivisions; they can only be further classified as lax or tense. The lack of an aspirated variant is an important feature of fricatives. What follows is an examination of fricatives similar to our earlier examination of stop sounds, bearing in mind that fricatives only have two subclassifications.

In the syllable structure of Korean, fricatives can only exist at the onset of a syllable, as there is a general principle in Korean that all syllable-final sounds should not be released after central closure. Korean fricatives therefore can only be observed in word-initial and word-medial positions.

4.2.2.1 Word-initial fricatives

Figure 4.6 shows the realisation of the Korean word-initial alveolar fricatives [s. s*] and also the glottal fricative [h] as represented on a spectrogram. In the picture, (a), (b) and (c) indicate the lax alveolar fricative, tense alveolar fricative and glottal fricative respectively. The difference in energy distribution frequency between alveolar and glottal fricatives is clearly visible. On the one hand, it is possible to observe energy distribution in the high frequency area of the alveolar fricative,[17] and on the other hand, strong energy can be seen in the formant of the vowel following the glottal fricative.[18]

Just by comparing (a) and (b) we can see differences in the articulation of the two alveolar fricatives. It is characteristic of both the lax alveolar fricative /s/ and also of the tense /s*/ that after starting from a low frequency with no energy, articulation is only accompanied by high frequency noise energy. However, a difference in phonation type can be seen at the offset of the fricative. Rather

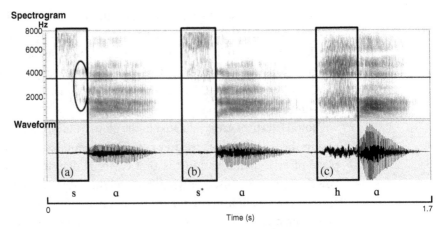

Figure 4.6   Spectrogram and waveform of fricatives in word-initial position

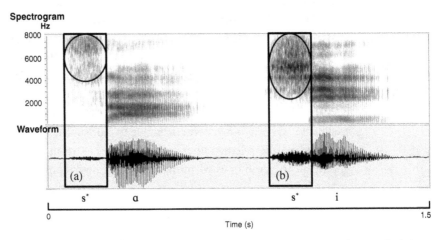

Figure 4.7   Spectrogram and waveform of a tense alveolar fricative followed by the vowels /ɑ/ and /i/ in word-initial position

like obstruents, the lax fricative in Korean is articulated with aspiration. In the diagram, the circled area indicates the aspiration that accompanies the articulation of the lax alveolar fricative.[19] However, such aspiration cannot be seen on the spectrogram of the articulation for /s*/.

As we have seen above, in Korean the vowel following a fricative can cause allophonic variation. In Figure 4.7 we can see the tense sound /s*/ followed by /ɑ/ and /i/. The areas on the diagram marked (a) and (b) indicate the friction duration of the two fricatives. The energy distribution of the two sounds differs greatly. The energy distribution of the friction noise of the sound has been circled. As can be seen, there is a big difference in the distribution of noise energy. When /s*/ is followed by /i/, frequency of noise energy is relatively

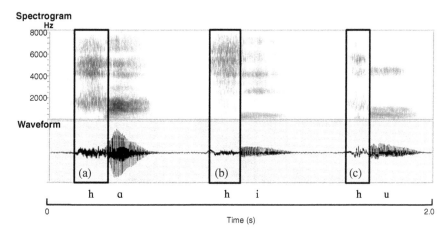

Figure 4.8   Spectrogram and waveform of a glottal fricative followed by the vowels /ɑ/, /i/, and /u/ in word-initial position

lower than when it is followed by /ɑ/. This is because alveolar fricatives are re-alised as alveolo-palatal fricatives when followed by /i/, as mentioned earlier.

Figure 4.8 shows /ɑ/, /i/ and /u/ with a preceding /h/ sound and the relevant waveforms. As can be seen, the distribution of noise energy of /h/ follows the pattern of the articulation of the following vowel sound.

4.2.2.2 Word-medial (intervocalic) fricatives

Figure 4.9 shows the three different Korean fricatives between two /ɑ/ sounds and the relevant spectrograms and waveforms. The figure shows patterns of energy distribution for alveolar and glottal sounds similar to those observed in word-initial position.

When alveolar fricatives in intervocalic position are compared to those in word-initial position, there is hardly any aspiration of the lax alveolar fricative.[20] Also, friction duration for the tense fricative is longer than for the lax frictive in word-medial position.[21] A difference can also be seen in the duration of the preceding vowel.[22] Similar phenomena have been observed in Korean obstruents.

Looking at (c) in Figure 4.9 it is very clear that /h/ becomes voiced when located between two vowels. Looking at the spectrogram of the intervocalic glottal fricative in Korean, we can see the voice bar at a lower frequency dur-ing the articulation of the consonant, as well as friction noise near the formant frequency of the neighbouring vowels.

Similar allophonic variation due to vowel sounds has been seen in word-initial position. The alveolar fricatives, both lax and tense, become alveolo-palatal

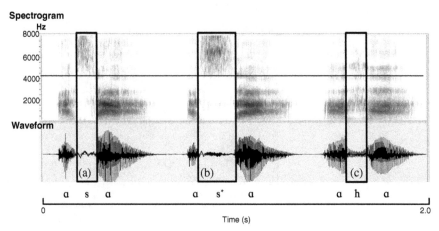

Figure 4.9   Spectrogram and waveform of fricatives in word-medial (intervocalic) position

fricatives when followed by /i/. The preceding vowel, however, has no effect on the place of articulation of the following fricatives. Glottal fricatives also tend to be influenced more by the vowel that follows them than by the one that precedes them.

4.2.2.3 Allophones and phonological identity of the lax fricative

As we move away from our previous discussion of lax and tense types of alveolar fricatives, it is necessary to question whether such a distinction is natural, given that Korean fricatives differ from other obstruents in having only two subclassifications. Kagaya (1974) and S.-J. Moon (1997) both point out that the distinction here is not between lax and tense, but between tense and aspirated. Kagaya (1974), the originator of this idea, used analyses of laryngeal gestures with a fibrescope to argue for an aspirated/tense distinction rather than a lax/tense distinction in Korean fricatives. This is because similarities were noticed between Korean lax alveolar fricatives and the aspirated types of other obstruents. In addition, S.-J. Moon (1997) posited that lax fricatives do not possess the same voicing quality as is observed in other lax obstruents and furthermore also have an aspirated quality.

However, such a discussion has two inherent problems. The first is that, as has been noted, phonological categories should be based on phonological behaviours rather than phonetic properties. Therefore, the focus of this discussion is whether lax fricatives share common phonological behaviours with other Korean lax obstruents. It is relatively easy to see that this is the case by looking at the process by which consonants become tense. As can be seen in (5a), /s/ is realised as [s*] after another obstruent, like the other lax obstruents

shown in (5b). If it were truly an aspirated consonant, then we would expect it
to undergo no change, like those seen in (5c).

(5) a. 가죽신 /katɕuk + sin/ → [katɕuksˀin]   'leather shoes'
         밥솥 /pap + sotʰ/ → [papsˀot]   'rice pot'
     b. 악보 /ak + po/ → [akpˀo]   'musical score'
         앞뒤 /apʰ + twi/ → [aptˀwi]   'the front and the rear'
         앞길 /apʰ + kil/ → [apkˀil]   'the road ahead'
         떡집 /tˀʌk + tɕip/ → [tˀʌktɕˀip]   'rice cake shop'
     c. 막판 /mak + pʰan/ → [makpʰan]   'the last round'
         집터 /tɕip + tʰʌ/ → [tɕiptʰʌ]   'housing site'
         집칸 /tɕip + kʰan/ → [tɕipkʰan]   'house unit'
         막차 /mak + tɕʰa/ → [maktɕʰa]   'the last train'

The second problem is that, compared to changes seen in some phonetic features, the differences between the fricatives under discussion and other lax obstruents do not seem as significant. As in both the discussion above of stops and also the discussion below of affricates, the lax variant either shows considerable aspiration in word-initial position or does not show any aspiration at all in word-medial position. Add to this the fact that only the fricatives under discussion do not undergo the voicing process in word-medial position and it becomes difficult to reach a definitive conclusion.[23] To sum up, fricatives do appear to share some features with other lax obstruents.[24] Therefore it is necessary to conclude that it is possible to see a distinction between lax and tense in Korean fricatives, but difficult to make a case for a distinction between aspirated and tense.

4.2.2.4 Major allophones of fricatives

On the basis of the preceding discussion it is possible to draw up a chart like that in Table 4.6. It follows from the table that the main factor in determining the allophonic variation of a fricative is the vowel sound that follows it.

DID YOU KNOW...?

Why are fricative sounds so difficult for Korean speakers?

In Korean, there are only three fricative sounds; the alveolar fricatives /s/, /sˀ/ and the glottal fricative /h/. In English, however, there are as many as nine fricative phonemes, as indicated in the table. They are the labiodental fricatives /f/, /v/, the dental fricatives /θ/, /ð/, the alveolar fricatives /s/, /z/, the palato-alveolar fricatives /ʃ/, /ʒ/, and the glottal fricative /h/.

	Labiodental	Dental	Alveolar	Palato-alveolar	Glottal
Voiceless	f	θ	s	ʃ	h
Voiced	v	ð	z	ʒ	

Consequently, it is not easy for native Korean speakers to distinguish between the fricative sounds in English and to pronounce them correctly. The first difficulty arises from the fact that, in English, fricative sounds are made in five different places, whereas in Korean, all fricatives are pronounced either in the alveolar or glottal positions. The second difficulty arises from the fact that, except for the glottal fricative, all other fricatives in English have a voiced and voiceless contrast. Because there are no voiced obstruents among Korean phonemes, they are difficult for Korean speakers to pronounce. In addition, fricatives show the longest duration among obstruents, which means that there must be a prolonged vibration of the vocal folds in order to make a voiced fricative sound. Due to these difficulties, in Korean /f/ is replaced by /pʰ/ ㅍ, /v/ by /p/ ㅂ, /θ/ by /s*/ ㅆ, /ð/ by /t/ ㄷ, /s/ by /s/ ㅅ or /s*/ ㅆ, /ʃ/ by /swi/ 쉬, and /ʒ/ by /tɕwi/ 쥐. We will come back to this issue when we discuss English loanwords in Chapter 10.

4.2.3 Affricates

As can be seen from Table 4.7, in Korean there is only one place of articulation for affricates, though there are three different phonation types. That this place of articulation is not shared by other obstruents is a particular feature of Korean.

Let's look at some minimal sets that can be used to determine the inventory of Korean affricates.

(6)   Minimal sets
      /tɕ/ : /tɕ*/ : /tɕʰ/   자다 /tɕata/ 'to sleep' : 짜다 /tɕ*ata/ 'to squeeze' :
      차다 /tɕʰata/ 'to kick'
      지다 /tɕita/ 'to be defeated' : 찌다 /tɕ*ita/
      'to steam' : 치다 /tɕʰita/ 'to hit'
      재다 /tɕɛta/ 'to measure' : 째다 /tɕ*ɛta/ 'to cut open' :
      채다 /tɕʰɛta/ 'to be kicked'

Table 4.6 Major allophones of fricatives

Category	Phoneme	Major allophone	Environment
Alveolar			
Lax	s	ç	before /j, i, wi/
		s	before all other vowels
Tense	s*	ç*	before /j, i/
		s*	before all other vowels
Glottal	h	ç	before /j, i/ in word-initial position
		x	before /ɯ/ in word-initial position
		ɸʷ	before /u, o/ in word-initial position
		h	before all other vowels in word-initial position
		j/ɣ/β/ɦ/	voiced counterparts in word-medial position

Table 4.7 Affricates

	Bilabial	Alveolar	Alveolo-palatal	Velar	Glottal
Lax			tç (ㅈ)		
Tense			tç* (ㅉ)		
Aspirated			tçʰ (ㅊ)		

족 /tçok/ 'trotter' : 쪽 /tç*ok/ 'indigo plant' :
촉 /tçʰok/ 'candle-power'

The place of articulation for affricates is the alveolo-palatal region, some-times also referred to as the prepalatal region, that is, where the palate meets the alveolar ridge. Korean alveolo-palatal affricates are articulated with the tip of the tongue either touching the lower teeth or both the lower teeth and the lower gums; the tongue blade briefly touches the front palate before air is released. After momentarily blocking airflow, the tongue blade is slightly lowered and the air passage slightly narrowed, creating turbulent airflow. The place of articulation for affricates is more or less the same as that for the allophonic variation of alveolar fricatives when articulated before the vowel /i/.

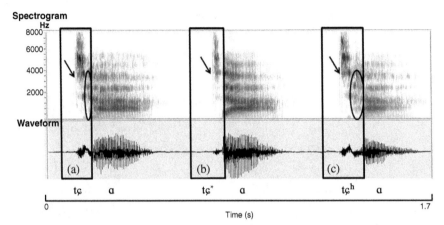

Figure 4.10   Spectrogram and waveform of lax, tense and aspirated affricates in word-initial position

The place of articulation for Korean affricates is different from that of English affricates, in the same way that the allophones of the Korean alveolar fricative [ɕ] and the English /ʃ/ differ, as described above. The English affricates /tʃ/ and /dʒ/ are articulated slightly further forward in the palato-alveolar region – the back of the alveolar ridge – than their Korean counterparts, and are always accompanied by protrusion of the lips. English affricates are produced in the same place as the English fricatives /ʃ, ʒ/, also with the lips protruding. English affricates are pronounced with the tip of the tongue touching only the lower gums. It is worth noting that English affricates are not articulated with the tip of the tongue touching the lower teeth; this is the biggest difference from their Korean counterparts.

Affricates can be classified as either lax, tense or aspirated sounds according to phonation type. All are voiceless. Just like fricatives, affricates can exist only in syllable-initial position. This is due to the fact that syllable-final sounds should not be released after central closure. In the following, we will discuss the phonetic characteristics of affricates in the word-initial and -medial positions.

4.2.3.1 Word-initial affricates

Figure 4.10 shows the word-initial realisation of /tɕ, tɕ*, tɕʰ/. (a), (b) and (c) indicate the realisations of the three different phonation types of affricates. Just as with other obstruents, where airflow is obstructed in sound production, the spectrogram of affricates shows vertical lines indicating the release of closure, indicated by arrows.[25] After the point indicated by the arrow, the kind of

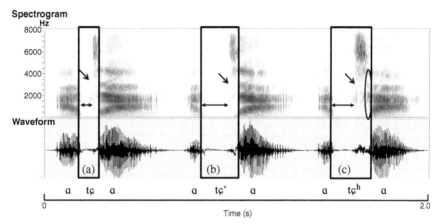

Figure 4.11   Spectrogram and waveform of lax, tense and aspirated affricates in word-medial (intervocalic) position

energy distribution associated with high-frequency friction noise can be identified. Aspiration of the lax and aspirated variants of the affricates is observed as with other obstruents, but the tense variant does not possess the same aspiration, as can be seen through the absence of a circled area on the diagram.

4.2.3.2 Word-medial (intervocalic) affricates

Figure 4.11 shows the three types of affricates in intervocalic position. In the diagram, the three types of affricates are labelled (a), (b) and (c), with a double-headed arrow indicating the duration of closure, and a diagonal arrow indicating the release of the closure. In word-medial position, friction is observed at the point of release, similar to what was found in word-initial position. However, in the case of tense and lax affricates the onset of the following vowel occurs immediately afterwards, whereas the release of the aspirated affricate is followed first by aspiration and then by the onset of the following vowel. Like other obstruents, the lax affricate in word-medial position is articulated with no aspiration, unlike in word-initial position.

It can be seen that the closure period, friction period and length of preceding vowel in affricates all vary according to phonation type.[26] This is a particular feature of word-medial affricates, and is also seen in other obstruents.

Another point to note is that in the examples in Figure 4.11, the lax affricates in intervocalic position are not realised as voiced sounds. The voice bars on the spectrogram and the periodic wave in the waveform which are usually

Table 4.8 Major allophones of affricates

Category	Phoneme	Allophone	Environment
Lax	tɕ	tɕ	Word-initial
		dʑ/d̥ʑ̥	Word-medial
Tense	tɕ*	tɕ*	Onset
Aspirated	tɕʰ	tɕʰ	Onset

observed with voiced sounds are not present. However, as noted above, lax affricates in Korean are not necessarily realised by all speakers as voiced sounds
in word-medial onset position. More importantly, in this environment, lax
sounds are not articulated with aspiration.

4.2.3.3 Major allophones of affricates

Table 4.8 shows the major allophones of Korean affricates. As can be seen, the
major allophones of affricates are similar to those of stop sounds.

4.3 Sonorants

Sonorants are sounds produced without any obstruction as airflow passes
through the vocal tract. Table 4.9 shows a list of sonorants in Korean. As
can be seen, sonorants in Korean can be further classified into (i) nasal and
(ii) liquid. There are three nasals in Korean, but only one liquid. All sonorants
are voiced consonants.

Let's look at some minimal sets which can help us to define the inventory
of sonorants in Korean. Velar nasals can only appear in syllable-final position, and not syllable-initial position, whereas lateral sounds cannot appear in
word-initial position, except in the case of loanwords. This means that minimal sets for sonorants need only focus on syllable-final position. The following
examples show minimal sets which differ in syllable-final position.

(7)   Minimal sets
       /m/ : /n/ : /ŋ/ : /l/
       담 /tam/ 'fence' : 단 /tan/ 'column' : 당 /taŋ/ 'party' : 달 /tal/ 'moon'
       맘 /mam/ 'heart' : 만 /man/ 'ten-thousand' : 망 /maŋ/ 'watch' :
       말 /mal/ 'language'
       밤 /pam/ 'night' : 반 /pan/ 'class' : 방 /paŋ/ 'room' : 발 /pal/ 'foot'

Table 4.9 Sonorants

	Bilabial	Alveolar	Alveolo-palatal	Velar	Glottal
Nasal	m (ㅁ)	n (ㄴ)		ŋ (ㅇ)	
Liquid		l (ㄹ)			

삼 /sɑm/ 'flax' : 산 /sɑn/ 'mountain' : 상 /sɑŋ/ 'table' : 살 /sɑl/ 'flesh'
쌈 /s*ɑm/ 'lettuce-wrapped rice' : 싼 /s*ɑn/ 'to be cheap (adnominal)' :
쌍 /s*ɑŋ/ pair : 쌀 /s*ɑl/ 'rice'
잠 /tɕɑm/ 'sleep' : 잔 /tɕɑn/ 'glass' : 장 /tɕɑŋ/ 'market' : 잘 /tɕɑl/ 'well'
탐 /tʰɑm/ 'greed' : 탄 /tʰɑn/ 'coal' : 탕 /tʰɑŋ/ 'soup' : 탈 /tʰɑl/ 'mask'
함 /hɑm/ 'box' : 한 /hɑn/ 'grudge' : 항 /hɑŋ/ 'item' : 할 /hɑl/
'percentage'

4.3.1 Nasals

Nasals in Korean can be pronounced in the bilabial (i.e. /m/), alveolar (i.e. /n/) and velar positions (i.e. /ŋ/). Bilabial and alveolar nasals can occur either in word-initial or word-final position, but the velar nasal can only appear in word-final position. Major phonetic characteristics of Korean nasals are weak nasality in word-initial position and weak nasalisation of preceding vowels in syllable-final position. For this reason, native speakers of French, Italian or Japanese often recognise word-initial nasals as voiced stops instead of nasals.[27]

As discussed earlier, in order to produce nasals, the velum needs to be lowered, so that air can flow through the nasal cavity without any friction. When a vowel precedes a nasal, native speakers automatically lower the velum. The point at which the velum is lowered varies cross-linguistically. In Korean, the velum is lowered very late, so that the articulation of the preceding vowel is not greatly affected. However, in English and Japanese, the velum is lowered early, so that the preceding vowels are strongly nasalised.[28]

DID YOU KNOW...?

Korean [mun] vs. English [mun]

As mentioned earlier, word-initial nasals in Korean are different from those in English, French, Italian or Japanese, all of which have voiced stops. Compared to those languages, Korean word-initial nasals are weak and short. Vowels preceding word-final nasals are nasalised, but the degree of nasalisation is weaker in Korean in comparison with English and Japanese.

(5)   Korean   English
      a. 문 /mun/   'door'   /mun/   'moon'
      b. 눈 /nun/   'eye'   /nun/   'noon'
      c. 맘 /mɑm/   'heart'   /mɑm/   'mom'

As noted above, the words listed are represented by the same symbols in IPA, but when one actually listens to the way they are pronounced, one can hear that the degree of nasality differs greatly between Korean and English. We can easily see that word-initial nasals in Korean are shorter and weaker than in English. At the same time, the nasality of the preceding vowels is also weaker in Korean than in English, as they are barely nasalised. This shows that even the same sequence of segments can be pronounced differently according to the coordination timing between vocal organs. Moreover, differences in coordination timing give rise to different co-articulation characteristics across languages.

4.3.1.1 Word-initial nasals

Figure 4.12 shows the spectrograms and waveforms of the bilabial nasal /m/ and alveolar nasal /n/ in word-initial position. The word-initial nasal is relatively short as noted earlier, and therefore has a low degree of nasality.

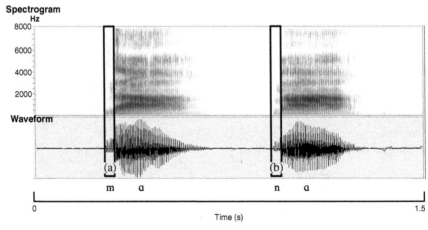

Figure 4.12   Spectrogram and waveform of bilabial and alveolar nasals in word-initial position

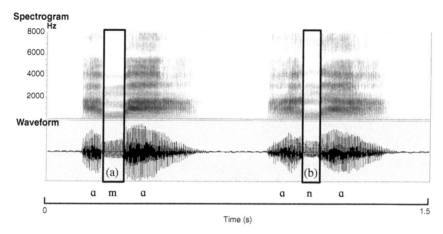

Figure 4.13   Spectrogram and waveform of bilabial and alveolar nasals in word-medial
(intervocalic) position

4.3.1.2 Word-medial (intervocalic) nasals

Now, let's see the spectrograms and waveforms of the bilabial nasal /m/ and
the alveolar nasal /n/ in word-medial intervocalic position. Figure 4.13 shows
how bilabial nasal /m/ and alveolar nasal /n/ are realised between /ɑ/ and
/ɑ/. Figure 4.13 shows that word-medial (intervocalic) nasals are longer than
word-initial nasals, and have a high degree of nasality.

4.3.1.3 Word-final nasals

The bilabial /m/, the alveolar /n/ and the velar /ŋ/ may all appear in word-
final position. Figure 4.14 shows the spectrograms and waveforms of the three
nasals in word-final position. They are pronounced much longer than in word-
initial or word-medial position. As in the case of other consonants, nasals in
word-final position are pronounced unreleased.

4.3.1.4 Major allophones of nasals

Table 4.10 shows the major allophones of Korean nasals. As can be seen, the
major allophones are realised within a syllable structure.

4.3.2 Liquids

4.3.2.1 Phonetic realisation of liquids

In the consonant inventory of Korean, there is only one liquid, /l/. However, phonetically speaking, two allophones of /l/ exist. That is, /l/ can be

Table 4.10 Major allophones of nasals

Phoneme	Major allophones	Environment
m n ŋ	m n	Onset
	m˺ n˺ ŋ˺	Coda

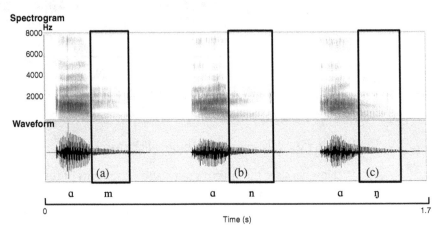

Figure 4.14   Spectrogram and waveform of bilabial, alveolar and velar nasals in word-final position

realised either as the alveolar lateral approximant [l], or as the alveolar tap [ɾ]. Figure 4.15 shows the spectrogram and waveforms of the liquid /l/ in four different phonetic environments: (a) word-initial, as in /la/, (b) inter-vocalic, as in /ala/, (c) word-final, as in /al/, and (d) after /l/, as in /alla/. /l/ is pronounced [ɾ] in word-initial and word-medial (intervocalic) position as shown in (a) and (b). In the case of (c) and (d), /l/ is pronounced [l] in word-final position, and when it occurs after another /l/ (i.e. in gemina-tion). However, although [l] and [ɾ] are very different phonetically, Korean native speakers do not regard them as two distinctive phonemes, but as allophones of /l/.

The use of /l/ in word-initial position is subject to restrictions. This is often called the Law of Initials. No pure Korean words begin with /l/, only loan-words. A syllable-initial /l/ can however occur in word-medial (intervocalic) position. Furthermore, /l/ cannot be realised after another consonant, unless that consonant is also /l/.[29]

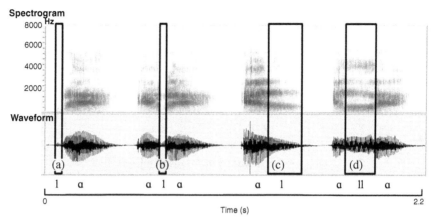

Figure 4.15   Spectrograms and waveforms of liquids in word-initial, word-medial (intervocalic), and word-final positions, and after /l/

DID YOU KNOW…?

Two 'lice' burgers please

Yuna went to a hamburger place in London with Henry. She saw a new burger made using rice instead of bread. She thought it would be a good idea to order it, since she wanted to eat rice. So, she said "two lice burgers please". The person in the shop looked puzzled and Henry could not help but laugh at her. This is one of the most common mistakes that native speakers of Korean make when learning English. They fail to distinguish between /r/ and /l/ sounds, which leads them to pronounce them the same. We will come back to this issue in Chapter 10.

4.3.2.2 Phonemic realisation of /l/

Previously, we have observed that /l/ is realised either as [l] or [ɾ] depending on the phonetic environment in which it is found. Table 4.11 shows the phonetic realisations of /l/.

Here a question arises as to why [l] is regarded as a phoneme, but not [ɾ]. What is the basis for this? To answer this question, we need to consider the phonological patterns of the liquid in Korean. Consider the following.

(8) a. 달나라 /tal + nala/ → [tallala]   'lunar world'
     들나물 /tɯl + namul/ → [tɯllamul]   'field herbs'

Table 4.11 Major allophones of the liquid

Phoneme	Major allophone	Environment
l	l	Coda and after /l/ (in gemination)
	ɾ	Word-initial and intervocalic

b. 난로 /nɑn + lo/ → [nɑllo]   'a stove'
   관료 /kwɑn + ljo/ → [kwɑlljo]   'a bureaucrat'
c. 비관론 /pi + kwɑn + lon/ → [pikwɑnnon]   'pessimism'
   흡인력 /hɯp + in + ljʌk/ → [hɯpinnjʌk]   'suction power or personal magnetism'

When /n/ and /l/ appear in a sequence either as /l/ + /n/ (8a) or /n/ + /l/ (8b), one of the sounds is assimilated into the other, as a sequence of /n/ and /l/ is not allowed in Korean phonology.[30] If [ɾ] were a phoneme and not [l], it would be hard to explain why the assimilation observed in (8a–c) occurs at all; why should the tap [ɾ] become a nasal? Phonetically, the most prominent difference between a tap and a nasal sound is the openness of the nasal cavity. However, this cannot be used as the sole criterion for distinguishing a tap from a nasal. For instance, this can also be used to distinguish a stop sound from a nasal. Hence, we are still unable to explain why [ɾ] is assimilated into the nasal [n].[31]

However, if we assume [l] as a phoneme, we can more easily explain this assimilation, since although [l] and [n] are both sonorants, only [l] has a lateral feature. If the lateral sound assimilates the nasal, then the sequences [ln] or [nl] will become [ll] as in (8a–b), and if the lateral sound loses the lateral feature, then the sequences will become [nn] as in (8c).[32]

DID YOU KNOW...?

What the sound of farting can tell us about the sounds of Korean?

The Korean language has a highly developed set of onomatopoeias. The list of onomatopoeic words that describe the sound of a fart alone is very extensive: /p*oŋ/ 뽕, /p*uŋ/ 뿡, /pʰik/ 픽, /pʰisisik/ 피시식, /p*ulɯlɯk/ 뿌르륵, /pulɯlɯk/ 부르륵. Of course, not all of these words are listed in the dictionary, but they are found in everyday use. By examining the onomatopoeic words used to describe the sound of farts, one discovers a very interesting phenomenon.

First, these onomatopoeic words can be divided into three general categories of sound: /p˚oŋ/, 뽕 and /p˚uŋ/ 뿡 denote the sound of loud, single farts (let's call these /p˚oŋ/ 뽕 type); /pʰisisik/ 피시식 the kind of farts that are more prolonged in length (let's call these /pʰisisik/ 피시식 type); and /p˚ulɯlɯk/ 뿌르특 and /pulɯlɯk/ 부르특 the kind of /p˚oŋ/ 뽕 type that is repeated at least twice (let's call these /p˚ulɯlɯk/ 뿌르특 type).

Different categories of onomatopoeia exist for the sound of farts because there are different ways in which the gas produced in the intestine exits through the anal passage. /p˚oŋ/ 뽕 type occurs when the gas that was trapped inside the intestine exits all at once, /pʰisisik/ 피시식 type when the gas inside the intestine exits through small crevices of the anus, creating air turbulence and /p˚ulɯlɯk/ 뿌르특 type when the /p˚oŋ/ 뽕 type is repeated more than twice.

These onomatopoeic sounds reflect patterns found in the articulation of consonants. The /p˚oŋ/ 뽕 type can be seen as stop sounds, the /pʰisisik/ 피시식 type as fricative sounds and the /p˚ulɯlɯk/ 뿌르특 type as trill sounds. The consonants in these onomatopoeic words, interestingly, reflect the acoustic characteristics of the farts themselves. The /p˚oŋ/ 뽕 type starts with the stop sound, /p˚/, which has no aspiration, and has only one syllable, expressing a momentary popping sound. The /pʰisisik/ 피시식 type starts with the stop sound /pʰ/ – which has strong aspiration – and the fricative /s/ that is repeated twice to create three syllables, expressing a continuing noise. In addition, the only vowel is the high vowel, /i/, which clearly emphasises the friction of the preceding consonants caused by vowel devoicing. The /p˚ulɯlɯk/ 뿌르특 type starts with an unaspirated stop sound, like the /p˚oŋ/ 뽕 type, but the liquid sound between the vowels is realised as a tap sound. This means that in two out of three syllables the tap sound [ɾ] is produced, which is the closest sound to a trill sound that can be pronounced in Korean. If there were trill sounds in Korean, the second syllable in /p˚ulɯlɯk/ 뿌르특 type would have been replaced by one.

The fact that the Korean onomatopoeic words for farts reflect the acoustic characteristics of the farts through the choice of consonants and the number of syllables is very interesting.

4.4 Features for consonants

Consider the Korean consonant charts again. As shown in Table 4.1, there are fifteen obstruents and four sonorants in Korean. Now we shall see how these nineteen consonants can be further classified by using phonological features.

4.4.1 Features for manner of articulation

Let's first consider the features related to manner of articulation. There are five ways of classifying consonants in Korean according to their manner of articulation. To classify the five groups (or categories), we need three features, as shown in (9).

(9)   Features for manner of articulation
      a. [+/−continuant]:
         [+continuant] sounds are produced without airflow being blocked where the primary constriction takes place, but continuing throughout the process of sound production.
      b. [+/−delayed release]:
         This feature is for sounds which are made with complete closure of the vocal tract. [+delayed release] sounds are produced without instantaneous release, as is the case with stops.
      c. [+/−lateral]:
         This feature is restricted to coronal consonants.[33] [+lateral] sounds are produced by lowering the mid section of the tongue at both sides or at only one side, thereby allowing air to flow out of the mouth in the vicinity of the molar teeth.

These three features can be used to distinguish five types of Korean consonants as shown in Table 4.12. Stops and affricates share [−continuant] and [−lateral] features, but they can be distinguished using the [delayed release] feature, as stops have the [−delayed release] feature, whereas affricates have the [+delayed release] feature.

FURTHER STUDY

[lateral] vs. [nasal]

Sonorant consonants in Korean can be divided into two categories, either nasal or lateral sounds. In this book, we have classified sonorants using the [lateral] feature. However, it is also possible to classify them by using the [nasal] feature. The result is that nasal sounds are classified as

Table 4.12 Classification of Korean consonants using a feature matrix

	Stop	Fricative	Affricate	Nasal	Lateral
[continuant]	−	+	−	−	−[a]
[delayed release]	−[b]		+	−	
[lateral][c]	−	−	−	−	+

[a] In some languages, lateral sounds have [+continuant] features, while in others, they have [−continuant] features. This is because although the central oral cavity, where airflow is blocked, is completely closed, the sides of the cavity are open. Given the closure of the central oral cavity, sounds may be described as having [−continuant] features, but if one considers that the sides of the cavity remain open, then the sound may be described as having [+continuant] features. Therefore, the phonological behaviours of lateral sounds need to considered further in order to determine whether they possess [+continuant] or [−continuant] features. For instance, one must consider how they behave when they occur with sounds which have [+continuant] or [−continuant] features. As we shall see in 8.1.1, in Korean, only seven consonants /p, t, k, m, n, ŋ, l/ can occur in the syllable-final position. Six of those sounds, /p, t, k, m, n, ŋ/, have the feature [−continuant]. It would be unnatural to assume that of these seven sounds, only the lateral has the feature [+continuant], and we therefore assume the lateral as having the feature [−continuant] in Korean.

[b] This is a feature limited to sounds created by closure of the vocal tract. Nasals, as sounds created by closure and immediate release of the vocal tract, possess the feature [−delayed release]. However this feature is not applicable to fricatives and laterals, which are not created by closure of the vocal tract, and it is not used with reference to them.

[c] As in the definition, the feature [lateral] is limited to consonants which are [+coronal]. Therefore, the feature [−lateral] is not accorded to all stops, fricatives, and nasals, but only those which are [+coronal]. As place of articulation is not shown clearly in this table, the three kinds of sound here are given the feature [−lateral].

[+nasal] and lateral sounds as [−nasal]; On the other hand, if sonorants are classified using the [lateral] feature, then lateral sounds come to be classified as [+lateral] and nasal sounds as [−lateral]. The reason why we have chosen the [lateral] over the [nasal] feature in this book is due to certain phonological behaviours that have been observed, as shown below. Consider the following examples:

(8) 겨울날   /kjʌul+nal/   [kjʌullal]   'winter days'
     과일나무   /kwail+namu /   [kwaillamu]   'fruit tree'
     달님   /tal+nim/   [tallim]   'moon'
     줄넘기   /tɕul+nʌm+ki/   [tɕullʌmkˀi]   'skipping'
     칼날   /kʰal+nal/   [kʰallal]   'blade of a knife'
     하늘나라   /hanɯl+nala/   [hanɯllala]   'heaven'

These examples display a phonological process known as lateralisation that we will discuss in Chapter 8. In the examples above, alveolar nasals become laterals due to the preceding lateral sound. If we were to replace the feature [lateral] with [nasal], this process could be understood as follows: lateral sounds with the [−nasal] features change sounds that have the [+nasal] feature into lateral sounds with the [−nasal] feature. This way of understanding Lateralisation may seem a little unnatural.

However, if we understand this process as lateral sounds with [+lateral] features changing following alveolar nasals with [−lateral] features into lateral sounds with [+lateral] features, the explanation seems more plausible. Moreover, when we explain Lateralisation using the [lateral] feature, we can understand why this happens only to alveolar nasals, since bilabial or velar nasals are not subject to the [lateral] features. As discussed earlier, only sounds with [+coronal] features are subject to the [lateral] features. However, bilabial and velar nasals are not coronal sounds. In other words, they are [−coronal].

4.4.2 Features for place of articulation

Consonants in Korean can also be classified according to their place of articulation. To distinguish each group, we need to postulate a different set of features, which is shown in (10).

(10) Features for place of articulation
   a. [+/−coronal]:
      [+coronal] sounds are produced with the blade of the tongue raised from the neutral position.
   b. [+/−anterior]:
      [+anterior] sounds are produced by an obstruction in the area forward of the palato-alveolar region of the mouth.

In order to understand the [coronal] feature, we must first understand what is meant by 'neutral position' of the tongue. The definition given for neutral position in SPE is shown in (11).

(11) Neutral position
   It can be observed that just prior to speaking, the subject positions his vocal tract in a certain characteristic manner. The velum is raised and the airflow through the nose is shut off. The body of the tongue, which in quiet breathing lies in a relaxed state on the floor of the mouth, is

Table 4.13 Features for place of articulation

	Bilabial	Alveolar	Alveolo-palatal	Velar	Glottal
[coronal]	−	+	+	−	−
[anterior]	+	+	−	−	−

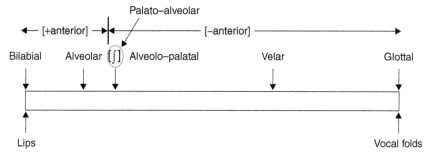

Figure 4.16   Place of articulation and feature value of the [anterior] feature

raised in the neutral position to about the level that it occupies in the articulation of the English vowel [e] in the word *bed*; but the blade of the tongue remains in about the same position as in quiet breathing.

Table 4.13 sums up how consonants can be further classified by features for place of articulation. As shown, bilabial and velar sounds are distinguished using the [+/−anterior] feature and bilabial and alveolar sounds are distinguished using the [+/−coronal] feature. Only alveolar and alveolo-palatal consonants have the [+coronal] feature since when these sounds are produced, the blade of the tongue is lifted up. This is not observed in any other consonants, which therefore have the [−coronal] feature. Bilabial and alveolar sounds share the [+anterior] feature since they are pronounced at the front of the mouth.

When alveolar and alveolo-palatal sounds are produced, the blade of the tongue is higher than when in the neutral position. Hence, they have the [+coronal] feature. However, when bilabial, velar or glottal sounds are produced, the blade of the tongue is lower than when in the neutral position. Hence, they have the feature [−coronal]. On the other hand, bilabial and alveolar sounds are produced closer to the front of mouth than palato-alveolar sounds, such as [ʃ]. Hence, they have the feature [+anterior], whereas alveolo-palatal, velar and glottal sounds, which are produced further back in the mouth, possess the feature [−anterior].

Table 4.14 Features for phonation type

	Lax	Tense	Aspirated
[tense]	–	+	+
[aspirated]	–	–	+

4.4.3 Features for phonation types

Table 4.14 shows the three-way contrast in stops and affricates in Korean. Alveolar fricatives also show a distinction between lax and tense types. To distinguish these consonants, we need two features, [+/−tense] and [+/−aspirated].

(12) Features for phonation type
  a. [+/−tense]:[34]
      [+tense] sounds are produced with tension in the vocal folds.
  b. [+/−aspirated]:[35]
      [+aspirated] sounds are produced with the two vocal folds far apart, and with subsequent opening of the glottis.

Table 4.15 Features for consonants in Korean

	p	p*	pʰ	t	t*	tʰ	k	k*	kʰ	s	s*	tɕ	tɕ*	tɕʰ	m	n	ŋ	l	h
Major class features																			
consonantal	+	+	+	+	+	+	+	+	+	+	+	+	+	+	+	+	+	+	+
syllabic	–	–	–	–	–	–	–	–	–	–	–	–	–	–	–	–	–	–	–
sonorant	–	–	–	–	–	–	–	–	–	–	–	–	–	–	+	+	+	+	–
Manner																			
continuant	–	–	–	–	–	–	–	–	–	+	+	–	–	–	–	–	–	–	+
delayed release	–	–	–	–	–	–	–	–	–			+	+	+	–	–	–		
lateral				–	–	–				–	–	–	–	–		–		+	
Place																			
coronal	–	–	–	+	+	+	–	–	–	+	+	+	+	+	–	+	–	+	–
anterior	+	+	+	+	+	+	–	–	–	+	+	–	–	–	+	+	–	+	–
Phonation types																			
tense	–	+	+	–	+	+	–	+	+	–	+	–	+	+	–	–	–	–	–
aspirated	–	–	+	–	–	+	–	–	+	–	–	–	–	+	–	–	–	–	+

Using these two features, phonation types can be classified as in Table 4.14.

Aspirated sounds and tense sounds shared the [+tense] feature, distinguishing them from lax sounds which have the [−tense] feature. Aspirated and tense sounds are distinguished from one another due to the fact that tense sounds do not possess the [+aspirated] feature.

Table 4.15 summarises the features relating to consonants in Korean.

DID YOU KNOW...?

Why is it unnecessary to posit a [voiced] feature in Korean?

Suppose you were in a mixed school. A [female] feature would be necessary to distinguish female students from male students. However, in a girls' school, this [female] feature would be redundant, because all the students are female. For the same reason, a [voiced] feature would be redundant in Korean, unlike in English or in Japanese.

This is because all three kinds of obstruent in Korean are voiceless sounds that do not entail vibration of the vocal folds, and all the sounds that can be classified as sonorant are voiced sounds, i.e. they are accompanied by vibration of the vocal folds. Therefore, in Korean consonants, all sonorant sounds are voiced, and all obstruents are voiceless.

4.5 Summary

In this chapter, we have discussed the consonants of Korean. Altogether, there are nineteen consonants in Korean. Four of them are sonorants and the rest are obstruents. Consonants in Korean can be further classified according to (i) place of articulation, (ii) manner of articulation and (iii) phonation types. The main characteristics of Korean consonants can be summarised as follows. First, Korean has a rich inventory of obstruents: fifteen out of nineteen consonants are obstruents. Second, Korean obstruents are all voiceless. Unlike English, Korean has no voiced obstruent in the inventory. Third, Korean shows a three-way contrast among stops and affricates. Cross-linguistically, such a three-way contrast is relatively rare.

The pronunciation of stops differs according to where they occur. The three-way contrast is neutralised in word-final or syllable-final position. We will discuss the reason why this is the case in more detail in Chapter 8. In contrast to stops, Korean has relatively few fricatives in comparison with English. In addition, only one liquid phoneme exists. Word-initial nasals in Korean are short and weak compared with English. In order to provide more natural explanations for consonant-related phonological processes, we need to classify each consonant as a set of features. Major features for consonants can either be those for manner of articulation (e.g. [+/–continuant], [+/–delayed release], [+/–lateral]) or place of articulation (e.g. [+/–coronal], [+/–anterior]). Consonants can also be classified according to phonation types (e.g. [+/–tense], [+/–aspirated]).

EXERCISES

1 Why is [pʰ] a phoneme in Korean but not in English? Explain with examples from Korean and English.

2 Circle the words which start with consonants articulated in the region specified.

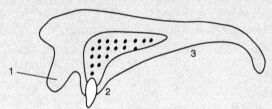

  a. Region 1: /pɑl/ 발 'foot', /t'ɑŋ/ 땅 'earth', /hanɯl/ 하늘 'sky', /maɯm/ 마음 'heart', /pʰoto/ 포도 'grape'
  b. Region 2: /kʌmi/ 거미 'spider', /tal/ 달 'moon', /kaŋ/ 강 'river', /salam/ 사람 'human', /pʰal/ 팔 'arm'
  c. Region 3: /tɕaŋkap/ 장갑 'gloves', /kaŋatɕi/ 강아지 'puppy', /tɕʰa/ 차 'car', /tʰatɕo/ 타조 'ostrich'

3 List examples which illustrate the three-way contrast (lax, tense and aspirated) among stops in Korean.

4 List examples which illustrate the three-way contrast (lax, tense and aspirated) among affricates in Korean.

5 Of lax, tense and aspirated stops, which are most commonly used in Korean?

6 Compare word-initial and word-final stops. What is the difference between them?

7 Compare word-initial and word-medial (intervocalic) stops. What is the difference between them?

8 How many liquids exist in Korean?

9 Explain the [lateral] feature and provide examples with the feature [+lateral].

10 What is the difference between bilabial and velar sounds? Explain using relevant features.

11 Discuss dialectal variations in Korean consonant pronunciation.

5 Vowels

In the previous chapter, we discussed consonants in Korean. In this chapter, we will discuss vowels in Korean. In particular, we will explore which vowels are phonemes in Korean and what their phonetic and phonological characteristics are. In 5.1, we will introduce the basic properties of vowels. In 5.2 and 5.3, we will examine in detail the phonetic and phonological characteristics of monophthongs (simple vowels) and diphthongs in Korean and 5.4 covers features for vowels. The chapter summary can be found in 5.5.

5.1 Phonological analysis of vowels

5.1.1 Monophthongs and diphthongs

A monophthong (or simple vowel) is a vowel consisting of one articulation from beginning to end. Likewise, a diphthong is a vowel made up of two articulations and a triphthong is a vowel made up of three articulations. Diphthongs can be further analysed into their constituent parts, glides and monophthongs. The articulation of a glide is similar to that of a vowel, but as it is pronounced much faster it does not remain stable during articulation, unlike vowels. Moreover, unlike a vowel, a glide cannot form a syllable by itself.

Diphthongs can be categorised as on-glide diphthongs or off-glide diphthongs according to the order in which the glide and monophthong are combined. An on-glide diphthong is one in which the glide precedes the monophthong, and an off-glide is one where the glide follows the monophthong. In Korean, only on-glide diphthongs exist.

5.1.2 Phonological status of the glide: consonant or vowel?

In the previous section, we said that a diphthong is seen as a combination of glides and monophthongs. A glide is also called a semivowel or an

/pʰil + jo/   /mil + wʌl/

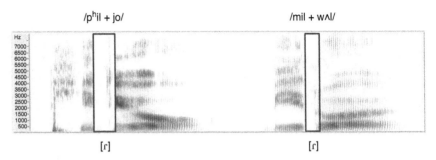

[ɾ]   [ɾ]

Figure 5.1   Allophonic realisation of /l/ followed by glides in Korean words /pʰil + jo/ 'necessity' and /mil + wʌl/ 'honeymoon'

approximant and has the properties of vowels as well as consonants. Because of this, glides are regarded as vowels in some languages but as consonants in others. In Korean, glides are classified as a type of vowel, yet in English they are regarded as consonants. For instance, the first sound /j/ in *yacht* [jɔt] in English and /j/ in /jo/ 요 'underquilt' in Korean is not so very different phonetically, but /j/ is a vowel in Korean and a consonant in English. In English, words starting with a glide such as *window* or *yacht* take the indefinite article *a* instead of *an*. This could be a piece of evidence which supports the analysis that an English glide is regarded as a consonant not a vowel.

In the case of Korean, it is difficult to use similar methods because grammatical morphemes are always attached at the end of a word and grammatical morphemes in Korean are only sensitive to the phonological category of the word-final sound. Also, as mentioned earlier, only on-glide diphthongs exist in Korean. This means that there are no words in Korean which end with a glide. However, we can confirm that a glide is a vowel by observing different phonetic realisations of /l/. As discussed in Chapter 4, /l/ is realised as [l] before a consonant or after /l/ but as [ɾ] before a vowel. If a glide is a vowel, /l/ before a glide should be realised as /ɾ/. But otherwise, /l/ should be realised as /l/. The words in (1) show that /l/ before a glide becomes [ɾ] as shown in Figure 5.1. This supports the case for glides being vowels.

(1)   a. /pʰil + jo/ 필요 'necessity'
        b. /mil + wʌl/ 밀월 'honeymoon'

DID YOU KNOW...?

Why do [twin] in Korean and [twin] in English sound different?

In Korean, [twin] is an adnominal of the verb {twi-} 튀- 'to spring', and means 'springing'. Although [twin] is represented identically in IPA in both

Korean and English as [twin], the English word *twin* [twin] and the Korean word 튄 [twin] sound different. Why is this the case?

The contrast in their pronunciation reflects two different methods of pronouncing the same combination of consonant and glide. When the Korean glide [w] follows a consonant, it makes the preceding consonant labialised, rather than being pronounced as an independent sound of its own. In English, on the other hand, although the succeeding glide labialises the preceding consonant to a certain extent, the glide, [w], is pronounced 'independently' with a noticeable duration of its own. Hence, [twin] in English is actually pronounced as [t^{w}win].

This helps to explain why native Korean speakers often make mistakes when pronouncing the sound /kw/, as found in such words as *queen* and *question*. Korean speakers have a particular tendency to pronounce /kw/ as [k^w] rather than [kw]. They therefore pronounce 'queen' and 'question' as [k^{w}in] and [k^{w}estʃən] rather than [kwin] and [kwestʃən], and this phenomenon arises from the fact that a combination of a consonant and a glide is pronounced differently in the two languages.

5.2 Monophthongs

In this section, we will discuss monophthongs in Korean. Unlike consonants, there is some noticeable difference between dialects with regard to vowels. In this book, we have focused on what is known as Standard Korean, which is based on the Seoul dialect.

Nevertheless, defining Standard Korean is not easy and in fact, what is referred to as 'Standard Korean Pronunciation' (SKP) is slightly different from Seoul speakers' real speech (or pronunciation), as we shall see in this section.

For instance, it is known that according to SKP, Standard Korean has ten monophthongs, yet as we shall see in 5.2.2, whether Korean has ten monophthongs or not is still debatable and in reality it is more likely that Korean has seven monophthongs instead of ten. In the following, we will first discuss the simple vowel system based on SKP and some problems of this system based on analysis of spontaneous speech.

5.2.1 How many are there?

According to SKP, Standard Korean has ten simple vowels as listed in Table 5.1.

Table 5.1   The ten monophthongs of SKP

	Front		Back	
	Unrounded	Rounded	Unrounded	Rounded
High	i (ㅣ)	y (ㅟ)	ɯ (ㅡ)	u (ㅜ)
Mid	e (ㅔ)	ø (ㅚ)	ʌ (ㅓ)	o (ㅗ)
Low	æ (ㅐ)		ɑ (ㅏ)	

Formant transition

[wɛ]   [wi]

Figure 5.2   Spectrogram of 외 'outside' and 위 'stomach'

5.2.1.1   Are there front rounded vowels in Korean?

As we can see, SKP postulates ten vowels, among which five are front vowels and five are back vowels. Both front and back vowels have roundedness/non-roundedness contrast and also can be classified into high, mid and low vowels according to the height of the tongue during articulation. This appears to be a systematic and stable vowel system, but perhaps doesn't quite reflect the reality of Korean vowels. In the following, we will discuss two aspects of the SKP system which reveal these problems.

Firstly, the two front rounded vowels /y/ and /ø/ are phonemes in SKP. However, in Seoul speakers' real speech, we do not observe the monophthongs /y/ and /ø/. Native speakers of Seoul Korean pronounce words with ㅟ and ㅚ spelling as diphthongs instead of monophthongs. The best way of finding out whether /ㅟ/ and /ㅚ/ are simple vowels or diphthongs is to pronounce words with ㅚ or ㅟ spelling such as 외 'outside, except' and 위 'stomach'. If the shape of mouth, that is, roundedness, is the same from the beginning to the end of articulation, then the vowel is a simple vowel. On the other hand, if the roundedness of the mouth disappears during the course of pronunciation, then it is a diphthong. Figure 5.2 shows the spectrogram for the two words 외 'outside' and 위 'stomach' by a female native Korean speaker. We can see

Table 5.2   Eight monophthongs of SKP (without /y/ and /ø/)

	Front	Back	
	Unrounded	Unrounded	Rounded
High	i	ɯ	u
Mid	e	ʌ	o
Low	æ	ɑ	

formant transition in both figures. This shows that /ㅚ/ and /ㅟ/ are diphthongs not monophthongs.

In fact, SKP also notices the dual nature of /ㅟ/ and /ㅚ/ and mentions that /ㅟ/ and /ㅚ/ 'can' be pronounced as diphthongs. However, in both natural and read speech, /ㅟ/ and /ㅚ/ are never pronounced as simple vowels but as diphthongs without exception. Based on this observation, we propose an eight simple-vowel system as in Table 5.2.

5.2.1.2   Are /e/ and /æ/ distinctive?

Let's move on to the next issue which is also controversial. Tables 5.1 and 5.2 (above) show that there are high, mid and low vowels in Korean, and that the definition of high, mid and low depends on the height of the tongue in articulation. However, it is not so obvious whether /e/ (front-mid vowel) and /æ/ (front-low vowel) are distinctive enough to native speakers of Standard Korean. Spellings corresponding to /e/ and /æ/ are ㅔ and ㅐ in Korean. Orthographically, 게 'crab' and 개 'dog' are different and often it is expected that the two words should sound different, given that /e/ and /æ/ are distinctive. In spontaneous speech, however, native speakers can't distinguish between the two sounds. H.-W. Choi (2002) shows that among 210 native speakers of Standard Korean between 20 and 80 years old, more than 80 per cent of the time participants pronounced the two sounds the same. That is, without any appropriate context, when (2) is heard, it can therefore refer to either (2a) or (2b). Not only in perception but also in production, native speakers can't distinguish the two sounds.

(2)   나는게/개를좋아한다.
  I like crabs.
  I like dogs.

Minimal pairs which show ㅔ and ㅐ contrast are given in (3). Native speakers will pronounce all words in (3a) and (3b) the same.

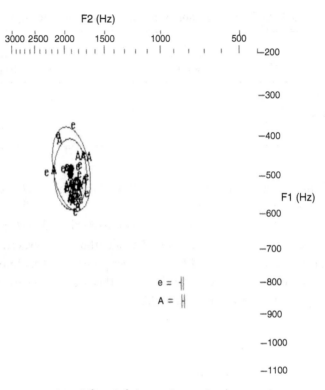

Figure 5.3   Formant plot of ㅔ and ㅐ (ten male speakers)

(3)   Minimal pairs having ㅔ and ㅐ
   a. words with ㅔ : 베 'hemp cloth',
      제적 'disenrolment', 네 'your'
   b. words with ㅐ : 배 'belly',
      재적 'enrolment', 내 'my'

Interestingly, because /e/ and /æ/ have become largely no longer distinctive, when there are two frequently used words with only an /e/ and /æ/ distinction, there is a tendency to use an alternative word to avoid any ambiguity (i.e., by replacing either the /e/ or /æ/ vowel or preceding consonant). For instance, in speech, 내 'my' and 네 'your' can be ambiguous and cause difficulty in the proper understanding of a sentence. To avoid this problem, native speakers tend to much prefer 니 /ni/ to 네 for the word 'your'. Also, except for words with ㅔ and ㅐ which are frequently used often in transcribing names, for example, people need to confirm the spelling because it is hard to tell which one is which.

Figures 5.3 and 5.4 confirm our observation. Both figures show the results of a study in which ten male and ten female native speakers took part. In this

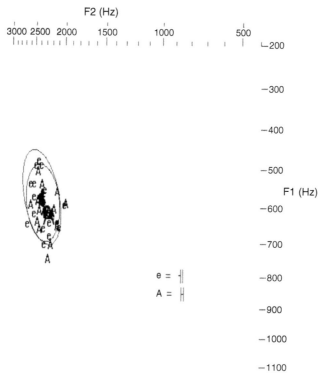

Figure 5.4   Formant plot of ㅔ and ㅐ (ten female speakers)

study, participants were asked to take part in a quiz, in which the answers to all of the questions were words which, orthographically speaking, contained either 에 or 애 followed by the {-ta} -다 ending. The test was repeated.

Figures 5.3 and 5.4 show the formant charts of / ㅔ / and / ㅐ / in terms of the formant-measures F1 and F2. No significant difference is observed between / ㅔ / and / ㅐ /. This indicates that native speakers of Korean cannot distinguish /e/ from /æ/.

5.2.2 The simple vowel system of Standard Korean

Table 5.3 sums up our observations and presents an updated version of the range of monophthongs available in Standard Korean, a total of seven sounds. From this table, it can be seen that there are more back vowels than front vowels in Korean. All back vowels except the low vowel /ɑ/ have a rounded and unrounded vowel pair and there is a symmetry between (high/mid) front vowels and (high/mid) back vowels.

Table 5.3 Monophthongs in Standard Korean

	Front	Back	
	Unrounded	Unrounded	Rounded
High	i	ɯ	u
Mid	ɛ	ʌ	o
Low		ɑ	

To confirm the accuracy of the above table, let us now turn to look at minimal pairs in Korean.

(4)　Minimal pairs
　　　Front vowels
　　　/i/ : /ɛ/　기미 /kimi/ 'freckles'　　개미 /kɛmi/ 'ant'
　　　　　　　미 /mi/ 'beauty'　　　　　매 /mɛ/ 'hawk'
　　　　　　　시 /si/ 'poetry'　　　　　새 /sɛ/ 'bird'
　　　　　　　시다 /sitɑ/ 'to be sour'　새다 /sɛtɑ/ 'to leak'

　　　Back vowels
　　　/ɯ/ : /ʌ/　글 /kɯl/ 'sentence'　　걸 /kʌl/ 'three points in a
　　　　　　　　　　　　　　　　　　　game of yut'

　　　　　　　들 /tɯl/ 'field'　　　　덜 /tʌl/ 'less'
　　　　　　　늘 /nɯl/ 'always'　　　널 /nʌl/ 'board'
　　　　　　　쓸다 /s*ɯltɑ/ 'to sweep'　썰다 /s*ʌltɑ/ 'to cut'
　　　/u/ : /o/　궁 /kuŋ/ 'palace'　　　공 /koŋ/ 'merit'
　　　　　　　숨 /sum/ 'breath'　　　솜 /som/ 'cotton'
　　　　　　　술 /sul/ 'tassel/liquor'　솔 /sol/ 'brush'
　　　　　　　굽다 /kuptɑ/ 'to be bent'　곱다 /koptɑ/ 'to be beautiful'
　　　/ɑ/ : /ʌ/　감 /kɑm/ 'persimmon'　검 /kʌm/ 'sword'
　　　　　　　가미 /kɑmi/ 'seasoning'　거미 /kʌmi/ 'spider'
　　　　　　　사기 /sɑki/ 'fraud'　　　서기 /sʌki/ 'clerk'
　　　　　　　감다 /kɑmtɑ/ 'to wind'　검다 /kʌmtɑ/ 'to be black'

5.2.3 The phonetic realisation of monophthongs

So far, we have observed the phonological aspects of the monophthong. In this section, we will discuss the phonetic realisation of the monophthong. Table 5.4 shows the results of a case-study investigation, in which ten male and female native Korean speakers were asked to pronounce the seven monophthongs outlined in Table 5.3 above. They were asked to pronounce the target vowels in a sequence of /h_tɑ/. Table 5.4 shows the mean and standard deviation

Table 5.4 Mean and standard deviation of F1 and F2 of ten male and female speakers' phonetic realisations of seven different monophthongs

	Male		Female	
	F1 (SD)	F2 (SD)	F1 (SD)	F2 (SD)
i	258.9 (40.0)	2065.9 (130.6)	291.2 (24.8)	2730.7 (133.8)
ɛ	489.5 (78.6)	1828.1 (121.2)	589.6 (108.5)	2309.2 (172.6)
ɑ	788.1 (55.3)	1406.9 (66.4)	990.9 (67.9)	1716.2 (103.7)
ʌ	560.4 (45.4)	1045.4 (94.3)	688.5 (107.6)	1293.4 (101.2)
ɯ	333.5 (71.7)	1517.6 (169.9)	322.2 (62.9)	1666.7 (171.0)
o	356.2 (42.8)	795.0 (116.7)	398.1 (63.1)	739.7 (110.9)
u	280.1 (37.0)	858.4 (146.6)	321.1 (24.8)	800.7 (112.9)

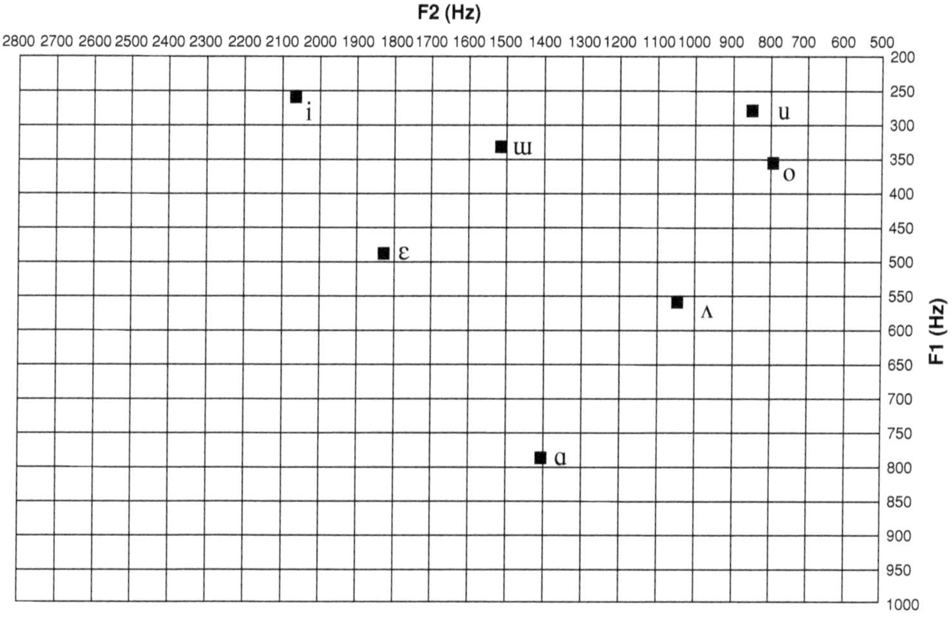

Figure 5.5   Formant chart (ten male speakers)

(SD) of F1 and F2 for seven monophthongs. Except the vowel /ɛ/, which has forty values (10 speakers × 2 times × 2 vowels (/ ㅔ / and / ㅐ /), all other vowels had twenty values (10 speakers × 2 times). In the case of / ㅔ / and / ㅐ /, native speakers were asked to pronounce words that are spelled ㅔ and ㅐ. Figures 5.5 and 5.6 show formant charts drawn from the same data that were summarised in Table 5.4.

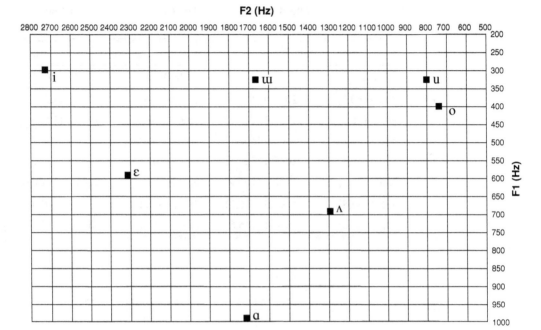

Figure 5.6   Formant chart (ten female speakers)

Figure 5.7 compares the formant charts of Standard Korean and English (RP).[1] The solid line represents Korean and the dotted line represents English. We can see that monophthongs in the two languages are quite different from each other. The number of monophthongs in Korean (seven) is smaller than in English (eleven) and the F2-value range of vowel pronunciation is smaller in Korean as a result. Interestingly, such a range difference is observed more significantly in terms of the front–back contrast than in terms of the high–mid–low contrast. Also, though /ɑ/ and /ʌ/ exist both in Korean and English, Figure 5.7 shows that the Korean /ɑ/ is lower than English /ɑ/ and also pronounced more at the front, whereas Korean /ʌ/ is pronounced further back than English /ʌ/ and the mouth is less open. Korean /ɯ/ is not found in English and English-speaking learners of Korean may find this sound unfamiliar.

In fact, not only English-speaking learners but learners of Korean in general find it very difficult to distinguish between /ɯ/ and /ʌ/, two back-unrounded vowels in Korean. In addition, /ɯ/ and /ʌ/ and /ʌ/ and /o/ are equally difficult to distinguish.

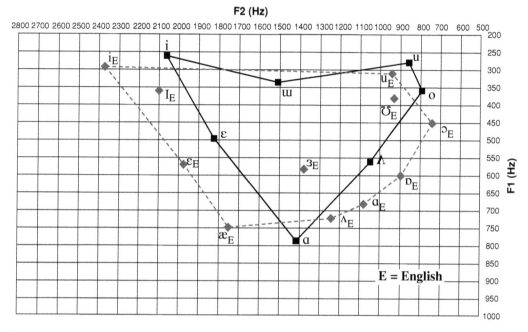

F2 (Hz)

Figure 5.7   Comparison of formant charts for English (RP) and Standard Korean

DID YOU KNOW…?

Are Korean taxi drivers still rip-offs?

Eric studies Korean at university. Wanting to improve his Korean, he decided to go to Korea, and finally arrived at Incheon International Airport. Thinking to himself that he could now finally practise his Korean as he wanted, he decided to take a cab to his friend's house, and got in a cab.

Eric: 기사님, 2호선신촌역으로가주세요.
          'I would like to go to the *Sinchon* station, please.'

Driver: 네, 알겠습니다. 한국어를아주잘하시네요.
          'Okay. You speak very good Korean.'

Having been complimented for his Korean shortly after his arrival, Eric felt very proud of himself for having studied so hard. According to his friend, *Sinchon* 신촌 was not very far from Incheon Airport. However, the taxi driver, despite having travelled quite far, did not seem to be stopping at all. Eric was a bit bewildered. Was the driver trying to rip him off? While Eric was thinking that the driver was a bit suspicious, the taxi driver spoke.

Driver: 손님, 다왔습니다. 7만 8천원 나왔습니다.
           'We have arrived. That will be 78,000 won.'

Eric: 네? 그럴리가요. 친구는 5만원이면 충분할거라고 하던데요.
           'Really? I can't believe that. My friend said it would cost about
           50,000 won at most.'

Driver: 친구가 잘못 안 모양이네요, 여기까지 5 만원에 절대
           올수없습니다.
           'He must be wrong. It is impossible to get here for 50,000 won.'

Eric thought to himself, "And they said there weren't any rip-off taxi
drivers in Korea anymore! Am I being completely ripped off by this guy?
Well, I suppose the fares are very cheap compared to England." Comforting
himself with this realisation, he looked for exit no. 4 from the subway
station. He had promised his friend to meet at a Burger King near exit
no. 4. But no matter where he looked, he couldn't find a Burger King next
to exit no. 4. While he was panicking, Eric saw that the subway station
read 신천역 *Sincheon* not 신촌역 *Sinchon*! He had mispronounced 신촌
[sintɕʰon], as 신천 [sintɕʰʌn], and so the taxi driver had dropped him off
at 신천 *Sincheon* station instead of 신촌 *Sinchon* station. "Distinguishing
/ʌ/ 어 from /o/ 오 in Korean is so hard! But I had better make sure of the
difference from now on", thought Eric.

DID YOU KNOW...?

The six-vowel system in the dialect of *Gyeongsang* Province

As mentioned earlier, the vowel system shows more discrepancies across
dialects than consonants do. Among the Korean dialects, the *Gyeongsang*
dialect has the smallest number of single vowels. Unlike Standard Korean,
the *Gyeongsang* dialect has a six-vowel system; this is because /ʌ/ and /ɯ/
are not distinct in this dialect.

Figure A compares the monophthongs of the *Daegu* dialect – a branch of
the *Gyeongsang* dialect – with those of the Seoul dialect. The data for
the *Daegu* dialect were drawn from ten male speakers in their forties,
while the data for the Seoul dialect were drawn from ten male speakers in
their twenties. The average F1 and F2 values of the seven monophthongs in
the Seoul dialect are indicated by the solid lines, while the average F1 and
F2 values of the *Daegu* dialect are indicated by the dotted lines. The

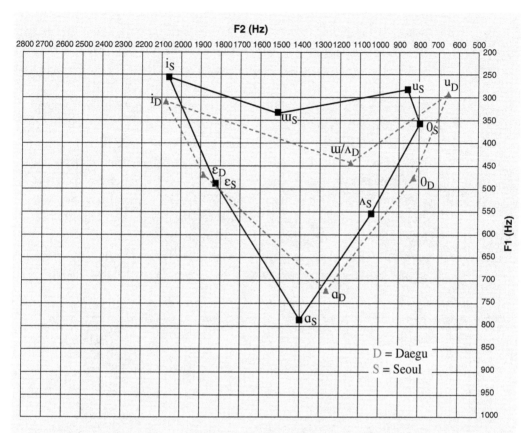

A: Comparison between Seoul and *Gyeongsang* (*Daegu*) dialects (ten male speakers of the *Daegu* dialect in their forties)

Daegu dialect speakers in their forties did not show a significant difference in their pronunciation of /ʌ/ and /ɯ/, and therefore the difference in the average F1 and F2 values of these two vowels is not statistically significant. The average value of the combined vowel is indicated in the chart as ɯ/ʌ$_D$. As the figure shows, the combined vowel is situated acoustically about halfway between /ʌ/ and /ɯ/ in the Seoul dialect.

It is interesting to observe that the combination of these two vowels influences the way that the other surrounding vowels are pronounced. This effect can be seen more distinctly with back vowels, rather than with front vowels. As the figure shows, *Daegu* dialect speakers tend to distinguish /u/ from /o/ far more clearly than Seoul dialect speakers. In particular, there is a noticeable difference in the way that /o/ is pronounced in these two dialects; in the *Daegu* dialect /o/ is pronounced with the mouth opened more widely than in the Seoul dialect. On the other hand, the open vowel /ɑ/ is *not* pronounced with the mouth opened as widely in the *Daegu* dialect as it is in the Seoul dialect. This is because the back unrounded vowels that result from the merging of the two unrounded vowels do not require the mouth to be open as wide as do back unrounded vowels in the Seoul dialect.

However, this vowel combination phenomenon was not observed among speakers in their twenties. According to H.-J. Jang and J.-Y. Shin (2006), *Daegu* dialect speakers in their twenties, regardless of gender, distinguish between seven monophthongs in the same way as speakers of the Seoul dialect, because of the influence of Standard Korean. Figure B is a chart that combines the data that H.-J. Jang and J.-Y. Shin (2006) drew from ten male *Daegu* dialect speakers in their twenties with the data drawn from ten male Seoul dialect speakers mentioned earlier in this book. As the *Daegu* dialect speakers in their twenties acquired a seven-vowel system, their overall vowel pronunciation patterns came to resemble those of Seoul dialect speakers.

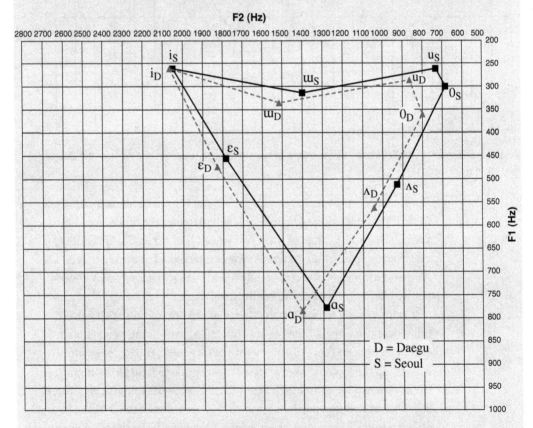

B: Comparison between Seoul and *Gyeongsang* (*Daegu*) dialects (ten male speakers of the *Daegu* dialect in their twenties)

Table 5.5 The eleven diphthongs of SKP

	i	e	æ	y	ø	ɯ	ʌ	ɑ	u	o
Glide										
j	–	je (ㅖ)	jæ (ㅒ)	–	–	ɯj (ㅢ)	jʌ (ㅕ)	jɑ (ㅑ)	ju (ㅠ)	jo (ㅛ)
w	–	we (ㅞ)	wæ (ㅙ)	–	–	–	wʌ (ㅝ)	wɑ (ㅘ)	–	–

Table 5.6 The ten diphthongs of Standard Korean (tentative)

	Monophthongs						
	i	ε	ɯ	ʌ	ɑ	u	o
Glide							
j	–	jε	ɯj (ㅢ)	jʌ	jɑ	ju	jo
w	wi	wε	–	wʌ	wɑ	–	–

5.3 Diphthongs

In this section, we will discuss diphthongs in Korean. According to SKP, there are eleven diphthongs as listed in Table 5.5.

However, if we adopt the seven-monophthong system, which assumes no distinction between /e/ and /æ/, /je/ and /jæ/ as well as /we/ and /wæ/ will also have no distinction. In addition, /wi/ should be categorised as a diphthong. This will give us a revised inventory of Korean diphthongs as shown in Table 5.6.

According to Table 5.6, we can observe one off-glide (ㅢ) along with nine on-glides in Korean. Is the diphthong /ㅢ/ the only off-glide in Korean? This will be discussed in the next section.

DID YOU KNOW...?

Is it 웬일 or 왠일?

People often confuse 웨 and 왜 and mistake the adnominal 웬 for 왠 in writing. For example, they often write 웬일이니 as 왠일이니, or 웬 말이냐 as 왠말이 냐. Alternatively, they make the opposite mistake, writing 왠지 as 웬지. These mistakes in orthography are due to the fact the two sounds are indistinguishable.

5.3.1 The diphthong /ㅢ/

5.3.1.1 Is /ㅢ/ an on-glide or off-glide?

Whether to treat /ㅢ/ in Korean as an on-glide or off-glide is one of the difficult problems in Korean phonology. Most researchers regard /ㅢ/ as an off-glide yet it is still debatable.

The problem is this: given that /ㅢ/ is a diphthong, one of the vowels should be the syllable nucleus and the other should be a glide. However, it is not easy to decide which one should be a syllable nucleus and which one should be a glide. If we analyse /ㅢ/ as /ɰj/, a /ɯ/ vowel plus a glide /j/, this yields a unique case of off-glide in Korean phonology. We can wonder if it is explanatorily adequate to postulate an off-glide sound in Korean to explain /ㅢ/. On the other hand, if we analyse /ㅢ/ as /ɰi/, where /i/ is a monophthong and /ɰ/ is attached to it as an on-glide, we won't have a unique off-glide. Nevertheless, this means we have an extra glide /ɰ/ in the inventory of Korean. In this book, we adopt the latter view and argue that /ɰ/ should be added in the list of glides in Korea.

There are two major reasons for this claim. First, if we assume that /ㅢ/ has an off-glide, we would have to change our assumption that diphthongs in Korean are falling. Moreover, we would need to explain why the glide /j/ combines in this way only with /ɯ/, but not with other vowels, as we can see from Table 5.6. On the other hand, if we assume that /ㅢ/ has an on-glide, then we avoid the problems outlined above, and simply state that the reason /ɰ/ combines only with /i/ in this way is due to the constraints placed on glide and monophthong combinations.

Second, Korean diphthongs have certain constraints placed on them with regard to preceding consonants. For instance, the glide /j/ cannot be combined with coronal consonants such as alveolar or alveolo-palatal sounds within a morpheme. As a result, in pure Korean words, coronal consonants can never be combined with /j/ and in Sino-Korean words, coronal obstruents can never be combined with /j/. On the other hand, /w/ cannot be combined with bilabial consonants.

(5)   *$/$sjo$/$ 쇼, *$/$sju$/$ 슈, *$/$tɕju$/$ 쥬, *$/$tɕ*ju$/$ 쮸, *$/$mwa$/$ 뫄

These constraints are only valid within a morpheme, though in cases where a sequence of morphemes is contracted, the constraints are not observed in the surface phonetic realisation. For instance, the phoneme /sjʌ/ is never observed as an independent morpheme, but is observed as the pronunciation of the contracted form of /hɑ- + -si- + -ʌ/, as shown in (6).

(6)   하시어 /ha- + -si- + -ʌ/ → [hasjʌ]

Morphologically, '의' cannot be preceded by a consonant. Although /의/ is preceded by a consonant in words such as 늴리리 (/nɰillili/), 흰색 (/hɰi+n+sɛk/) and 무늬 (/munɰi/), in the actual pronunciation, /의/ is pronounced as /i/ in all of these words. Of course, /의/ can be combined with consonants in its surface form. Standard Seoul Korean speakers will therefore pronounce 법의학 (/pʌp # ɰihak/) 'legal medicine' or 흔들의자 (/huntul # ɰitɕa/) 'rocking chair' as [pʌ.pɰi.hak] and [hun.tu.lɰi.tɕa].

In sum, if we assume /의/ to be a falling diphthong (i.e. a diphthong with an off-glide), we have to postulate a new combining constraint for falling diphthongs in general. On the other hand, if we assume /의/ to be a rising diphthong (i.e., a diphthong with an on-glide), we can say that the combining constraint observed above is not applicable to all rising diphthongs, but only the glide /의/ is combined with certain consonants. This is more plausible, as this constraint is universal to all languages.

5.3.1.2   The phonetic realisation of /의/

In spontaneous speech, /ɰi/ is realised as [ɰi] only when it appears as the first syllable of a free morpheme. Otherwise, /ɰi/ is realised as [i] in general as in (7) below. The only exception is when the first segment of the first syllable is a consonant as in (7c) below.

(7)   a. 의사 /ɰisa/ [ɰisa] 'doctor', 의자 /ɰitɕa/ [ɰitɕa] 'chair'
         여의사 /jʌ # ɰisa/ [jʌɰisa] 'female doctor',
         흔들의자 /huntul # ɰitɕa/ [huntulɰitɕa] 'rocking chair'

      b. 민주주의 /mintɕutɕuɰi/ [mintɕutɕui] 'democracy', 강의 /kaŋɰi/ [kaŋɰi] 'lecture'

      c. 희망 /hɰimaŋ/ [himaŋ] 'hope'
         (# = word boundary)

If /mintɕutɕuɰi/ 민주주의 and /kaŋɰi/ 강의 in (7b) are pronounced as [mintɕutɕuɰi] or [kaŋɰi] instead of [mintɕutɕui] and [kaŋi], it sounds very unnatural. Interestingly, however, genitive {ɰi} 의 is pronounced not as [ɰi] but as [ɛ] in general. For instance, /(suni + -ɰi) (sin)/ 순이의 신 'Suni's shoes' is more naturally pronounced as [suniɛsin] instead of [suniɰisin].

Table 5.7 Diphthongs in Standard Korean

	i	ɛ	ɑ	ɯ	u	ʌ	o
Glide							
j	–	jɛ	jɑ	–	ju	jʌ	jo
w	wi	wɛ	wɑ	–	–	wʌ	–
ɰ	ɰi	–	–	–	–	–	–

DID YOU KNOW…?

No courtesy in the *Jeolla* dialect?

There are discrepancies across dialects even in the list of diphthongs. The *Jeolla* dialect is a prime example of this. In the *Jeolla* dialect, unlike in Standard Korean, the glide /j/ cannot be combined with any front vowel. Thus, neither /jɛ/ nor /ji/ exists in its list of diphthongs. The diphthong /ɰi/ does not exist in the *Jeolla* dialect either.

Because of this, the /jɛ/ of standard Korean is replaced by /ɛ/ in the *Jeolla* dialect, and /ɰi/ by /ɯ/. Therefore, while /jɛɰi/ 'courtesy' is pronounced as [jɛi] in Standard Korean, it is pronounced as [ɛɯ] in *Jeolla* dialect. In other words, this means that there is no [jɛɰi], or courtesy, in the *Jeolla* dialect.

5.3.2 The diphthongal system of Standard Korean

Table 5.7 provides a further revised chart for diphthongs in Korean. Altogether it has ten vowels, which are indeed the combination of seven monophthongs and three glides. As we can see from the gaps in the chart, not all glides can combine with all monophthongs and not all monophthongs can combine with all glides. There are some restrictions in diphthong formation as in (8).

(8) Some constraints in diphthong formation in Korean

    a. All diphthongs in Korean have a structure of a glide plus a monophthong, where a glide precedes and does not follow the monophthong (i.e. on-glides). No glides can occur after a monophthong (i.e. no off-glides).

    b. No glide can be attached to /ɯ/.

c. /j/ can't be attached to /i/ and /w/ can't be attached to /u/ and /o/. This shows that the possible combinations are restricted when the two sounds are too similar.

d. /ɰ/ can be attached to /i/ only.

We will conclude this section by discussing the benefit of considering the diphthong in Korean as a combination of two phonemes instead of one independent phoneme. Economy and simplicity of the system is the first reason. If we regard each diphthong as an independent phoneme, we will have 19 consonants, 7 monophthongs and 10 diphthongs, which altogether are 36 phonemes. But, if we consider a diphthong as the combination of a monophthong and a glide, we will have 19 consonants, 7 monophthongs, and 3 glides, which is 29 altogether. Not only this, we can also provide a systematic explanation for why only certain diphthongs can exist as we discussed above.

DID YOU KNOW...?

Knowing how to pronounce things correctly can save your life!

Some sparrows were sitting in a row on an electric line and chatting away. Then, suddenly, another sparrow flew over and said urgently to the perched sparrows, "Guys, we're in big trouble! There's a hunter in town! But, apparently, he asks you where your hometown is first, then, he kills all the sparrows from *Gyeongsang-do* and spares all the rest!"

The sparrow from *Gyeongsang-do* was overcome with fear at the news. However, he considered himself lucky to have been warned in good time. He figured that as long as he lied about his hometown, he would be spared.

Then one day, the hunter appeared before the sparrow from *Gyeongsang-do*. Just as it was rumoured, the hunter asked the sparrow where he was from.

Hunter: (pointing the gun towards the sparrow) Where is your hometown?

Sparrow: (speaking as calmly as possible) [kɛŋkito] 갱기도!

Needless to say, the hunter shot the sparrow straight away.

The story above can be very funny with just a little background knowledge about the *Gyeongsang* dialect. In the *Gyeongsang* dialect, the C + /jʌ/ of Standard Korean corresponds to C + /ɛ/; *Gyeongsang* dialect speakers therefore pronounce [kjʌŋtɕɛ] 경제, [mjʌŋtɕɛ] 명제, and [pjʌŋ]

평 in Standard Korean as [kɛŋtɕɛ], [mɛŋtɕɛ], [pɛŋ] respectively. It was inevitable that the sparrow from 경상도 *Gyeongsang-do* would pronounce [kjʌŋkito] in Standard Korean as [kɛŋkito]. 🎧

In the end, the false hometown that the sparrow had decided on revealed most clearly the phonemic characteristics of the dialect of his true hometown. If this sparrow had been more knowledgeable about the differences in pronunciation across dialects, he would have been spared his life!

DID YOU KNOW...?

Triphthongs found in Korean

As noted above, the vowel system of Korean consists of seven monophthongs and ten diphthongs. However, if one examines the surface level phonetics carefully, one finds that there are not only diphthongs but also triphthongs. Triphthongs are not found within morphemes, but observed only in particular cases of the joining of morphemes. In particular, this sound can be heard only in the contraction that occurs when a stem that ends with /wi/ is combined with an ending that starts with /ʌ/. Of course, this cannot be observed in the writing itself, but only in speech. There is as yet no letter in Korean orthography that can represent this sound.

Some examples are as follows:

바꿔어 /pak*wi ('to change') + ʌ/ → [pak*wjʌ]/[pak*jʌ]
사귀어 /sakwi ('to make friends with') + ʌ/ → [sakwjʌ]/[sakjʌ]
쉬어 /swi ('to rest') + ʌ/ → [swjʌ]/[sjʌ]
뉘어 /nwi ('to lie down') + ʌ / → [nwjʌ]/[njʌ]
뛰어 /t*wi ('to run') + ʌ/ → [t*wjʌ]/[t*jʌ]

As these examples show, when the diphthong, /wi/, in the word stem meets the /ʌ/ word ending, it sometimes results in the contraction, [wjʌ], or sometimes the [w] drops out to form [jʌ]. The omission of the semivowel [w] occurs most commonly when it is located in the second syllable or after.

The question arises, therefore, of how the triphthong, which exists in Korean phonetics, ought to be represented in the Korean phonemic inventory. Whilst it is true that triphthongs exist in surface level phonetics, this sound cannot be observed within a morpheme, but only where contraction occurs between particular morphemes. The triphthong therefore cannot acquire the status of a phoneme, since this sound only occurs as a by-product of common speech (and does not exist in the foundations of Korean phonology).

The above is similar to the phenomenon in which the alveolar affricative [ts], although absent from the list of English phonemes, is heard in surface level phonetics, in words such as /sports/ or /texts/. The alveolar affricative, /ts/, does not exist in the foundational phoneme system of English. However, when /t/ and /s/ are brought together by a combination of certain morphemes, the alveolar affricative, /ts/, can be observed in the surface level phonetics.

To conclude, the alveolar affricative [ts] in English, and the triphthong [wjʌ] in Korean, are not necessarily included in the phoneme inventory of those languages; rather, they are observed as surface level sounds that occur through the bridging of the phonemes /t/ and /s/, and /wi/ and /ʌ/.

Table 5.8 Features for vowels

	i	ɛ	ɯ	ʌ	u	o	ɑ
[high]	+	−	+	−	+	−	
[low]	−	−	−	−	−	−	+
[back]	−	−	+	+	+	+	+
[round]	−	−	−	−	+	+	−

5.4 Features for vowels

There are three factors that play an important role in the articulation of a vowel: (i) roundedness (lip protrusion), (ii) tongue backness and (iii) tongue height. The first factor is related to the lips and the second and third are related to the body of the tongue. Vowels are articulated mostly by using the body of the tongue, but consonants are articulated in general by using the tip or blade of the tongue. This is why most features for vowels are related to the body of the tongue. To distinguish seven monophthongs in Korean, we need four features as given in Table 5.8.

Table 5.9 Features for vowels and glides

	i	ɛ	ɰ	ʌ	u	o	ɑ	j	w	ɥ
[syllablic]	+	+	+	+	+	+	+	−	−	−
[high]	+	−	+	−	+	−	−	+	+	+
[low]	−	−	−	−	−	−	+	−	−	−
[back]	−	−	+	+	+	+	+	−	+	+
[round]	−	−	−	−	+	+	−	−	+	−

Let's think briefly about the four features used in the table. Of these, three features relate to the body of the tongue, namely [high], [low] and [back], while the feature [round] relates to the lips. Each feature is explained in (9).

(9) Features for vowels
    a. Features related to the body of the tongue
        (i)   [+/−high]:
            [+high] sounds are produced by raising the body of the tongue above the level that it occupies in the neutral position.[2]
        (ii) [+/−low]:
            [+low] sounds are produced by lowering the body of the tongue below the level that it occupies in the neutral position.
        (iii) [+/−back]:
            [+back] sounds are produced by retracting the body of the tongue from the neutral position.
    b. Features related to the lips
        (i)   [+/−round]:
            [+round] sounds are produced with the lips narrowed.

Glides and vowels share the same features, except for the feature [syllabic]: vowels possess the feature [+syllabic], whereas glides are [−syllabic]. This means that /j, w, ɥ/ are exactly the same was /i, u, ɥ/ except for the value of their syllabic features, as shown in Table 5.9.

5.5 Summary

In this chapter, we have discussed vowels in Korean. There are three types of vowels in Korean: monophthongs (simple vowels), diphthongs and glides. Glides are consonants in English, but it is better to view them as vowels in Korean. We demonstrated that all diphthongs in Korean are on-glides, that is, made up of glides preceding monophthongs. Monophthongs can be classified by the height and backness of the tongue and by the roundedness of the lips. Some vowel distinctions in Korean, such as the one between /e/ and /æ/, no longer seem to exist. Taking into account the lack of true distinction between /e/ and /æ/, we have shown that there are seven monophthongs in Korean, and ten diphthongs, which are combinations of these seven monophthongs with the three glides. In order to provide more natural explanations for vowel-related phonological processes, we need to classify each vowel as a set of features. Of the four major features for vowels, three are related to the position of the body of the tongue (e.g. [+/−high], [+/−low], [+/−back]), and one is related to the flat or rounded shape of the lips (i.e. [+/−round]).

EXERCISES

1 Define monophthongs, diphthongs and glides.
2 Is a glide a consonant or a vowel in Korean? Explain why with relevant examples.
3 Are /ㅚ/ and /ㅟ/ monophthongs or diphthongs?
4 Is there any difference between /e/ and /æ/ in contemporary Korean?
5 State whether the following pairs of words form minimal pairs in Korean and explain why. Also, write down the Korean letter(s) as the relevant phoneme(s).
   a. 금 'gold', 곰 'bear'
   b. 개미 'ant', 거미 'spider'
   c. 골 'brain', 굴 'cave'
   d. 굽다 'curve', 곱다 'to be pretty'
   e. 나 'I', 너 'you'
   f. 국 'soup', 곡 'song'
6 Which monophthong(s) can be found in Korean, but not in English?
7 What is the difference between English diphthongs and Korean diphthongs?
8 Discuss dialectal differences in Korean vowels.
9 Classify the seven monophthongs in Korean using the features [high], [low], [back] and [round].

6 Frequency trends of Korean sounds

In Chapters 4 and 5, we have discussed the phonetic and phonological characteristics of consonants and vowels in Korean. However, not all of the sounds which exist are found frequently in Korean, and some are used more often than others. In this chapter, we would like to explore the frequency of sounds in Korean to find out which sounds are frequently used and which are used less. We will try to find the answers by looking at dictionary data and spontaneous speech data. In addition, we will compare the frequency of sounds in Korean with that of sounds in English.

There are 19 consonants and 7 monophthongs in Korean, along with 10 diphthongs made from 7 monophthongs and 3 glides. Therefore, 36 sounds exist in total in the Korean sounds inventory. In the previous chapter, we considered a diphthong as a combination of a monophthong and a glide. This view can provide a better explanation because it doesn't increase the number of phonemes unnecessarily. In addition, this can capture the phonetic similarity between the corresponding monophthong and the glide and hence increase explanatory adequacy in accounting for the behaviours of speech sounds.

However, in terms of explaining phoneme frequency, it is better to analyse diphthongs as one discrete phoneme instead of a combination of two phonemes. By doing so, we can easily observe the frequency difference between diphthongs as well as monophthongs. Therefore, in this chapter we will regard diphthongs as one phoneme. As a result, the number of phonemes in Korean increases from 29 to 36 (19 consonants, 7 monophthongs, 10 diphthongs).

The organisation of this chapter is as follows: in 6.1, we will look at how the data under discussion have been collected; in 6.2 and 6.3, we will

Table 6.1 Sound distribution (dictionary)

Lexemes	47,401
Syllables	122,761
Sounds	
Vowels	122,761 (42.3%)
Consonants	
Onset	110,015 (65.7%)
Coda	57,355 (34.3%)
Subtotal	167,370 (57.7%)
Total	290,131

discuss phoneme and syllable frequency respectively. In 6.4, we will compare sound frequency in Korean with that of English, and the conclusion follows in 6.5.

6.1 Database

6.1.1 Dictionary

We have chosen the *Yonsei Korean Language Dictionary* (henceforth 'dictionary') for our discussion in this section. Compared to other dictionaries, the Yonsei dictionary better reflects 'real' usage in selecting word entries. Among the 49,553 entries in the Yonsei dictionary, we have excluded those entries that are not found in the *Standard Korean Language Dictionary*.[1] This leaves us with 47,401 entries. Table 6.1 shows the statistics for those entries.

6.1.2 Spontaneous speech

To investigate sound distribution in spontaneous speech, we have used a database called SLILC (Spoken Language Information Lab Corpus), established by one of the authors (J.-Y. Shin 2008). To create this database, 57 native speakers' dialogue was recorded and subsequently transcribed. Of those 57 speakers, 28 were male and 29 female; their ages ranged from 19 to 32; and all 57 spoke Seoul Korean. Recording took place in a phonetic booth, and three people participated in each conversation. The total length of recorded material amounts to approximately 23 hours. Table 6.2 shows the statistics for the sounds occurring in the database.

Table 6.2 Sound distribution (speech)

Speakers (M, F)	57 (28, 29)
Utterances	35,439
Syllables	403,605
Sounds	
Vowels	403,605 (47.0%)
Consonants	
Onset	345,128 (75.9%)
Coda	109,779 (24.1%)
Subtotal	454,907 (53.0%)
Total	858,512

6.2 Phoneme frequency

Based on the database established in 6.1, in this section, we will investigate phoneme frequency. As mentioned, there are 36 sounds in Korean, consisting of 19 consonants, 7 monophthongs and 10 diphthongs. In the following, while discussing phoneme frequency, we will treat the diphthong as an independent phoneme instead of as a combination of a monophthong and a glide, for simplicity of discussion. In 6.2.1, we will discuss overall phoneme frequency and in 6.2.2 and 6.2.3, we will discuss the distribution of consonants and vowels in the dictionary and in spontaneous speech, respectively.

6.2.1 Overall phoneme frequency

Table 6.3 shows the rankings of phoneme frequency found in the dictionary. Likewise, Table 6.4 shows the rankings of phoneme frequency as found in spontaneous speech. We can see that in both databases, /ɑ/ is the most frequently used phoneme and /ɰi/ is the least frequently used phoneme.

As can be seen in Figure 6.1, not all phonemes appeared with similar frequency. 'DIC' indicates dictionary data and 'SP' indicates spontaneous speech. In other words, in both the dictionary and in speech, some phonemes were much more frequently used than others. In the dictionary, the four most highly ranked phonemes constituted 30.90% of total distribution, and the eight most highly ranked phonemes constituted 51.86%. However, the bottom 16 phonemes constituted only 9.82%. Phoneme distribution becomes even more asymmetric in the case of spontaneous speech. Here, the top three phonemes constituted 30.43% of total distribution, and the top seven constituted 55.78% of total distribution, whereas the bottom 18 phonemes constituted only 9.95%.

Table 6.3 Phoneme frequency (dictionary)

Rank	Phoneme	Frequency	%	Cumulative (%)	Rank	Phoneme	Frequency	%	Cumulative (%)
1	ɑ	28,844	9.9	9.90	19	tɕʰ	5,290	1.8	89.04
2	k	22,284	7.7	17.62	20	pʰ	3,289	1.1	90.18
3	n	19,385	6.7	24.30	21	tɕ*	2,922	1.0	91.18
4	i	19,133	6.6	30.90	22	k*	2,784	1.0	92.14
5	ŋ	16,726	5.8	36.66	23	wɛ	2,772	1	93.10
6	l	16,090	5.5	42.21	24	s*	2,726	0.9	94.04
7	ʌ	14,783	5.1	47.30	25	wɑ	2,662	0.9	94.96
8	tɕ	13,205	4.6	51.86	26	tʰ	2,609	0.9	95.85
9	s	12,818	4.4	56.27	27	kʰ	2,361	0.8	96.67
10	o	12,817	4.4	60.69	28	t*	1,821	0.6	97.30
11	u	12,557	4.3	65.02	29	jo	1,529	0.5	97.83
12	m	11,802	4.1	69.09	30	ju	1,329	0.5	98.28
13	h	11,224	3.9	72.96	31	jɑ	1,232	0.4	98.71
14	p	10,161	3.5	76.46	32	p*	1,216	0.4	99.12
15	ɛ	9,309	3.2	79.67	33	wi	998	0.3	99.47
16	t	8,657	3.0	82.65	34	wʌ	997	0.3	99.81
17	ɯ	6,882	2.4	85.02	35	jɛ	314	0.1	99.92
18	jʌ	6,373	2.2	87.22	36	ɰi	230	0.1	100.00

6.2.2 Consonant frequency

In this section, we will discuss phonemic distribution with respect to consonants. Section 6.2.2.1 will show overall distribution and then examine the distribution of consonants with regard to their position within the syllable; in 6.2.2.2 we will examine consonant distribution in syllable-initial, or onset, position, and in 6.2.2.3 we will look at consonant distribution in syllable-final, or coda, position.

6.2.2.1 Overall consonant frequency

Figure 6.2 shows overall consonant frequency as observed in the dictionary. The most frequently used consonant was /k/, followed by /n/, /ŋ/, /l/ and /tɕ/.

Table 6.4 Phoneme frequency (speech)

Rank	Phoneme	Frequency	%	Cumulative (%)	Rank	Phoneme	Frequency	%	Cumulative (%)
1	ɑ	95,853	11.17	11.17	19	k^*	11,355	1.32	91.38
2	n	92,621	10.79	21.95	20	s^*	10,638	1.24	92.62
3	k	72,756	8.47	30.43	21	t^*	8,873	1.03	93.65
4	i	60,318	7.03	37.45	22	$tɕ^*$	7,480	0.87	94.52
5	l	54,253	6.32	43.77	23	jɑ	6,640	0.77	95.29
6	ʌ	52,381	6.11	49.88	24	$tɕ^h$	6,349	0.74	96.03
7	ɯ	50,704	5.91	55.78	25	t^h	6,229	0.73	96.76
8	ɛ	50,024	5.83	61.61	26	k^h	5,553	0.65	97.41
9	m	36,132	4.21	65.82	27	wɛ	3,792	0.44	97.85
10	o	31,268	3.64	69.46	28	wɑ	3,628	0.42	98.27
11	t	30,704	3.58	73.04	29	p^h	3,399	0.4	98.67
12	tɕ	27,076	3.15	76.19	30	jo	2,874	0.33	99.00
13	u	24,061	2.8	79.00	31	p^*	2,457	0.29	99.29
14	ŋ	23,874	2.78	81.78	32	wʌ	2,345	0.27	99.56
15	s	22,827	2.66	84.44	33	jɛ	1,614	0.19	99.75
16	h	16,494	1.92	86.36	34	ju	1,165	0.14	99.88
17	jʌ	15,915	1.85	88.21	35	wi	905	0.11	99.99
18	p	15,837	1.84	90.05	36	ɯi	85	0.01	100.00

The above five consonants constituted 52.4% of total consonant distribution. On the other hand, the bottom seven consonants, shown in the right-hand box, constituted just 9.8% of the total consonant distribution. It is worth noting that both /k/ and /ŋ/ are highly ranked in the distribution. Given that it occurs only in syllable-final position, the fact that /ŋ/ is the third most frequently used consonant is particularly significant.

Figure 6.3 shows overall consonant frequency as observed in spontaneous speech. The most frequently used consonant here was /n/, followed by /k/, /l/, /m/, /t/, and /tɕ/. On the other hand, the least frequently used consonant was /p*/. The top three consonants constituted 48.3% of total distribution, whereas the bottom nine constituted only 13.7%.

The results show that in both the dictionary and in spontaneous speech, obstruent consonants were more frequently used than sonorant consonants and among obstruents, lax obstruents were more frequently used than their tense or aspirated counterparts.

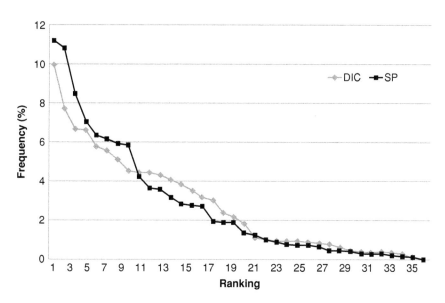

Figure 6.1   Frequency trends by rank (all phonemes, dictionary vs. speech)

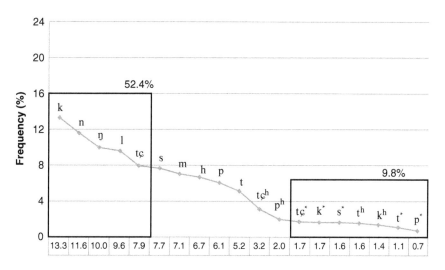

Figure 6.2   Consonant frequency (dictionary)

Figure 6.4 shows the frequency ranking of consonants found in the dictionary and in speech. As the figure shows, the curve was smoother in the dictionary than in speech. In other words, in the dictionary, the distribution of consonants is even, rather than being concentrated on a limited set of sounds, as in speech.

Figure 6.5 shows a comparison between the data from the dictionary and from spontaneous speech. The boxed areas show cases where the distributional

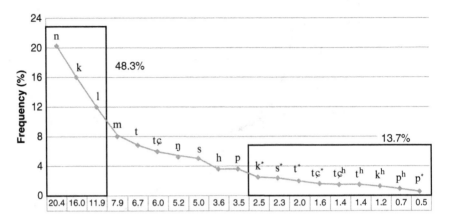

Figure 6.3   Consonant frequency (speech)

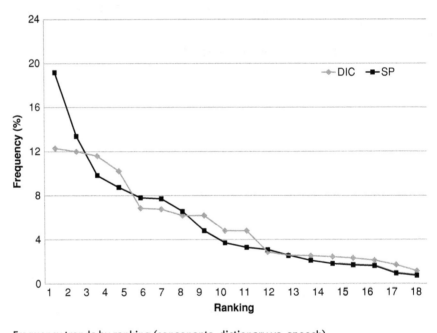

Figure 6.4   Frequency trends by ranking (consonants, dictionary vs. speech)

difference between the dictionary and spontaneous speech is either greater than 5% (solid box) or between 3% and 5% (dashed box). Of all the conso-nants, the distribution of /n/, which was used 8.8% more frequently in sponta-neous speech than in the dictionary was most asymmetric. On the other hand, /ŋ/ and /h/ were used more frequently in the dictionary than in spontaneous speech: /ŋ/ was used 4.8% more in the dictionary than in speech and /h/ was used 3.1% more in the dictionary than in speech. In short, /n/ was found fre-quently in speech and /ŋ/ and /h/ were found frequently in the dictionary.

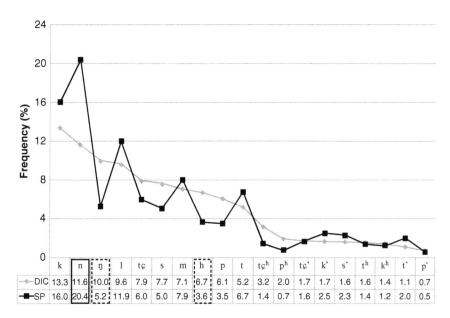

	k	n	ŋ	l	tɕ	s	m	h	p	t	tɕʰ	pʰ	tɕʼ	kʼ	sʼ	tʰ	kʰ	tʼ	pʼ
DIC	13.3	11.6	10.0	9.6	7.9	7.7	7.1	6.7	6.1	5.2	3.2	2.0	1.7	1.7	1.6	1.6	1.4	1.1	0.7
SP	16.0	20.4	5.2	11.9	6.0	5.0	7.9	3.6	3.5	6.7	1.4	0.7	1.6	2.5	2.3	1.4	1.2	2.0	0.5

Figure 6.5   Consonant frequency differences (dictionary vs. speech)

The fact that /k/ is used less frequently in speech while /n/ is used very frequently is related to the use of grammatical morphemes. Indeed /n/ is the most frequently used sound among grammatical morphemes and constituted of 29.8% of all consonants found in them. For instance, grammatical morphemes such as –는, a topic or adnominal particle, or the verbal ending –니, are both used very frequently, and both contain /n/.

Tables 6.5–6.7 show consonant distribution classified according to obstruents vs. sonorants (Table 6.5), place of articulation (Table 6.6) and manner of articulation (Table 6.7).

Table 6.5 shows that in both the dictionary and spontaneous speech, obstruents are used more frequently than sonorants. In particular, in speech, obstruents occurred 7.2% more often than in the dictionary. Among obstruents, tense consonants were observed 5.2% more often in speech than in the dictionary, while aspirated consonants were observed 5.4% less frequently in speech than in the dictionary.

Consider Table 6.6. When consonants were classified according to place of articulation, the most significant difference between speech and the dictionary was observed in alveolar sounds. Alveolar sounds were observed 11.4% more frequently in speech than in the dictionary. Now consider Table 6.7 for differences in manner of articulation. When consonants were classified according to manner of articulation, the most significant difference between speech and the

Table 6.5 Type and token Frequency of consonants (sonorants vs. obstruents and phonation types)

	Type (%)	Token (%)		
		DIC	SP	Δ
Sonorants	21.1	38.2	45.5	−7.2
Obstruents	78.9	61.8	54.5	7.2
Lax	35.7	72.8	73.1	−0.2
Tense	35.7	12.4	17.6	−5.2
Aspirated	28.6	14.7	9.3	5.4

Table 6.6 Type and token frequency of consonants by place of articulation

	Type (%)	Token (%)		
		DIC	SP	Δ
Bilabial	21.1	15.8	12.7	3.1
Alveolar	36.8	38.3	49.7	−11.4
Alveolo-palatal	15.8	12.8	9.0	3.8
Velar	21.1	26.4	25.0	1.4
Glottal	5.3	6.7	3.6	3.1

Table 6.7 Type and token frequency of consonants by manner of articulation

	Type (%)	Token (%)		
		DIC	SP	Δ
Stop	47.4	33.0	34.5	−1.6
Fricative	15.8	16.0	11.0	5.0
Affricate	15.8	12.8	9.0	3.8
Nasal	15.8	28.6	33.6	−4.9
Liquid	5.3	9.6	11.9	−2.3

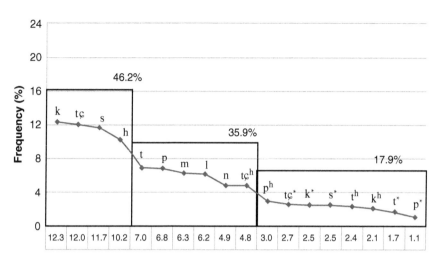

Figure 6.6   Onset frequency (dictionary)

dictionary was observed in fricatives and nasals, which were observed 5.0% more and 4.9% less frequently respectively in the dictionary than in speech.

6.2.2.2 Onset frequency

In this section, we will look at consonant distribution in syllable-initial position. As discussed in Chapter 4, only eighteen consonants can appear in this position. Figure 6.6 shows the data observed for dictionary usage. In the dictionary, /k/ was most frequently used, while /p*/ was least frequently used. Figure 6.6 shows the consonants grouped according to their frequency. The three groups were divided at points where frequency drops significantly. The left-most group consists of high-frequency consonants; the middle group consists of mid-frequency consonants; and the right-most group consists of the consonants least frequently used.

Along with /k/, /tɕ, s, h/ appear in the high-frequency consonant group. Except for /k/, all of these consonants are either fricatives or affricates. The mid-frequency consonants include /t, p, m, l, n, tɕʰ/. Except for /tɕʰ/, all were either lax stops or sonorants. In both the dictionary and in speech, /pʰ, tɕ*, k*, s*, tʰ, kʰ, t*, p*/ appear in the low-frequency group, and these consonants are all either tense or aspirated consonants.

Next, we will discuss the data from spontaneous speech. Figure 6.7 shows the data from speech. In speech, the most frequently used syllable-initial consonant was /k/ (19.2%). The least frequently used consonant was /p*/ (0.7%). As shown in Figure 6.7, the top four consonants constituted 51.2% of the

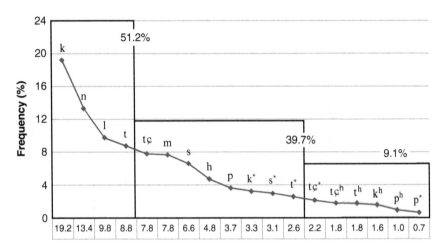

Figure 6.7   Onset frequency (speech)

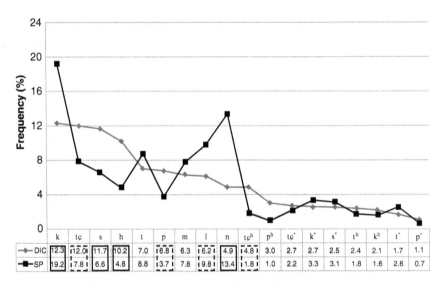

Figure 6.8   Onset frequency differences (dictionary vs. speech)

overall distribution of syllable-initial consonants, while the bottom six constituted just 9.1% altogether.

Figure 6.8 shows a comparison between the data from the dictionary and
from speech. The boxed areas show cases where the distributional difference
between the dictionary and spontaneous speech is either greater than 5% or
between 3% and 5%. Consonants which show a difference greater than 5% in
both speech and the dictionary include /k/ (6.9% more in speech), /s/ (5.1%
more in the dictionary), /h/ (5.4% more in the dictionary), and /n/ (8.5% more
in speech). Furthermore, consonants which show a difference between 3% and

Table 6.8 Type and token frequency of onsets (sonorants vs. obstruents and phonation types)

	Type (%)	Token (%)		
		DIC	SP	Δ
Sonorants	16.7	17.3	31.0	−13.7
Obstruents	83.3	82.7	69.0	13.7
Lax	35.7	68.6	71.9	−3.3
Tense	35.7	14.4	18.4	−4.0
Aspirated	28.6	17.0	9.7	7.3

Table 6.9 Type and token frequency of onsets by place of articulation

	Type (%)	Token (%)		
		DIC	SP	Δ
Bilabial	22.2	17.2	13.2	4.0
Alveolar	38.9	36.1	46.1	−9.9
Alveolo-palatal	16.7	19.5	11.9	7.6
Velar	16.7	17.0	24.1	−7.1
Glottal	5.6	10.2	4.8	5.4

5% include /tɕ/ (4.2% more in the dictionary), /p/ (3.1% more in dictionary), /l/ (3.6% more in speech), and /tɕʰ/ (3% more in the dictionary).

This data shows that in syllable-initial position, /n/, /k/ and /l/ are used relatively more frequently in speech than in the dictionary, while /h/, /s/, /tɕ/, /p/, /tɕʰ/ are used relatively more frequently in the dictionary than in speech.

Tables 6.8–6.10 show consonant distribution classified according to obstruents vs. sonorants (Table 6.8), place of articulation (Table 6.9) and manner of articulation (Table 6.10).

Table 6.8 shows that in both the dictionary and spontaneous speech, obstruents are used more frequently than sonorants. In particular, obstruents occurred 13.7% more often in the dictionary. Among obstruents, in both the dictionary and in spontaneous speech, lax consonants were much more frequently used than their tense and aspirated counterparts. Aspirated consonants, which account for 17.0% of total distribution in the dictionary, only accounted for 9.7% in speech.

Table 6.10 Type and token frequency of onsets by manner of articulation

		Token (%)		
	Type (%)	DIC	SP	Δ
Stop	50.0	38.9	42.7	−3.8
Fricative	16.7	24.3	14.5	9.9
Affricate	16.7	19.5	11.9	7.6
Nasal	11.1	11.2	21.1	−10.0
Liquid	5.6	6.2	9.8	−3.7

Table 6.9 shows that alveolar sounds are the most frequently used, both in the dictionary and in speech, but were much more frequently used in speech than in the dictionary. Table 6.10 shows that stops are the most frequently used in both the dictionary and in speech. Fricatives and affricates were more frequent in the dictionary than in speech, but on the other hand, nasals were more frequent in speech than in the dictionary.

6.2.2.3 Coda frequency

In the following section, we will discuss the distribution of syllable-final consonants, that is, codas. As discussed in Chapter 4, only seven consonants can appear in this position. Figure 6.9 shows the data from the dictionary for syllable-final consonants. Among syllable-final consonants, /ŋ/ was the most frequently used (29.1%), whereas the alveolar stop /t/ was the least frequently used (1.8%). Along with /ŋ/, /n/ was frequently used, and together the two consonants account for 53.6% of overall distribution. The three consonants that occurred least frequently, i.e. /m, p, t/, only account for 15.0% of overall distribution.

Figure 6.10 shows the data from speech. Again, as in the dictionary, /n/ was the most frequently used syllable-final consonant (42.3%), while the alveolar stop /t/ was the least frequently used (0.3%). Next to /n/, /ŋ/ was most frequently used, and together the two consonants account for 64% of overall distribution. The three consonants that occurred least frequently, i.e. /k, p, t/, only account for 9% of overall distribution.

Consider Figure 6.11. The boxed areas show cases where the distributional difference between the dictionary and spontaneous speech is greater than 5%. Among these, /ŋ/ was observed 7.4% more frequently in the dictionary than

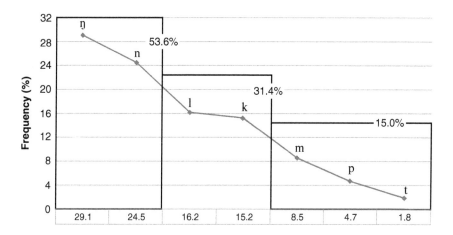

Figure 6.9   Coda frequency (dictionary)

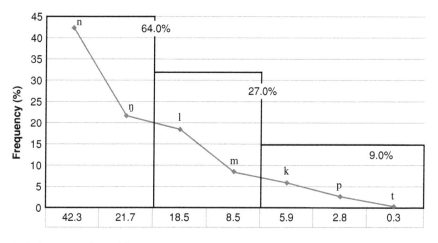

Figure 6.10   Coda frequency (speech)

in speech, /n/ was observed 17.8% more frequently in speech than in the dictionary, and /k/ was observed 9.3% more frequently in the dictionary than in speech.

Tables 6.11–6.13 show consonant distribution in codas classified according to obstruents vs. sonorants (6.11), place of articulation (6.12), and manner of articulation (6.13).

Table 6.11 shows that in both the dictionary and in spontaneous speech, sonorants were more frequently used than obstruents in syllable-final (coda) position. In particular, in speech, sonorants accounted for 91.0% of overall distribution, 12.7% higher than in the dictionary, where sonorants accounted for 78.3% of consonants in syllable-final position.

Table 6.11 Type and token frequency of codas (sonorants vs. obstruents)

	Type (%)	Token (%)		
		DIC	SP	Δ
Sonorants	57.1	78.3	91.0	−12.7
Obstruents	42.9	21.7	9.0	12.7

Table 6.12 Type and token frequency of codas (place of articulation)

	Type (%)	Token (%)		
		DIC	SP	Δ
Bilabial	28.6	13.2	11.3	1.9
Alveolar	42.9	42.5	61.1	−18.6
Velar	28.6	44.3	27.6	16.7

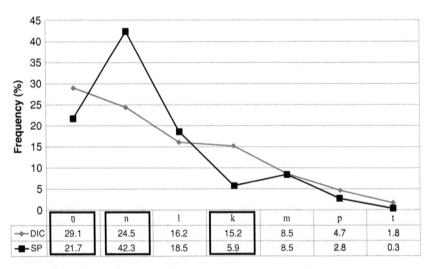

	ŋ	n	l	k	m	p	t
DIC	29.1	24.5	16.2	15.2	8.5	4.7	1.8
SP	21.7	42.3	18.5	5.9	8.5	2.8	0.3

Figure 6.11   Coda frequency differences (dictionary vs. speech)

Table 6.12 shows that alveolar and velar sounds appear frequently, while the frequency of bilabial sounds is low. In particular, in speech, alveolar sounds accounted for 61.1% of overall distribution. This is 18.6% higher than in the dictionary, where alveolar sounds accounted for 42.5% of consonants in syllable-final position.

Table 6.13 Type and token frequency of codas (manner of articulation)

	Type (%)	Token (%)		
		DIC	SP	Δ
Stop	42.9	21.6	9.0	12.7
Nasal	42.9	62.1	72.5	−10.4
Liquid	14.3	16.2	18.5	−2.3

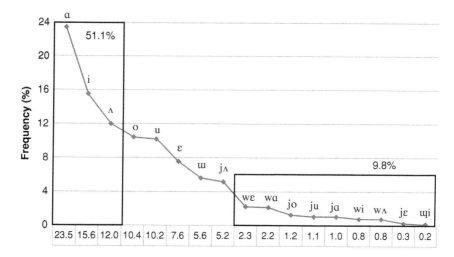

Figure 6.12   Vowel frequency (dictionary)

Table 6.13 shows that in both the dictionary and in speech, nasals are dominant. In the dictionary, the proportion of stops was relatively higher than in speech, while the proportion of nasals was higher in speech than in the dictionary. No significant difference is observed in the distribution of liquids between the dictionary and speech.

6.2.3 Vowel frequency

In this section, we will discuss the phonemic distribution of vowels. Figure 6.12 shows vowels ranked according to the frequency with which they appear in the dictionary. The most frequently observed vowel was /ɑ/ (23.5%), followed by, /i/, /ʌ/, and /o/. It is worth noting that the top seven vowels, which amount to 85.0% of all vowel occurrences, are all monophthongs. This is much higher than the total for diphthongs (15.0%). The three most frequently used

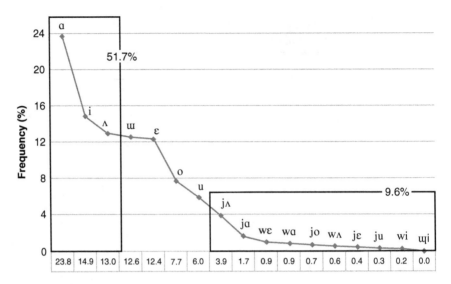

Figure 6.13   Vowel frequency (speech)

vowels constituted 51.1% of overall distribution, whereas the nine least used vowels accounted for only 9.8% of the total. Of monophthongs, /ɯ/ was the least frequently observed and of diphthongs, /jʌ/ was the most frequently observed.

Figure 6.13 shows vowels according to their frequency in speech. The most frequently observed vowel was /ɑ/ (23.8%). Following this, /i/, /ʌ/, /ɯ/, /ɛ/ were most frequent. Just as in the dictionary, the seven most frequently used vowels are all monophthongs. The three most frequently used vowels constitute 51.7% of overall distribution, whereas the ten least used vowels constitute only 9.6% of the total. Among monophthongs, /u/ was least observed and among diphthongs, /jʌ/ was most frequently observed.

Consider Figure 6.14. Unlike in the case of consonants, distributional patterns for vowels were similar both in speech and in the dictionary. That is, it cannot be said that distributional asymmetry was more marked in speech than in the dictionary.

Figure 6.15 shows a comparison between the data from the dictionary and from speech. The only vowel which shows a frequency difference between speech and dictionary greater than 5% is /ɯ/ (7% more in speech). Vowels which show a difference between 3% and 5% include /u/ (4.3% more in the dictionary) and /ɛ/ (4.8 % more in the dictionary). While /ɯ/ is frequent in speech, /u/ and /ɛ/ are frequent in the dictionary. Overall, diphthongs are even less frequently observed in speech than in the dictionary.

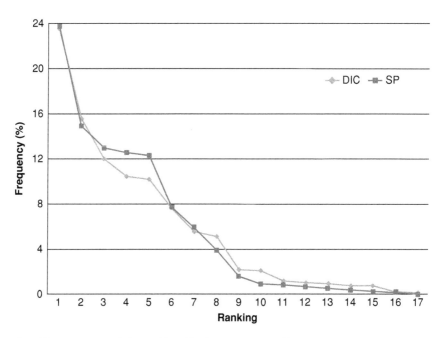

Figure 6.14   Vowel frequency trends by ranking (dictionary vs. speech)

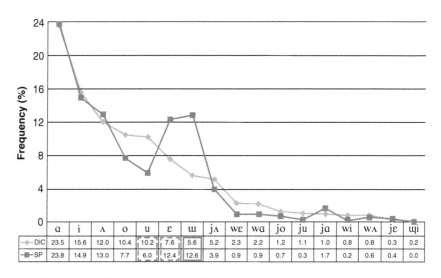

	ɑ	i	ʌ	o	u	ɛ	ɯ	jʌ	wɛ	wɑ	jo	ju	jɑ	wi	wʌ	jɛ	ɰi
DIC	23.5	15.6	12.0	10.4	10.2	7.6	5.6	5.2	2.3	2.2	1.2	1.1	1.0	0.8	0.8	0.3	0.2
SP	23.8	14.9	13.0	7.7	6.0	12.4	12.6	3.9	0.9	0.9	0.7	0.3	1.7	0.2	0.6	0.4	0.0

Figure 6.15   Vowel frequency (dictionary vs. speech)

Tables 6.14–6.17 show the classification of vowels. The results in Table 6.14 show that monophthongs are much more frequently used than diphthongs. In particular, monophthongs are more frequently used than diphthongs in speech, where they accounted for 90.4% of total distribution. In the dictionary, monophthongs accounted for 85.0% of total distribution.

Table 6.14 Type and token frequency of vowels (monophthongs vs. diphthongs)

	Type (%)	Token (%)		
		DIC	SP	Δ
Monophthong	41.2	85.0	90.4	−5.4
Diphthong	58.8	15.0	9.6	5.4

Table 6.15 Type and token frequency of vowels by vowel height

	Type (%)	Token (%)		
		DIC	SP	Δ
High	42.9	37.0	37.1	−0.1
Mid	42.9	35.4	36.6	−1.2
Low	14.3	27.6	26.3	1.3

Table 6.16 Type and token frequency of vowels by tongue backness

	Type (%)	Token (%)		
		DIC	SP	Δ
Front	28.6	27.3	30.2	−2.9
Back	71.4	72.7	69.8	2.9

Table 6.17 Type and token frequency of vowels by roundedness

	Type (%)	Token (%)		
		DIC	SP	Δ
Rounded	28.6	24.3	15.2	9.1
Unrounded	71.4	75.7	84.8	−9.1

Table 6.15 shows that tongue height does not appear to have a major impact on vowel distribution. Table 6.16 shows that in both the dictionary and in speech, back vowels were more frequently used than front vowels. Table 6.17 shows that in both the dictionary and in speech, unrounded vowels were more frequently used than rounded vowels.

6.3 Syllable frequency

6.3.1 High-frequency syllables

In the dictionary, 1,283 syllable types were observed in total. Among these, the most frequently used syllable was /hɑ/, which was observed 5,414 times. The syllables /li/ and /tɕi/ were also frequently used. The reason why /hɑ/ was so frequent is related to the widespread use of the verbal suffix /-ha-/ -하- 'to do' in Korean.

Table 6.18 shows 82 syllable types which constitute more than 50% of overall usage. It is significant that the usage of these 82 syllable types, just 6.39% of all observed 1,283 syllable types, constitute 50.29% of the total distribution. High-frequency syllable structures are in general either of the V type or CV type. Among seven possible V types, five are found in the high-frequency group. In addition, among 127 observed CV types, 45 are found in the high-frequency group. On the other hand, although approximately 778 structures of the CVC type have been observed, only 21 are found in the high-frequency group.

In speech, 1,212 syllable types were observed in total. Of these, the most frequently-used syllable was /kɯ/, which was observed 13,755 times, constituting 3.41% of the overall distribution. /kɑ/ and /i/ were also frequently used. There were 36 syllable types which together accounted for approximately half of the total distribution. In other words, this means that just 2.97% of all observed structure types accounted for 50% of the syllables used in speech. Table 6.19 shows a list of the 36 most frequently used syllables. Most of those 36 were either V or CV types. Of seven possible V types, four appear in the high-frequency group. In addition, of 126 possible CV type syllable structures, 28 appear in the high-frequency group. On the other hand, although there are 712 observed structures of the CVC type, only two, /nɯn/ and / mjʌn/, appear in the high-frequency group.

Table 6.20 shows a list of the high-frequency syllables that comprise more than 50 per cent of total distribution, as found both in the dictionary and in speech. These 27 syllables were found both in the 82 most frequently used syllables in the dictionary as well as in the 36 most frequently used syllables in speech.

Of the 27 syllables in Table 6.20, /tɕi/ and /i/ ranked among the top ten both in the dictionary and in speech. Some of the syllables, such as /kɯ/, /lʌ/, /ni/ occurred more frequently in speech than in the dictionary, whereas others, such as /si/ and /sɑ/, /to/ and /tɕɑ/ occurred more frequently in the dictionary than in speech. The distributions of /tɛ/, /i/, /lɑ/ and /nɛ/ were similar both in the dictionary and in speech.

Table 6.18 Syllable frequency (dictionary)

Rank	Syllable	Frequency	%	Cumulative (%)	Rank	Syllable	Frequency	%	Cumulative (%)
1	hɑ	5,414	4.41	4.41	33	tɕo	635	0.52	31.24
2	li	1,808	1.47	5.88	34	toŋ	634	0.52	31.76
3	tɕi	1,642	1.34	7.22	35	tɕ*ʌk	596	0.49	32.25
4	i	1,629	1.33	8.55	36	pʰa	588	0.48	32.73
5	ki	1,627	1.33	9.87	37	sʌ	584	0.48	33.20
6	sɑ	1,389	1.13	11.00	38	nɑ	581	0.47	33.67
7	tɕʌk	1,367	1.11	12.12	39	sʌŋ	579	0.47	34.15
8	twɛ	1,209	0.98	13.10	40	tɑ	563	0.46	24.60
9	tɕɑ	1,198	0.98	14.08	41	in	560	0.46	35.06
10	si	1,175	0.96	15.04	42	koŋ	550	0.45	35.51
11	su	1,154	0.94	15.98	43	mi	546	0.44	35.95
12	tɛ	1,095	0.89	16.87	44	nɛ	543	0.44	36.40
13	kɑ	1,065	0.87	17.74	44	sɯ	543	0.44	36.84
14	tɕʌŋ	1,011	0.82	18.56	46	po	542	0.44	37.28
15	pu	1,006	0.82	19.38	47	ma	533	0.43	37.71
16	tɕɛ	949	0.77	20.15	48	sin	519	0.42	38.14
17	kʰɑ	946	0.77	20.92	49	sɛ	517	0.42	38.56
18	ko	904	0.74	21.66	50	ʌ	512	0.42	38.97
19	sɑŋ	881	0.72	22.38	51	mul	500	0.41	39.38
20	kɛ	880	0.72	23.09	52	ɑ	498	0.41	39.79
21	tɕɑŋ	860	0.70	23.79	53	lɑ	487	0.40	40.18
22	hwɑ	850	0.69	24.49	54	ni	481	0.39	40.58
23	tɕu	847	0.68	25.18	55	mun	480	0.39	40.97
24	to	836	0.68	25.86	55	kʰi	480	0.39	41.36
25	mu	827	0.67	26.53	57	sʌn	467	0.38	41.74
26	tɕʌn	815	0.66	27.19	58	mo	464	0.38	42.12
27	pi	784	0.64	27.83	59	tɕʰɛ	462	0.38	42.49
28	ku	781	0.64	28.47	60	il	458	0.37	42.87
29	so	750	0.61	29.08	61	wʌn	450	0.37	43.23
30	tɕʰi	711	0.58	29.66	62	s*ʌŋ	449	0.37	43.60
31	ju	659	0.54	30.20	63	kjʌŋ	446	0.36	43.96
32	kʌ	652	0.53	30.73	64	kɯ	438	0.36	44.32

Table 6.18 (*cont.*)

Rank	Syllable	Frequency	%	Cumulative (%)	Rank	Syllable	Frequency	%	Cumulative (%)
65	mjʌŋ	438	0.36	44.68	74	lɛ	405	0.33	47.75
66	u	434	0.35	45.03	75	pul	399	0.33	48.08
67	sil	433	0.35	45.38	76	tɕʰa	395	0.32	48.40
68	jʌn	428	0.35	45.73	77	kjo	392	0.32	48.72
69	tɕʌ	420	0.34	46.07	78	tʰa	388	0.32	49.03
70	tɕuŋ	419	0.34	46.41	79	kwan	387	0.32	49.35
71	pal	414	0.34	46.75	79	tan	387	0.32	49.66
71	paŋ	414	0.34	47.09	81	san	386	0.31	49.98
73	lʌ	409	0.33	47.42	82	o	381	0.31	50.29

Table 6.19 Syllable frequency (speech)

Rank	Syllable	Frequency	%	Cumulative (%)	Rank	Syllable	Frequency	%	Cumulative (%)
1	kɯ	13,755	3.41	3.41	19	ko	4,880	1.21	34.60
2	ka	12,386	3.07	6.48	20	ku	4,632	1.15	35.75
3	i	10,920	2.71	9.18	21	s*ʌ	4,591	1.14	36.89
4	na	9,609	2.38	11.56	22	la	4,530	1.12	38.01
5	tɛ	9,362	2.32	13.88	23	lɛ	4,283	1.06	39.07
6	nɯn	8,606	2.13	16.02	24	ja	4,272	1.06	40.13
7	ni	8,143	2.02	18.03	25	ma	4,143	1.03	41.16
8	kʌ	7,114	1.76	19.80	26	tɕa	4,044	1.00	42.16
9	a	6,608	1.64	21.43	27	ɛ	3,763	0.93	43.09
10	tɕi	6,100	1.51	22.94	28	jʌ	3,659	0.91	44.00
11	kɛ	5,815	1.44	24.38	29	ʌ	3,386	0.84	44.84
12	ha	5,476	1.36	25.74	30	si	3,236	0.80	45.64
13	lʌ	5,459	1.35	27.09	31	k*a	3,229	0.80	46.44
14	sʌ	5,279	1.31	28.40	32	hɛ	3,018	0.75	47.19
15	ta	5,146	1.28	29.68	33	tɯ	2,909	0.72	47.91
16	ki	5,131	1.27	30.95	34	to	2,888	0.72	48.62
17	li	4,958	1.23	32.18	35	mjʌn	2,794	0.69	49.32
18	nɛ	4,914	1.22	33.39	36	sa	2,762	0.68	50.00

Table 6.20 High-frequency syllables (dictionary and speech)

Syllable	Ranking (DIC)	Ranking (SP)	Syllable	Ranking (DIC)	Ranking (SP)
ha	1	12	kʌ	32	8
li	2	17	sʌ	37	14
tɕi	3	10	na	38	4
i	4	3	ta	40	15
ki	5	16	nɛ	44	18
sa	6	36	ma	47	25
tɕa	9	26	ʌ	50	29
si	10	30	a	52	9
tɛ	12	5	la	53	22
ka	13	2	ni	54	7
ko	18	19	kɯ	64	1
kɛ	20	11	lʌ	73	13
to	24	34	lɛ	74	23
ku	28	20			

6.3.2 Syllable type frequency

Table 6.21 shows the distribution of syllable types. In the dictionary, of eight possible syllable structures, the CV type was the most frequently used, comprising 42.8% of all occurring syllable types. The GV type, on the other hand, was the least frequently used, accounting for only 2.1% of all occurrences. CVC types comprise 60.6% of all observed syllable types, yet accounted for only 36.1% of the syllables in the dictionary. This contrasts with the CV type, which comprises 9.9% of possible syllable types, but accounts for 42.8% of all occurrences.

In speech too, the CV type was the most frequently used, comprising 59.1% of all syllable types. Unlike in the dictionary, the CGVC type was the least frequently used, comprising only 2.3% of all occurrences. CVC types comprise 58.8% of all possible syllable types, yet were used in only 21% of occurrences in the dictionary. This again contrasts with the CV type, which comprises 10.4% of all possible syllable types, but is used 59.1% of the time.

The most significant difference between the dictionary and speech was found in the frequency of CV and CVC types. The CV type was used 16.3% more in speech than in the dictionary. On the other hand, the CVC type was

Table 6.21 Token and type frequency of syllable types (dictionary vs. speech; C = consonant, G = glide, V = vowel)

	Token (%)			Type (%)		
	DIC	SP	Δ	DIC	SP	Δ
V	3.2	7.2	−4.0	0.6	0.6	0.0
GV	2.1	3.4	−1.4	0.8	0.8	0.0
CV	42.8	59.1	−16.3	9.9	10.4	−0.5
CGV	5.3	3.1	2.3	7.7	8.3	−0.5
VC	2.9	3.0	−0.1	3.7	3.9	−0.2
GVC	2.3	0.9	1.4	2.6	3.3	−0.7
CVC	36.1	21.0	15.1	60.6	58.8	1.9
CGVC	5.4	2.3	3.1	14.2	14.0	0.2
Total	100.0	100.0	0.0	100.0	100.0	0.0

Table 6.22 Token and type frequency of syllable types with/without onsets

	Token (%)			Type (%)		
	DIC	SP	Δ	DIC	SP	Δ
With onset	89.6	85.5	4.1	92.5	91.4	1.0
Without onset	10.4	14.5	−4.1	7.6	8.6	−1.0

found to occur 15.1% more in the dictionary than in speech. This shows that the frequency of the CVC type was relatively higher in the dictionary than in speech, whereas the frequency of the CV type was relatively higher in speech than in the dictionary. No significant difference was observed in terms of possible types of syllables between the dictionary and speech. In both, the frequency of syllables including glides, i.e. GV, CGV, GVC, CGVC, was low both in terms of type and token frequency. In the dictionary, the type and token frequencies of syllables including a glide were 25.3% and 15.0% respectively. In speech, the type and token frequencies of syllables including a glide were 26.4% and 9.7% respectively.

Table 6.22 shows the frequencies of syllables with and without onsets. In both the dictionary and in speech, the majority of syllables (92.5% of syllables in the dictionary and 91.4% of those in speech) had onsets. As we can see in the distribution, syllables with onsets accounted for 89.6% in the dictionary and 85.5% of those in speech.

Table 6.23 Token and type frequency of syllables with/without codas

	Token (%)			Type (%)		
	DIC	SP	Δ	DIC	SP	Δ
Without coda	53.4	72.8	−19.4	19.0	20.0	−1.0
With coda	46.6	27.2	19.4	81.0	80.0	1.0

Table 6.23 shows the frequency of syllables with and without codas. In both the dictionary and in speech, the majority of syllable types did not have codas – that is, they were open syllables – and this was mirrored in the actual distribution. Syllables without codas, – that is, open syllables – were observed far more frequently. The type frequency of open syllables was 19.0% in the dictionary and 20.0% in speech. On the other hand, the token frequency of open syllables was 53.4% in the dictionary and 72.8% in speech. In terms of type frequency, no significant difference was observed between speech and the dictionary. However, in terms of token frequency, open syllables occurred 19.4% more frequently in speech than in the dictionary.

6.4 Comparison with phoneme frequency in English

In this section, we will briefly discuss phoneme frequency in English in comparison with Korean. From language to language, it is not only the sound inventory, but also the frequency of occurrence of those sounds that differs. This section contains the frequency of phonemes found in Received Pronunciation (RP), based on the 70,646 entries found in the *Oxford Advanced Learner's Dictionary* by John Higgins. The data is available at http://linguistlist.org/issues/4/4–294.html#1. It also contains the frequency of phonemes found in speech, based on Crystal (1995)'s work which originates from Fry (1947).

6.4.1 Consonant frequency in English

Consider Figures 6.16 and 6.17. These figures show consonant frequency as observed in the dictionary (Figure 6.16) and in speech (Figure 6.17). In the dictionary, /t/ was the most frequently used, followed by /s/, /n/, /l/, /r/, /k/, /d/, /z/. On the other hand, in speech, /n/ was most frequently used, followed by /t/, /d/, /s/, l/, / ð /, r/.

Tables 6.24–6.26 show observed types of consonants and their actual realisation in the dictionary and in speech. As shown in Table 6.24, obstruents were

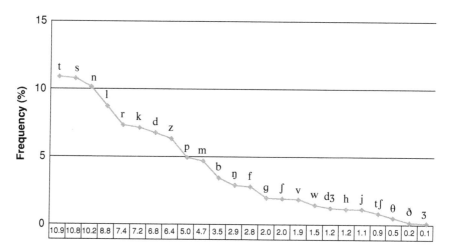

Figure 6.16   Consonant frequency of English (dictionary)

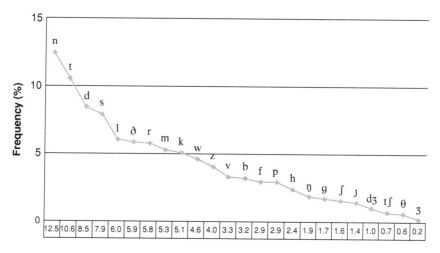

Figure 6.17   Consonant frequency of English (speech)

more frequently used than sonorants both in the dictionary and in speech. Among the obstruents, voiceless sounds were more frequent than voiced sounds. This distinction is, however, less pronounced in speech than in the dictionary.

Table 6.25 shows that both in the dictionary and in speech, alveolar sounds are more frequent than bilabials, and that bilabials are more frequent than velars. Alveolar sounds, which account for 29.2% of the possible sound types, occurred most often, accounting for 61.3% of occurrences in the dictionary and 55.2% of occurrences in speech.

Table 6.26 shows that in terms of manner of articulation, both in the dictionary and in speech, stop sounds were most frequent, accounting for 35.4%

Table 6.24 Type and token frequency of English consonants (sonorants vs. obstruents)

	Type (%)	Token (%)		
		DIC	SP	Δ
Sonorants	29.2	36.6	37.5	−0.9
Obstruents	70.8	63.4	62.5	0.9
Voiceless	47.1	65.1	55.5	9.5
Voiced	52.9	34.9	44.5	−9.5

Table 6.25 Type and token frequency of English consonants by place of articulation

	Type (%)	Token (%)		
		DIC	SP	Δ
Bilabial	12.5	13.2	11.5	1.7
Labial-velar	4.2	1.5	4.6	−3.2
Labiodental	8.3	4.7	6.2	−1.5
Dental	8.3	0.7	6.5	−5.8
Alveolar	29.2	61.3	55.2	6.1
Palato-alveolar	16.7	4.2	3.4	0.8
Palatal	4.2	1.1	1.4	−0.3
Velar	12.5	12.1	8.7	3.4
Glottal	4.2	1.2	2.4	−1.2

Table 6.26 Type and token frequency of English consonants by manner of articulation

	Type (%)	Token (%)		
		DIC	SP	Δ
Stop	25.0	35.4	32.0	3.4
Fricative	37.5	25.9	28.8	−2.9
Affricate	8.3	2.1	1.7	0.4
Nasal	12.5	17.9	19.7	−1.8
Lateral	4.2	8.8	6.0	2.7
Approximant	12.5	10.0	11.8	−1.9

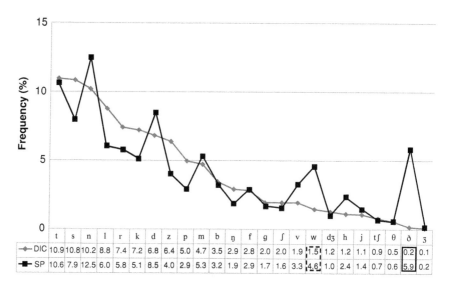

	t	s	n	l	r	k	d	z	p	m	b	ŋ	f	g	ʃ	v	w	dʒ	h	j	tʃ	θ	ð	ʒ
DIC	10.9	10.8	10.2	8.8	7.4	7.2	6.8	6.4	5.0	4.7	3.5	2.9	2.8	2.0	2.0	1.9	1.5	1.2	1.2	1.1	0.9	0.5	0.2	0.1
SP	10.6	7.9	12.5	6.0	5.8	5.1	8.5	4.0	2.9	5.3	3.2	1.9	2.9	1.7	1.6	3.3	4.6	1.0	2.4	1.4	0.7	0.6	5.9	0.2

Figure 6.18   Differences in English consonant frequency (dictionary vs. speech)

of occurrences in the dictionary and 32.0% in speech, followed by fricatives and nasals. Fricatives were found only 25.9% of the time in the dictionary, but 28.8% of the time in speech. Nasals were found 17.9% of the time in the dictionary, and 19.7% of the time in speech. Both in the dictionary and in speech, affricates occurred least frequently, accounting for 2.1% of occurrences in the dictionary and 1.7% in speech.

Finally, Figure 6.18 shows a comparison between consonant frequency in the dictionary and in speech. The boxed areas show cases where the difference between the dictionary and speech is greater than 5% (solid box) or between 3% and 5% (dashed box). We can see that /ð/ and /w/ show a difference greater than 3%. It is noticeable that /ð/, which is used only 0.2% of the time in the dictionary, is found 5.9% of the time in speech. Along with /ð/, /w/ is also used only 1.5% of the time in the dictionary, but is observed 4.6% of the time in speech.

6.4.2 Vowel frequency in English

Figures 6.19 and 6.20 show vowel frequency in English as observed both in the dictionary and in speech. The most frequently used vowel in the dictionary was /ɪ/, followed by /ə/, /æ/, /e/, /eɪ/. On the other hand, /ə/ was used most frequently in speech, followed by /ɪ/, /e/, /aɪ/, /ʌ/. Both in the dictionary and in speech, the two most frequently used vowels accounted for the majority of the total vowel distribution (46.0% in the dictionary and 48.6% in speech).

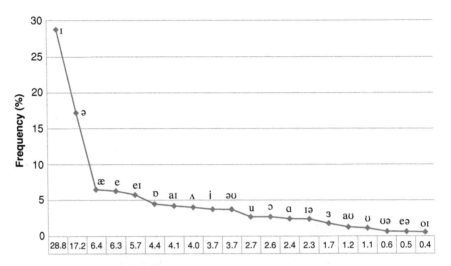

Figure 6.19   Vowel frequency in English (dictionary)

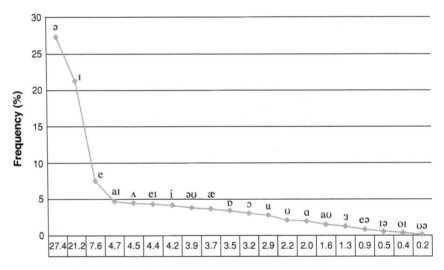

Figure 6.20   Vowel frequency in English (speech)

Tables 6.27–6.30 show the classification of vowels. The results shown in Table 6.27 reveal that monophthongs are much more frequently used than diphthongs. Table 6.28 shows that mid and high vowels appeared more frequently than low vowels. Table 6.29 shows that front vowels appeared more frequently than back vowels. Table 6.30 shows that unrounded vowels appeared more frequently than rounded vowels.

Figure 6.21 shows a comparison between vowel frequency in the dictionary and in speech. The boxed areas show cases where the difference between

Table 6.27 Type and token frequency of English vowels (monophthongs vs. diphthongs)

	Type (%)	Token (%)		
		DIC	SP	Δ
Monophthong	60.0	81.4	83.7	−2.3
Diphthong	40.0	18.6	16.3	2.3

Table 6.28 Type and token frequency of English vowels by vowel height

	Type (%)	Token (%)		
		DIC	SP	Δ
High	33.3	44.6	36.5	8.1
Mid	41.7	39.1	52.5	−13.4
Low	25.0	16.3	11.0	5.3

Table 6.29 Type and token frequency of English vowels by backness

	Type (%)	Token (%)		
		DIC	SP	Δ
Front	33.3	55.6	43.9	11.7
Central	25.0	28.2	39.7	−11.5
Back	41.7	16.2	16.4	−0.2

Table 6.30 Type and token frequency of English vowels by roundedness

	Type (%)	Token (%)		
		DIC	SP	Δ
Rounded	33.3	13.3	14.0	−0.7
Unrounded	66.7	86.7	86.0	0.7

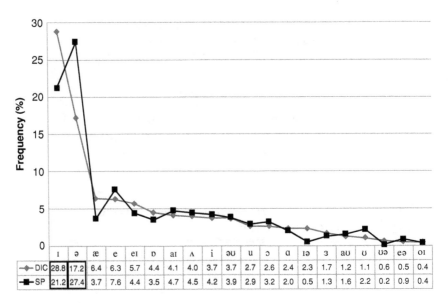

	I	ə	æ	e	eɪ	ɒ	aɪ	ʌ	i	əʊ	u	ɔ	ɑ	ɪə	ɜ	aʊ	ʊ	ʊə	eə	ɔɪ
DIC	28.8	17.2	6.4	6.3	5.7	4.4	4.1	4.0	3.7	3.7	2.7	2.6	2.4	2.3	1.7	1.2	1.1	0.6	0.5	0.4
SP	21.2	27.4	3.7	7.6	4.4	3.5	4.7	4.5	4.2	3.9	2.9	3.2	2.0	0.5	1.3	1.6	2.2	0.2	0.9	0.4

Figure 6.21   Vowel frequency in English (dictionary vs. speech)

the dictionary and speech is greater than 5%. /ɪ/ and /ə/ show a difference of greater than 5% between dictionary and speech usage. In the dictionary, /ɪ/ is the most frequently used vowel, comprising 28.8% of the total distribution, whereas in speech, /ə/ is the most frequently used vowel, comprising 27.4% of the total distribution.

To sum up, we can observe the following characteristics in our comparison of phoneme frequency in English and Korean. First, let's look at the frequency of /t/, /k/, /s/. In Korean, /t/ occurred 5.2% of the time and ranked tenth in the dictionary, and in speech, it occurred 6.7% of the time and ranked fifth. However, in English, /t/ was found to be the most frequently used consonant in the dictionary (10.9%) and the second most frequently used consonant in speech (10.6%). In Korean, on the other hand, /k/ was found to be the most frequently used consonant in the dictionary (13.3%) and the second most frequently used consonant in speech (16.0%). In English, /k/ occurred 7.2% of the time and ranked sixth in the dictionary, and in speech, it occurred 5.1% of the time and ranked ninth. The distribution of /s/ also differed. In Korean, /s/ occurred 7.7% of the time and ranked sixth in the dictionary, and in speech, it occurred 5.0% of the time and ranked eighth. However, in English, /s/ was ranked second in the dictionary (10.8%) and ranked fourth in speech (10.6%). The results are summarised in Table 6.31.

In other words, in Korean velars occur more frequently than alveolar sounds. In English, all of the five most frequently used consonants are alveolars, whereas in Korean only two of the most frequently used consonants in

Table 6.31 Comparison of phoneme frequency in Korean and English

	Korean (rank/%)		English (rank/%)	
	Dictionary	Speech	Dictionary	Speech
/t/	10th / 5.2%	5th / 6.7%	1st / 10.9%	2nd / 10.6%
/k/	1st / 13.3%	2nd / 16.0%	6th / 7.2%	9th / 5.1%
/s/	6th / 7.7%	8th / 5.0%	2nd / 10.8%	4th / 10.6%

Table 6.32 Comparison of consonant frequency in Korean and English

	Korean		English	
	Dictionary	Speech	Dictionary	Speech
Fricatives	16.0%	11.0%	25.9%	28.8%
Affricates	12.8%	9.0%	2.1%	1.7%
Nasals	28.6%	33.6%	17.9%	19.7%

the dictionary and three in speech are alveolars. On the other hand, in English no velar sounds were frequently used, whereas in Korean two of the five most frequently used consonants in the dictionary were velars, and one in speech.

In terms of manner of articulation, the distribution of fricatives, affricates and nasals is significantly different in Korean and English. In short, fricatives were less frequent in Korean than in English, while nasals and affricates were more frequent in Korean than in English. Table 6.32 summarises these results.

THINK MORE!

How would English sound to Koreans? And how would Korean sound to you?

Although these words are not officially listed in the dictionary, how English sounds to Korean people who do not speak English is represented as 솰라솰라 (or 쏼라쏼라; although 솰라솰라 is more commonly found in writing, it is more commonly pronounced as 쏼라쏼라) or 샬라샬라 (or 쌸라쌸라). Why do Korean people think that English sounds like 솰라솰라, 쏼라쏼라, 샬라샬라, 쌸라쌸라? Might these onomatopoeic expressions be related to the sounds characteristic of the language in question, or its high-frequency phonemes?

This hypothesis is not totally ungrounded if we pay attention to the alveolar, the alveolar fricative, or the lateral sounds that are characteristically found frequently in English pronunciation. And, conversely, what would people who heard Korean, but did not understand it, think that Korean sounded like?

6.5 Summary

In this chapter, we have examined the frequency of phonemes and syllables in Korean, based on dictionary and spontaneous speech data. The result shows that overall, /ɑ/ was used most frequently and /ɰi/ used least frequently. Among consonants, /k/ and /n/ were most frequently used. Overall frequency of obstruents is higher than sonorants. In terms of place of articulation, alveolar sounds were most frequent and in terms of manner of articulation, stops were most frequent. Of the vowels, monophthongs were much more frequent than diphthongs. As for syllable frequency, CV types were more frequently found than CVC types. Comparisons with English were also discussed. In terms of place of articulation, velars were frequently observed in Korean but not in English. On the other hand, alveolars were frequently observed in English than in Korean. In terms of manner of articulation, fricatives were frequent in English, but not in Korean. Both affricates and nasals were more frequent in Korean than in English.

EXERCISES

1   What are the most and least frequently used consonants in Korean, both in the dictionary and in speech?

2   What are the most and least frequently used vowels in Korean, both in the dictionary and in speech?

3   Is there any difference, in terms of consonant distribution, between word-initial and word-final positions?

4   Which syllable structures are frequently used in Korean?

5   Compare phoneme frequency in Korean and English. What is the significant difference?

6   How does Korean sound to you? State which sounds are most frequently heard by you when you listen to the Korean language.

7 Prosody

So far, we have observed Korean sounds at the segmental level. In particular, we have considered the phonetic characteristics of each sound. However, the same sound can have different phonetic realisations; for instance, /ɑ/ can be produced either with high pitch or low pitch, as a long vowel or a short vowel, and sometimes loudly or quietly. This is not only the case for individual sounds but also for sequences of sounds or segments. Hence, the same sequence of sounds (or segments) may be realised with a different pitch, loudness or length, and these are known as 'supra-segmental features' or 'prosodic features'. The term 'supra-segmental features' emphasises the sound 'unit' in which those features appear. By contrast, the term 'prosodic features' draws emphasis to the sound properties that are manifested within the sequence of segments. We will use the term 'prosodic features' throughout this chapter, since we are more interested in the nature of sound properties than the sound units bearing these properties.

In this chapter, we will discuss the prosody of Korean: in 7.1, we will examine the linguistic function of prosody; 7.2 will provide an overview of the prosodic structure of Korean; 7.3–7.6 look at each of the linguistic units which comprise the prosodic structure of Korean from the syllable, the smallest unit, to the phonological word, phonological phrase, and finally the intonational phrase; and in 7.7, we conclude.

7.1 Linguistic function of prosody

Prosody includes such variables as pitch, loudness, length and pause. Of course, pitch, loudness, length and pause all have their corresponding physical reality, such as fundamental frequency for pitch, intensity for loudness, duration for length and silence duration for pause; for instance, high-pitch sounds have a higher fundamental frequency than lower-pitch sounds. Likewise, loud sounds will be more intense than quiet sounds; long sounds will have a longer duration than short sounds; pauses naturally grow longer as silence duration becomes longer. However, native speakers are not typically conscious of properties such as pitch, loudness, length and pause, for they are naturally attuned to the music of their language.

Across all languages, even when there might be no difference in sound at a segmental level, different meanings can be expressed through variation in prosody: for instance, Mandarin Chinese is a tonal language, and so even when a group of words all have exactly the same sound properties at a segmental level, the differences in pitch yield words with different meanings. An example of this phenomenon is presented below.

(1) a. [ma] with high level tone: 'mother' 媽
     b. [ma] with high rising tone: 'hemp' 麻
     c. [ma] with low falling-rising tone : 'a horse' 馬
     d. [ma] with high falling tone: 'to scold' 罵

Let's consider the case of Korean.

(2) a. 가 [ka] with rising pitch
     b. 가 [ka] with falling pitch

To Korean speakers, (2a) and (2b) sound different. Though the sound sequence is exactly the same, when the sequence /ka/ is pronounced at the end of a sentence in a rising tone, it turns the sentence into a question, whereas the same sequence in a falling tone makes the sentence declarative or imperative. Does this mean that Korean is a tonal language like Chinese? The answer is no. In the case of (2), the difference in pitch marks a difference in mood; that is, a rising pitch makes the sentence interrogative, whereas a falling pitch makes the sentence declarative or imperative. In terms of word meaning, however, /ka/ in (2) means the same thing, 'to go'. In other words, in the case of Korean, unlike languages such as Chinese, variation in pitch contributes to the meaning of a *sentence*, but not to the meaning of a *word*.[1]

Now then, what about the duration of sound? According to SKP, the meanings of individual words can change according to the vowel length. Listed in (3) are minimal pairs which demonstrate this: for instance, /nu:n/ 눈 meaning 'snow' is pronounced with a longer vowel than /nun/ 눈 meaning 'human eyes', and /pa:m/ 밤 meaning 'chestnut' is pronounced with a longer vowel than /pam/ 밤 meaning 'night'. Likewise, /ma:l/ 말 meaning 'language' is pronounced with a longer vowel than /mal/ 말 meaning 'horse'.

(3) a. 눈 /nuːn/ 'snow'   눈 /nun/ 'eye'
     b. 밤 /paːm/ 'chestnut'   밤 /pɑm/ 'night'
     c. 말 /mɑːl/ 'language'   말 /mɑl/ 'horse'
     d. 발 /pɑːl/ 'blind'   발 /pɑl/ 'foot'

However, in everyday language usage, duration of sound alone doesn't play an important role in distinguishing the meaning of one word from another. It is indeed hard to find any word that has relatively long vowels in contemporary spoken Korean. Neither does loudness or pause play a role in distinguishing between words.

DID YOU KNOW...?

Is length distinctive in Seoul Korean?

SKP assumes length as a distinctive feature in Korean. However, this is far from what is observed in 'real' contemporary spoken Korean. S.-N. Lee (1960) argued that from his own observation (he is a native Seoul Korean speaker and a renowned Korean phonologist), length is becoming less and less distinctive and indeed has almost disappeared in his time. He also claimed that a view of length as a distinctive feature is not based on real spoken data but purely based on dictionary knowledge. About half a century has passed since S.-N. Lee (1960), but normative pronunciation still assumes that length is a distinctive feature in Seoul Korean.

In short, in the case of Korean, prosody doesn't distinguish one word from another. What, then, is the linguistic function of prosody in Korean? To understand this, one must consider linguistic units higher than a word. Consider (4).

(4) 산에 가요 [sɑ.nɛ. kɑ.jo]
     (. = syllable boundary)

As we saw in (2), prosody determines the mood of a sentence. It is difficult to recognise the meaning of sentence (4) without an awareness of the prosody of the final syllables. For instance, a falling tone would make the sentence either declarative or imperative, whilst a rising tone would make it a yes/no question. In this way, prosody plays a crucial role in realising grammatical and pragmatic information. Listen carefully to the utterances in (5).

(5) a. [ɑ. pʌ. tɕi. kɑ. pɑŋ. ɛ. tɯ. lʌ. kɑ. sin. tɑ.]
     b. [ɑ. pʌ. tɕi. kɑ. pɑŋ. ɛ. tɯ. lʌ. kɑ. sin. tɑ.]
     c. [ɑ. pʌ. tɕi. kɑ. pɑŋ. ɛ. tɯ. lʌ. kɑ. sin. tɑ.]
         (. = syllable boundary)

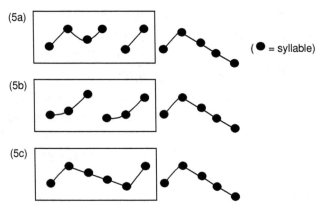

Figure 7.1   Stylised pitch movements in (5a–c)

(6) a. (아버지가)(방에)(들어가신다)
        [ɑ. pʌ. tɕi. kɑ | pɑŋ. ɛ| tɯ. lʌ. kɑ. sin. tɑ.]
    b. (아버지)(가방에)(들어가신다)
        [ɑ. pʌ. tɕi| kɑ. pɑŋ. ɛ| tɯ. lʌ. kɑ. sin. tɑ.]
    c. (아버지가방에)(들어가신다)
        [ɑ. pʌ. tɕi. kɑ. pɑŋ. ɛ| tɯ. lʌ. kɑ. sin. tɑ.]
        (. = syllable boundary, | = minor break boundary)

Although all the examples in (5) consist of the same syllables, in the same order (and therefore of the same segments), the meaning of each sentence is different according to the way in which the syllables are grouped together. When pronounced, (6a) means '(my) father goes into a room', but (6b) means '(my) father goes into a bag', and (6c) means '(somebody who is older than me) goes into (my) father's bag'. The different interpretations result from different phrasing. We will come back to this issue in 7.5.

Before going further, let's look closely at the prosodic differences between the three utterances in (5). As noted, although the three utterances have the same sequences of segments, prosodically, they are all different. The most prominent difference is observed in pitch pattern, as we can see in Figure 7.1. Consider the boxed areas in Figure 7.1.

In (5a), the first syllable has a low pitch, the second has a high pitch, the third is a little lower again, and then the fourth syllable has a high pitch. After that, the pitch drops radically at the fifth syllable and in the sixth syllable, the pitch rises again, as in the fourth syllable.

On the other hand, in (5b), the first syllable has a low pitch as in (5a), but the second syllable does not have a high pitch, unlike (5a). However, the pitch rises suddenly in the third syllable and then falls down again in the fourth syllable. The pitch rises a little in the fifth syllable, similar to the second syllable. The pitch rises further in the sixth syllable until it is as high as the third syllable.

Finally in (5c), the first syllable has a low pitch, rising to the second syllable and then descending in the third, fourth and fifth syllables, before rising again suddenly in the sixth syllable.

Different pitch movements cause native speakers to group the same segments differently and subsequently cause a difference in meaning. In (5a) in Figure 7.1, different pitch patterns cause the first four syllables to be grouped together and the other two syllables to be grouped separately. Likewise, in (5b) in Figure 7.1, pitch patterns cause the first three syllables to be grouped as one and the following three syllables to be grouped together. In (5c) in Figure 7.1, the pitch pattern causes all six syllables to form one group. While difference in pitch movement is one of the easiest things to notice, there are of course other prosodic differences to be found in different utterances.

7.2 Prosodic structure of Korean

Listen carefully to the following sentence, spoken at a normal speed.

(7) 미영이는붓을사는데나영이는먹을산다.
   (mijʌŋ + -i + -nɯn) (pus + -ɯl) (sa- + -nɯntɛ), (najʌŋ + -i + -nɯn)
   (mʌk + -ɯl) (sa- + -nta).
   (+ = morpheme boundary, ( ) = *eojeol* unit)

The sentence in (7) has six word phrases (i.e. *eojeols*). Listen again and this time, try to figure out where the longest and shortest pauses are located. A native speaker of Korean would be able to tell that the longest pause is between the third and fourth word phrases, and that there are breaks between the second and third word phrases, as well as between the fifth and sixth word phrases, as demonstrated in (8). In (8), one bar (|) refers to a shorter pause, compared to two bars (‖) denoting a longer pause.

(8) 미영이는| 붓을사는데 ‖ 나영이는| 먹을산다 ‖
   [(mijʌŋ + -i + -nɯn)| (pus + -ɯl) (sa- + -nɯntɛ)‖ (najʌŋ + -i + -nɯn)|
   (mʌk + -ɯl) (sa- + -nta)]
   (+ = morpheme boundary, ( ) = *eojeol* unit)

The bracketing in (8) shows how each segment forms a prosodic or phonological unit. These prosodic units then build up a larger prosodic/phonological structure. The way in which the actual prosodic structure is built up

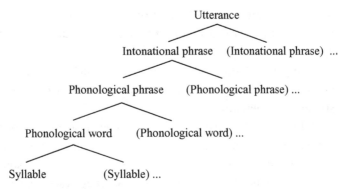

Figure 7.2   Prosodic structure of Korean

differs from language to language. Figure 7.2 shows the prosodic structure of Korean.

As shown in Figure 7.2, the smallest prosodic unit is a syllable and the largest possible unit is an utterance. In Korean, an utterance contains at least one *intonational phrase* (IP), and an intonational phrase contains at least one *phonological phrase* (PP).[2] A phonological phrase contains at least one *phonological word* (PW), and a phonological word contains at least one syllable. In the following sections, we will discuss each prosodic structure in more detail.

7.3 Syllable

A '*syllable*' is the smallest unit within the prosodic structure of Korean.[3] A syllable is formed of phonemes, and syllables can be made up of different numbers of phonemes. For instance, the word /utɕusʌn/ 우주선 'spaceship' has six segments: /u/, /tɕ/, /u/, /s/, /ʌ/, /n/. These six segments can be grouped into three syllables as in [u], [tɕu], [sʌn]. However, each syllable has a different number of segments: the first syllable [u] has one segment, the second syllable [tɕu] has two segments, and the third syllable [sʌn] has three segments. Any native Korean speaker will agree with this way of grouping syllables. A syllable is an abstract, psychological unit, not a concrete, physical unit, and it differs from language to language. Hence, even when the same string of sounds is heard, native speakers of other languages will group the segments differently. For example, the English word *strike* is recognised as a one-syllable word by native English speakers, but as a five-syllable word by native Korean speakers.

DID YOU KNOW...?

How many syllables does *milk* have?

Syllable structures differ from language to language. Hence, even the same sequence of segments will be grouped differently. Let's try an experiment. Ask an English native speaker to pronounce *milk*. And then, ask English, Korean and Japanese speakers to clap their hands according to the number of syllables *milk* has. You will see that English speakers clap once, Koreans twice and Japanese three times. This is due to the different syllable structures of the three languages.

In English, *milk* is syllabified as one syllable because consonant clusters such as /lk/ are allowed in word-final position. On the other hand, in Korean, consonant clusters are not allowed in any position and therefore, /lk/ is pronounced as [lkɯ], with an additional default vowel /ɯ/ after /k/. This makes Koreans regard *milk* as a two-syllable word. On the other hand, Japanese, which is a CV language, cannot have any consonant at all in word-final position, except for nasals. Therefore, /l/ and /k/ can only occur in word-initial position with the added default vowel /u/. Hence, the English /milk/ is recognised as a three-syllable word, /miruku/. We will come back to this in Chapter 10.

7.3.1 Syllable structure

A syllable consists of a syllable nucleus and a syllable margin. Just as a cell must have a cell nucleus, each syllable must have a syllable nucleus. This is the same in any language, but the inventory of the possible sounds that can act as a syllable nucleus or a syllable margin differs from language to language, as does syllable structure.

In the following section, we will briefly discuss the syllable nucleus. Often, it is simply called 'nucleus', and forms the core part of a syllable. These syllable nuclei can only be formed of syllabic sounds. These are sounds that can form a syllable on their own without a syllable margin. In the case of Korean, only vowels are syllabic, but in other languages there are syllabic consonants; in English, for instance, sonorant consonants such as /n/ and /l/ are syllabic and can form a separate syllable as in *button* [bʌ-tn̩] and *jungle* [dʒʌŋ-gl̩]. *Button* and *jungle* are therefore considered two-syllable (disyllabic) words in English.

A glide can be attached to the nucleus either before or after the vowel. In contemporary Korean, as we discussed in Chapter 5, a glide can only precede

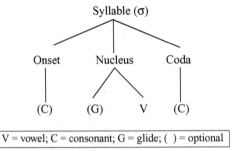

Figure 7.3   Syllable structure of Korean

the vowel in a syllable nucleus. In short, a syllable nucleus in Korean consists of an obligatory vowel and optional glide preceding the vowel.

Unlike the syllable nucleus, a syllable margin is optional and can precede or follow the syllable nucleus. Syllable margins are formed of consonants. A consonant that precedes a nucleus is an *onset* and one that follows is a *coda*. Which particular sounds can be onset or coda, and how many of them are allowed to form one syllable, differs across languages. In contemporary Korean, only one consonant can appear before or after the syllable nucleus, meaning consonant clusters are not possible. Figure 7.3 summarises the syllable structure of Korean.

As mentioned earlier, every language has a unique syllable structure. This is why English can have one-syllable (monosyllabic) words containing as many as three consonants in the onset position, but a maximum of four consonants in the coda position, such as *strike* [stɹɑɪk] and *texts* [tɛksts]. In the case of Japanese, only one consonant is allowed in the onset position and only nasal sounds at the coda.

FURTHER STUDY

Cross-linguistic differences in syllabic structure

A language can be classified as either a CV or CVC language, depending on whether or not its syllable structure allows consonants in the coda position. For example, Japanese, Italian and Spanish are CV languages, while English, German and Mandarin Chinese are CVC languages. Korean is a CVC language because we can easily find Korean words with a CVC syllable structure, such as /각/ or /밥/. Due to different syllable structures, the same loanwords may therefore be adopted differently. For instance, the English words *tile* and *helmet* have been adopted in Japanese as *tairu* and *herumetto*, but as *tʰail* and *helmet* in Korean. We will get back to this issue in Chapter 10.

A different way of pronouncing coda sounds

In languages like French, coda sounds must be released after central closure. Hence, the third person, feminine pronoun *elle* should be pronounced not as [ɛlˀ], but as [ɛl]. This is in contrast to Korean, where coda sounds must never be released after central closure.

On the other hand, this tendency does not exist in English. Therefore, English native speakers will recognise the pronunciations [kætˀ] with closure, or [kæt] with release of the closure, as the same one-syllable word, *cat*.

What would the syllable structure of fifteenth-century Korean have been like?

As a language changes, so too does its syllable structure. One complete character in Hangeul 한글 forms one syllable. Hence, as noted above, it is easy to count syllables in Korean. In fact, when it was first invented, Hangeul orthography was more faithful to actual pronunciation than to morphological information. Therefore, it is easy to reconstruct the syllabic structure of fifteenth-century Korean by looking at the documents in this period. Fifteenth-century Korean displays a different syllable structure from that of contemporary Korean. Most significantly, glides can not only precede, but also follow vowels. In fifteenth-century Korean ㅐ and ㅔ were regarded as a combination of ㅏ /a/ plus ㅣ /j/ and ㅓ /ʌ/ plus ㅣ /j/, that is, ㅣ /j/ following simple vowels such as ㅏ and ㅓ. ㅐ and ㅔ can be then understood as the combination of a glide attached before and after the simple vowel.

In addition, consonant clusters existed in both syllable-initial (onset) and syllable-final (coda) positions. Fifteenth-century documents allow consonant clusters of up to three consonants. For example, 둙 ᄣᅢ found in 훈민정음 해례 *Hunminjeongeum Haerye* 'Explanation and Examples of *Hunminjeongeum*', has three consonants at the coda of the first syllable and three at the onset of the second syllable. Some scholars argue that the words like 둙 'chicken' are clear evidence of the existence of an /lk/ sequence in fifteenth-century Korean. Moreover, in fifteenth-century Korean, 조 'millet' combines with ᄡᆞᆯ 'rice' to produce 좁ᄊᆞᆯ 'millet'. The ㅂ after 조 is the result of ᄡᆞᆯ being at that time. Similar words are listed below.

햅쌀 'newly-harvested rice'   입쌀 'unglutinous rice'
찹쌀 'glutinous rice'   멥쌀 'nonglutinous rice'

7.3.2 Syllable types

In this section, we will discuss the various syllable types possible in Korean. Based on the syllable structure of Korean given in Figure 7.3, we can think of about eight possible syllable types in Korean, as shown in (9). Here, C refers to a consonant, V refers to a vowel and G refers to a glide:

(9) Type 1: A syllable with one vowel: V, e.g. /i/ 'tooth'
    Type 2: A syllable with a glide and a vowel: GV, e.g. /jo/ 'underquilt'
    Type 3: A syllable with a consonant and a vowel: CV, e.g. /no/ 'oar'
    Type 4: A syllable with a consonant, a glide and a vowel: CGV, e.g. /mwʌ/ 'what'
    Type 5: A syllable with a vowel and a consonant: VC, e.g. /ok/ 'jade'
    Type 6: A syllable with a glide, a vowel and a consonant: GVC, e.g. /jok/ 'abuse'
    Type 7: A syllable with a consonant, a vowel and a consonant: CVC, e.g. /nok/ 'rust'
    Type 8: A syllable with a consonant, a glide, a vowel and a consonant: CGVC, e.g. /pjʌk/ 'wall'

This confirms that: (i) all syllable types have a vowel as a syllable nucleus; (ii) glides can only precede the vowel as in types 2, 4, 6 and 8 in (9); (iii) only one consonant can precede or follow the vowel as in types 3, 4, 5, 6, 7 and 8 in (9).

FURTHER STUDY!

Body vs. rhyme structure

The syllable structure given in Figure 7.3 is a flat structure, but two more syllable structures are available in which the onset and nucleus or nucleus and coda form a sub-structure first.

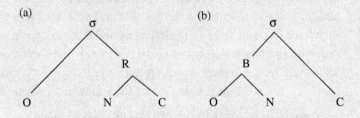

σ = syllable; R = rhyme; B = body; O = onset; N = nucleus; C = coda

The former is called a rhyme structure, and languages such as English follow this pattern of syllable structure formation. The latter is called a body structure. It is not easy to decide whether Korean has a body or rhyme structure. The following examples suggest that Korean has a body structure rather than a rhyme structure.

a. 딱-따닥 /t*ak-t*atak/, 빵-빠방 /p*aŋ-p*apaŋ/, 쿵-쿠궁 /kʰuŋ-kʰukuŋ/, 뽕-뾰봉 /p*oŋ-p*opoŋ/, 뿡-뿌붕 /p*uŋ-p*upuŋ/
b. 파닥-파다닥 /pʰatak-pʰatatak/, 푸닥-푸다닥 /pʰutak-pʰutatak/, 후닥-후다닥 /hutak-hutatak/
c. 두-둥실 /tu-tuŋsil/

On the other hand, the following examples suggest that Korean has a rhyme structure.

d. 울퉁-불퉁 /ultʰuŋ-pultʰuŋ/, 올록-볼록 /ollok-pollok/, 울룩-불룩 /ulluk-pulluk/

Recent studies in psycholinguistics suggest that Korean has a body structure, rather than a rhyme structure, but more research is needed to confirm this (see Yoon and Derwing, 2001 for more discussion).

7.3.3 Building a syllable structure

In this section, we will discuss how segments are built up into a syllable in Korean. The most important principle in this is the onset-first principle. This principle states that as many of the margins (consonants) as possible should be included as onsets preceding the nucleus, and then any margins that remain should be included as the coda, after the nucleus. Figure 7.4 shows how the syllable structures in /halapʌtɕi/ 할아버지 'grandfather', /halmʌni/ 할머니 'grandmother' and /tɕoŋihak/ 종이학 'paper crane' are built up.

As shown in stage (a), the first thing to do is to find the syllable nucleus and build a skeleton. Then afterwards, as in stage (b), as many of the consonants as possible should be incorporated into that nucleus following the onset-first principle. Finally, as in stage (c), any remaining segments need to be linked to the coda.

7.3.4 Syllabification and phonological processes

In Korean, those consonants that can appear in the onset position are different from those that appear in the coda position. All consonants except /ŋ/, and

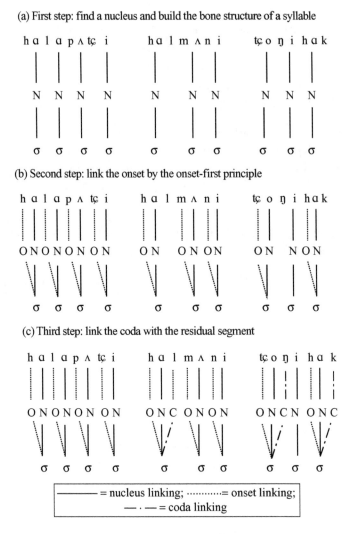

(a) First step: find a nucleus and build the bone structure of a syllable

(b) Second step: link the onset by the onset-first principle

(c) Third step: link the coda with the residual segment

Figure 7.4   Syllable structures for /halapʌtɕi/, /halmʌni/ and /tɕoŋihak/

therefore eighteen out of nineteen consonants, can occur in the onset position. These sounds are pronounced with no change in their basic pronunciation. However, only seven of the nineteen consonants (i.e. /k, n, t, l, m, p, ŋ/) can appear in the coda position. All other sounds are therefore substituted by one of these seven sounds; in other words, the same consonant is pronounced differently depending on the position in which it occurs within a syllable structure. Why is this the case?

It is because all coda sounds in Korean must be a 'stop' sound involving the closure of the mouth, and cannot simply be released, as we discussed in

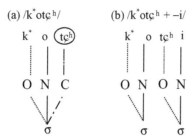

Figure 7.5   Syllabification of /k*otɕʰ/ and /k*otɕʰ + -i/

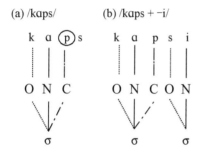

Figure 7.6   Syllabification of /kɑps/ and /kɑps + -i/

4.2.1.3. Due to this restriction, those sounds which end with a release of air instead of 'closure', are changed into sounds produced with complete closure. Hence, fricatives and affricatives are changed into the 'stop' sounds that are produced in the same manner of articulation. We will come back to this issue in Chapter 8. Put simply, all syllables in Korean should end with the central closure of the oral cavity. If these coda sounds were fricative, they would be regarded as the onset of the next syllable instead of the coda of the current syllable. For instance, /tɕʰ/ is pronounced differently in /k*otɕʰ/ 꽃 and /k*otɕʰ + -i/ 꽃 + 이]: /tɕʰ/ is pronounced as [t] in /k*otɕʰ/, but as [tɕʰ] in /k*otɕʰ + -i/. The reason behind this is the difference in syllabification. As shown in Figure 7.5, /tɕʰ/ is in the coda position in /k*otɕʰ/ 꽃, whereas in /k*otɕʰ + -i/ 꽃 + 이], it is in the onset position of the second syllable.

Another phonological process related to syllable structure is consonant-cluster simplification. In Korean, although consonant clusters can be expressed orthographically, only one of these sounds is pronounced because only one consonant can appear in the coda position. This is why in /kɑps/ 값 only /p/ is pronounced, so it becomes [kɑp] as in Figure 7.6a. However, in /kɑps + -i/ 값 + 이] where a subject particle is attached, there are two syllable nuclei, so the second consonant /s/ can also be pronounced, as it becomes the onset of the second syllable, as shown in Figure 7.6b. Further discussions on consonant-cluster simplification will be given in Chapter 8.

7.4 Phonological words

Syllables are grouped together to form a *phonological word*, which is different from a *morphological word*. In morphology, a word is defined as the smallest independent, indivisible unit that contains no pause. In most cases, a morphological word and a phonological word are the same. However, we also find examples of morphological words that don't coincide with phonological words. Consider (10): the syllables bracketed together are recognised as forming one phonological word within an utterance, yet this same unit can consist of more than one morphological word.

(10) a.   (갈) (수)$_\omega$없었다. (kɑl) (su)$_\omega$ (ʌpsʌsʼtɑ)$_\omega$
             '(I) could not go there'
             (먹을) (것)$_\omega$찾는다. (mʌk- + -ɯl) (kʌs)$_\omega$ (tɕʰɑtɕ- + -nɯn + -tɑ)$_\omega$
             'I am searching for something to eat'
             (그럴) (리)$_\omega$없어. (kɯlʌ- + -l) (li)$_\omega$ (ʌps- + ʌ)$_\omega$
             'I doubt it'
      b.   그 사람 (어됬니)$_\omega$? (kɯ) (salam)$_\omega$ (ʌtisʼ- + -ni)$_\omega$
             ← (어디) (있니) (ʌti)$_\omega$ (isʼ- ± -ni)$_\omega$
             'where is he?'
             자, (여깄다)$_\omega$. (tɕa)$_\omega$ (jʌkisʼ- + -ta)$_\omega$
             ← (여기) (있다) (jʌki)$_\omega$ (isʼ- + -ta)$_\omega$
             'here it is'
      c.   (범$_\omega$민족적$_\omega$) (pʌm-$_\omega$# mintɕoktɕʌk$_\omega$)
             'cross-national'
             (초$_\omega$호화판$_\omega$) (tɕʰo-$_\omega$#hohwapʰan$_\omega$)
             'extra-luxurious'
             (반$_\omega$민주주의$_\omega$) (pan-$_\omega$# mintɕutɕuɥi$_\omega$)
             'anti-democracy'
             (맹$_\omega$활약상$_\omega$) (mɛŋ-$_\omega$# hwaljaksaŋ$_\omega$)
             'playing extremely well'
             (역$_\omega$차별주의$_\omega$) (jʌk-$_\omega$# tɕʰapjʌltɕuɥi$_\omega$)
             'counter-differentia'

             (+ = morpheme boundary, ( ) = *eojeol* unit, ω = phonological word boundary # = word boundary)

For instance, in (10a), when the first two words are pronounced, they are always found as one whole unit without any pause in between. Although morphologically each sound unit forms two individual words, phonologically they form one word. Shown in (10b) are other cases where two morphological words have been contracted into one phonological word. In (10c), however, the words listed are morphologically recognised as one word, but phonologically regarded as two. This is because these words are formed of a prefix and a stem. Since there is a strong pause between the prefix and stem, it is natural to regard them phonologically as two separate words.

7.5 Phonological phrases

Phonological words form *phonological phrases*. An understanding of phonological phrases is crucial in explaining various phonological processes in Korean. Consider (11).

(11) $(\text{mat}\varphi\text{imak})_\omega$ $(\text{salam} + \text{-tul} + \text{-i})_\omega$ $(\text{mok} + \text{soli} + \text{-nun})_\omega$
$(\text{alumtaw-} + \text{-}\Lambda\text{jo})_\omega$
마지막 사람들이 목소리는 아름다워요.
'The last group of people have beautiful voices.'

The sentence in (11) has four phonological words and can therefore be uttered in four different ways, as in (12). The pronunciation of these sentences is given in (13).

(12) a. $(\text{mat}\varphi\text{imak})_\omega|$ $(\text{salam} + \text{tul} + \text{-i})_\omega|$ $(\text{mok} + \text{soli} + \text{-nun})_\omega|$
$(\text{alumtaw-} + \text{-}\Lambda\text{jo})_\omega$
마지막|사람들이|목소리는|아름다워요.
　 b. $(\text{mat}\varphi\text{imak})_\omega$ $(\text{salam} + \text{-tul} + \text{-i})_\omega|$ $(\text{mok} + \text{soli} + \text{-nun})_\omega$
$(\text{alumtaw-} + \text{-}\Lambda\text{jo})_\omega$
마지막사람들이|목소리는아름다워요.
　 c. $(\text{mat}\varphi\text{imak})_\omega|$ $(\text{salam} + \text{-tul} + \text{-i})_\omega|$ $(\text{mok} + \text{soli} + \text{-nun})_\omega$
$(\text{alumtaw-} + \text{-}\Lambda\text{jo})_\omega$
마지막|사람들이|목소리는아름다워요.
　 d. $(\text{mat}\varphi\text{imak})_\omega$ $(\text{salam} + \text{-tul} + \text{-i})_\omega|$ $(\text{mok} + \text{soli} + \text{-nun})_\omega|$
$(\text{alumtaw-} + \text{-}\Lambda\text{jo})_\omega$
마지막사람들이|목소리는|아름다워요.

(13) a. 마지막|사람들이|목소리는|아름다워요.
[ma.tɕi.mak| sa.lam.tɯ.li| mok.sʼo.li.nɯn| a.lɯm.ta.wʌ.jo]

b. 마지막사람들이|목소리는아름다워요.
   [ma.tɕi.mak.sʼa.lam.tɯ.li| mok.sʼo.li.nɯ.na.lɯm.ta.wʌ.jo]
c. 마지막|사람들이|목소리는아름다워요.
   [ma.tɕi.mak| sa.lam.tɯ.li| mok.sʼo.li.nɯ.na.lɯm.ta.wʌ.jo]
d. 마지막사람들이|목소리는|아름다워요.
   [ma.tɕi.mak.sʼa.lam.tɯ.li| mok.sʼo.li.nɯn| a.lɯm.ta.wʌ.jo]

In (13), when /s/ in /salamtɯli/ 사람들이 is phrased together with the preceding word /matɕimak/ 마지막 which ends with /k/, /s/ is tensified to become /sʼ/ as in (13b) and (13d). However, when /s/ in /salamtɯli/ 사람들이 is *not* phrased together with the preceding word /matɕimak/ 마지막, /s/ is not tensified, as in (13a) and (13c). For the same reason, /s/ in /moksoli/ 목소리 is tensified and thus pronounced [moksʼoli]. These examples show that whether the segment is to be tensified or not depends on where the sound occurs within the same prosodic structure. (We will discuss Post-obstruent Tensification in more detail in 8.2.1.)

Words found in the same phonological phrase form a smooth, unbroken pitch curve. Figure 7.7 shows how a female Seoul Korean speaker pronounces the sentence in (14). When there is a boundary between two phonological words as in (14b), there is a clear drop in pitch between the last syllable of the first word [nɛ] and the first syllable of the second word [ʌ]. (See Figure 7.7a.) Yet, when there is no such boundary between the two words, there is no sudden drop in pitch between the two words, as in (14c). (See Figure 7.7b.)

🎧 (14) a.   미연이네어머니는나연이를미워하니?
         (mijʌninɛ)ω (ʌmʌninɯn)ω (najʌnilɯl)ω (miwʌhani)ω?/
         'Does Mi.yeon's mother hate Nayeon?'
      b.   (미연이네) (어머니는) 나연이를미워하니?
         [mijʌninɛ|ʌmʌninɯn| najʌnilɯl| miwʌhani]
      c.   (미연이네어머니는) 나연이를미워하니?
         [mijʌninɛ ʌmʌninɯn| najʌnilɯl| miwʌhani]

Let's consider the different pitch curves that can be found in phonological phrases. In Seoul Korean, the two most common pitch patterns for four-syllable words are LHLH and HHLH (L = low and H = high).

Whether the first syllable of a phonological phrase is produced with a high pitch or a low pitch depends on the syllable-initial phoneme. Phonological phrases in which the initial consonant is one of the following: /pʼ, tʼ, kʼ, tɕʼ, sʼ, pʰ, tʰ, kʰ, tɕʰ, h, s/ (i.e. tensed or aspirated stops and affricates, or any type of fricative) tend to start with a high pitch as in HHLH. Otherwise, they start with a low pitch as in LHLH. From now on, we will call those phonemes that

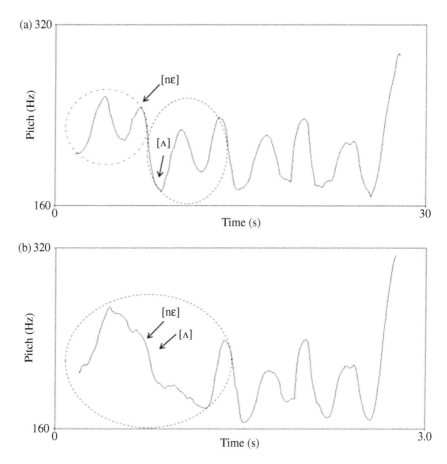

Figure 7.7   Two pitch curves of /(mijʌninɛ)ω (ʌmʌninɯn)ω (najʌnilɯl)ω (miwʌhani)ω?/ spoken by a female speaker of Standard Korean

are responsible for high pitch in syllable-initial position *high-tone group pho-nemes*, and those that are responsible for low pitch in syllable-initial position *low-tone group phonemes*. Consider (15).

(15)   까다로운|어머니는|하는 일이|너무너무|많다고는|하시더냐?
       /(kʼataloun)ω| (ʌmʌninɯn)ω| (hanɯn)ω (ili)ω| (nʌmunʌmu)ω|
       (mantʰakonɯn)ω| (hasitʌnja) ω?/
       'Does your picky mother complain that she has lots of things to do?'

Figure 7.8 shows a pitch curve extracted from the utterances of a female Seoul Korean speaker. This utterance contains six phonological phrases. Consider the four circles in Figure 7.8, which show the first four phonological phrases. As expected, when the first phoneme is a high-tone phoneme, as in the first and third phonological phrases, HHLH pitch curves are observed.

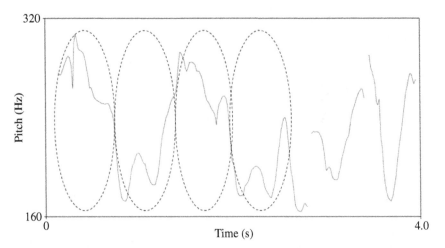

Figure 7.8   A pitch curve of /(kʼataloun)_ω| (ʌmʌninɯn)_ω| (hanɯn)_ω (ili)_ω| (nʌmunʌmu)_ω| (mantʰakonɯn)_ω| (hasitʌnja) _ω?/ spoken by a female speaker of Standard Korean

However, when the first phoneme is a low-tone phoneme, as in the second and fourth phonological phrases, LHLH pitch curves are observed. Based on this observation, we can conclude that the basic pitch curve for four-syllable words in Korean is T(High/Low) HLH.[4] Whether an initial syllable is produced with a high or a low tone is determined by the syllable-initial phonemes. Figure 7.9 captures this.

What, then, of words made up of fewer than four syllables, or more than four syllables? In either case, what determines the pitch pattern of a phonological phrase is the first and last tone of a phonological phrase, leaving the number of syllables irrelevant. Let's consider cases where a word has three syllables or less. In such cases, the second or third tones of a phonological phrase will not be realised. Hence, THH, TLH, THL, and TLL are all possible pitch patterns. Figure 7.10 shows the typical pitch patterns of phonological phrases with less than four syllables.

What about a phonological phrase that has more than four syllables? There is no difference in pitch patterns between four-syllable words and five-syllable words. The difference between the two is simply which particular syllable tone is realised.

In principle, the first syllable will have the first tone and the second syllable will have the second tone. The third tone will then be realised from the second syllable from the end. All other syllables which are not assigned any particular tone will show a 'between-pitch', or interpolation. As the distance between the second pitch and the third pitch increases, the between-pitch or interpolation slope will be smooth as in Figure 7.11.

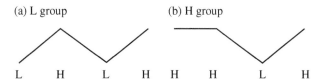

Figure 7.9   Typical pitch patterns of phonological phrases with four syllables in Standard Korean

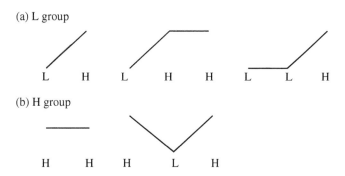

Figure 7.10   Typical pitch patterns of phonological phrases with fewer than four syllables in Standard Korean

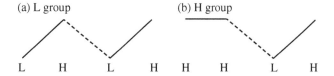

Figure 7.11   Typical pitch patterns of phonological phrases with more than four syllables in Standard Korean

In other words, those words with more than four syllables will show the same tonal pattern as four-syllable words. The fewer syllables the word has, the stiffer the slope will be and vice versa.

The next question which comes to mind is how many syllables a phonological phrase in Korean has on average? Is it limitless? Figure 7.12 shows the results drawn from a study of the spontaneous speech of 57 adult native Korean speakers, involving some 122,912 phonological phrases, as well as a study of one female speaker's reading of 3,000 sentences, which contains 33,719 phonological phrases.[5] In the former study, up to 13 syllables were observed within a phonological phrase, and in the latter study, up to 11 syllables were observed. As we can see, the most frequently observed were 3-syllable PPs, which constituted 32% of the spontaneous speech that was studied, and 25.3% of the female speaker's read speech. PPs of 2–5 syllables were also frequent; in spontaneous speech, they constituted about 80.9%, and as for the speech

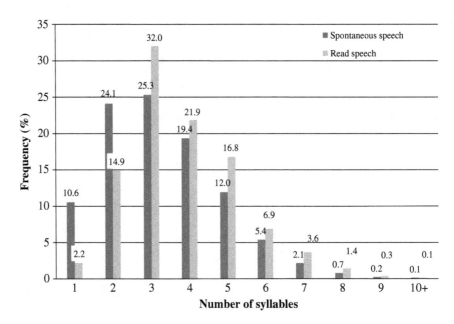

Figure 7.12   Number of syllables per phonological phrase in spontaneous and read speech

read aloud, they constituted about 85.5% of the total PPs. In both read speech and spontaneous speech, native Korean speakers tend to produce phonological phrases of 2–5 syllables.

Interestingly, Figure 7.12 shows that the proportion of 1 or 2-syllable PPs in read speech (17.1%) was half that of spontaneous speech (34.7%). This is because of the frequent use of interjections and shortened forms in spontaneous speech. In addition, phonological phrases with more than 6 syllables were rare in both spontaneous speech (8.5%) and in read speech (12.3%).

7.6 Intonational phrases

Phonological phrases form an *intonational phrase*. The intonational phrase is where intonation is realised. Like phonological phrases, intonational phrases are responsible for various phonological processes. Consider the following sentence (16):

(16) 미역국 누가 먹니?
     /(mijʌk + kuk)_ω (nu + -kɑ)_ω (mʌk- + -ni)_ω?/
     'Who is having seaweed soup?'

The sentence in (16) has three phonological words and they can be phrased as in (17).

🎧 (17) a. 미역국|누가|먹니?

   / (mijʌk + kuk)_ω| (nu + -ka)_ω| (mʌk- + -ni)_ω?/

   [mi.jʌ.kʼuŋ| nu.ka| mʌŋ.ni]

 b. 미역국 ‖ 누가| 먹니?

   /(mijʌk + kuk)_ω‖ (nu + -ka)_ω| (mʌk- + -ni)_ω?/

   [mi.jʌ.kʼuk‖ nu.ka| mʌŋ.ni]

 c. 미역국|누가먹니?

   /(mijʌk + kuk)_ω| (nu + -ka)_ω (mʌk- + -ni)_ω?/

   [mi.jʌ.kʼuŋ| nu.ka.mʌŋ.ni]

 d. 미역국 ‖ 누가먹니?

   /(mijʌk + kuk)_ω‖ (nu + -ka)_ω (mʌk- + -ni)_ω?/

   [mi.jʌ.kʼuk‖ nu.ka.mʌŋ.ni]

According to the way the phonological word is incorporated into the larger phonological structure, the pitch pattern or the actual pronunciation of each segment can change as in (17a). When there is an intonational phrase boundary between the first and second word as in (17b, d), the final segment of the first phonological word /k/ is realised as [k], following its basic pronunciation. However, when there is no intonational phrase boundary between the first and second phonological word as in (17a, c), the final segment of the first phonological word /k/ is nasalised and pronounced as [ŋ] because of the following nasal sound /n/. This process is called *Nasalisation*. The key thing here is that whether to nasalise /k/ into [ŋ] or not depends on the existence of an intonational phrase boundary.

How, then, does one identify an intonational phrase? What are the criteria for determining whether a phrase is intonational or not? The lengthening of the final syllable followed by a pause or distinctive pitch pattern is called an *intonational phrase boundary tone*, and this can be used as an important cue in detecting an intonational phrase. As mentioned earlier, the intonational phrase is also the unit where intonation is realised. Intonation plays an important role in determining the grammatical and pragmatic meaning of a sentence. Consider (18):

🎧 (18) 미연이는|친구들을|미워해요.

   [mijʌninɯn|tɕʰinkutɯlɯl| miwʌhɛjo] (RISING /FALLING)

   'Miyeon hates her friends.'

Even if the sentence (18) has three phonological phrases and they are phrased together as in (18), the mood of the sentence can vary according to the intonation pattern, particularly in the last phonological phrase. In Figure 7.13, we can see that the pitch curves of the two figures are similar, except for the last

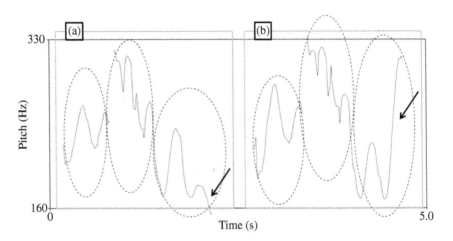

Figure 7.13   Pitch curves of two types of intonation patterns of [mijʌninɯnl tɕʰinkutɯlɯl miwʌhɛjo] 'Miyoen hates her friends'

phonological phrases: both utterances have an LHLH pitch pattern for the first phonological phrase, HHLH for the second, and LHL for the third. At the final syllable, however, Figure 7.13a has a low tone – falling pitch; and Figure 7.13b has a high tone – rising pitch. This difference means the same sentence can either be made declarative (Figure 7.13a), or interrogative (Figure 7.13b).

As discussed in Chapter 1, intonation plays an important role in realising mood (e.g. declarative, interrogative, imperative, propositive, etc.). Particularly in informal speech, the most frequently used sentence-final enders such as -ʌ(a) –어/아 and -ʌ(a)jo –어/아요 [6] can be used to express all moods. The specific mood is determined solely by the intonation of the last syllable in the final intonational phrase; for instance, in (19), -ʌ(a) and -ʌ(a)jo can be used as endings for declarative, interrogative, imperative, propositive and exclamatory sentences.

(19) Intonation and Mood
    /(pap + -ɯl) (mʌk- + -ʌ + -jo)/
    a. Declarative: low tone   '(I) am having a meal.'
    b. Interrogative: high tone   'Are (you) having a meal?'
    c. Imperative: short low tone   'Have a meal!'
    d. Propositive: low-high tone   'Let's have a meal.'
    e. Exclamatory: high-low tone   '(You) are having a meal!'

Finally, Table 7.1 shows some statistical information on prosodic units in Korean based on data gathered from the spontaneous speech of 57 adult Korean speakers. The 35,439 utterances that were analysed contain a total of 55,927

Table 7.1 Statistical information relating to prosodic units

Utterance	
Intonational phrase	1.58
Phonological phrase	3.47
Syllable	11.39
Phoneme	24.22
Intonational phrase	
Phonological phrase	2.20
Syllable	7.22
Phoneme	15.35
Phonological phrase	
Syllable	3.28
Phoneme	6.98
Syllable	
Phoneme	2.13

intonational phrases, 12,919 phonological phrases, and 403,605 syllables. This means that, on average, one utterance contains 1.58 intonational phrases, 3.47 phonological phrases, 11.39 syllables, and 24.22 phonemes. One intonational phrase has an average of 2.20 phonological phrases, 7.22 syllables and 15.35 phonemes. One phonological phrase has 3.28 syllables and 6.98 phonemes. One syllable has an average of 2.13 phonemes.

DID YOU KNOW...?

Why is it hard for Koreans to pronounce 'www'?

You may notice something very interesting when you listen closely to Korean people read out website addresses. Despite there clearly being three 'w's, they may commonly only pronounce two. Why do Koreans pronounce 'www.' as [tˀʌpullju|tˀʌpulljutɕˀʌm], instead of [tˀʌpullju|tˀʌpu llju|tˀʌpulljutɕˀʌm]? Of course, people who are used to the internet know that there are three 'w's in a web address, and may assume they heard three 'w's even though only two may have been pronounced.

The reason for this may be twofold. The first is to do with production and rhythm. In a URL, the 'www.' part contains comparatively more syllables than other parts separated by dots. For example, www.korea.

ac.kr or www.naver.com are each [tˀʌpullju|tˀʌpullju| tˀʌpulljutɕˀʌm ‖ kʰoliɑtɕˀʌm‖ ɛisˀitɕˀʌm‖ kʰɛial] (10, 4, 4, 3 syllables respectively), and [tˀʌpullju| tˀʌpullju| tˀʌpulljutɕˀʌm‖ nɛipʌtɕˀʌm‖ kʰʌm] (10, 4, 1 syllables respectively), making the 'www.' segment unusually long. Pronouncing this unusually long segment in full will disrupt natural speech rhythm. Reducing one 'w' still makes it the longest with seven syllables, but there is a considerable metrical difference between a seven-syllable and ten-syllable segment in the Korean language. This brings us to the second reason.

As seen in Table 7.1, Korean intonational phrases are comprised of an average of 2.20 phonological phrases and 7.22 syllables. Therefore, while reducing one 'w' will still leave this segment with the most syllables, it will be much easier to pronounce as it still conforms to Korean rhythmic patterns. Therefore it is thought that one 'w' is dropped in order to make the phrase better fit the pattern of Korean intonational phrases.

DID YOU KNOW...?

Men, don't speak!

There was an academic conference to be held in *Busan*, so some students from Seoul decided to take a trip. They all took taxis. One male student and two female students from Seoul ended up taking one taxi together. After stating their destination to the taxi driver, the three students began talking amongst themselves. Suddenly, the taxi driver interrupted them in a *Busan* dialect.

"Young man, please stop speaking! You sound like a coward. Please just let the women speak!"

People from *Gyeongsang* province often say that the Seoul accent sounds cloying, effeminate and feeble. This is why people from the *Gyeongsang* province, especially the men, consider the Seoul accent ill-suited and unbecoming for men. On the other hand, people from Seoul say that the 경상 *Gyeongsang* dialect sounds blunt, brusque and angry. So people from Seoul consider people from the *Gyeongsang* province impolite and bad-mannered. Why might this be?

Prosodically, the *Gyeongsang* dialect (which includes the *Busan* dialect) always has a low tone at the end of a sentence. Also, the last syllable in an utterance is never lengthened, making the end of a sentence abrupt;

even yes/no questions do not have a rising tone. In contrast to the Seoul dialect, the mood of a sentence is decided not by prosodic factors, but by morphological markings such as grammatical particles.

The fact that the end of an utterance is always short, coupled with the quickly falling tone, makes speakers of Seoul or Standard Korean think that people from *Gyeongsang* province sound angry and rude. In addition, in the Seoul dialect, abrupt speech endings are associated with commands, stubbornness and sternness. Lengthened speech endings and smooth pitch movement on the other hand represent kindness, fondness, and affection.   🎧

DID YOU KNOW...?

Learning the prosody of a second language

Prosody is one of the first features acquired in one's mother tongue, but one of the last learned in foreign language acquisition. Let's think about some examples. Firstly, Japanese learners of Korean often realise the last syllable of an intonational phrase as too short. This is because there is no final lengthening in Japanese. As in the *Gyeongsang* dialect, short-ending at the end of an utterance may sound abrupt. Conversely, Korean speakers of Japanese tend to over-lengthen the final syllable of an utterance.   🎧

What about English learners of Korean? Let's think about the case of yes/no questions. In both Korean and English, the end of a question has a rising tone. However, how much of the question is spoken in a rising tone differs between the two languages. In Korean, only the last syllable of an utterance is raised. In English, however, it is often the case that the whole sequence of sounds after the accented syllable of the last word is raised. If you are curious as to whether this is really true, ask a Korean friend to say the sentence below.

🎧 한국 음식 먹어 봤었니?

One of the most difficult parts of language acquisition for second language learners is acquiring the prosody of the target language. This is especially true for Korean and English, languages that differ significantly in prosody. In Korean, there is no lexical stress, whereas there is a lexical stress to each word in English. Due to this difference, in Korean each syllable tends to be pronounced with similar length or weight.

7.7 Summary

In this chapter, we have discussed the prosodic characteristics of Korean. Prosody includes the notions of pitch, loudness and length of a sound as well as pause. These are psychological rather than physical notions which are realised onto a sequence of segments. Different prosody can lead to a different interpretation of a word or a sentence. Although rising and falling tone in a Korean sentence make it either a question or a statement, it cannot be said that Korean is a tonal language like Chinese, since tone does not cause any changes in lexical meaning for individual words. Having a syllable structure with an onset, a nucleus and a coda is universal in all languages. Nevertheless, how actual syllable structure is formed and realised differs from language to language. Onset and coda consonants are optional, whereas a vowel as a syllable nucleus is obligatory in syllable structures. In Korean, we observed that there are eight possible syllable structures. Korean also has a prosodic structure where a single syllable, or a sequence of syllables, forms a phonological word, and a single phonological word, or a sequence of phonological words, form a phonological phrase. Furthermore, a single phonological phrase, or a sequence of phonological phrases, may form an intonational phrase. An utterance is formed by a single intonational phrase, or a sequence of intonational phrases.

EXERCISES

1   Explain why the same English word is adopted differently in Korean and Japanese, as in the case of the word *milk*, which was discussed earlier.

2   Discuss why Korean native speakers perceive the words below as having a different number of syllables from the number of syllables in English.
    news, boat, strike, silk, tractor, graph

3   Listen carefully to the following words in Korean and write down how many syllables they have. 🎧

4   Is Korean a tonal language? Answer the question with relevant examples.

5   Listen carefully to the following sentence and describe it using musical notes. 🎧

6   Listen carefully. How many phonological phrases or intonational phrases can you hear in this sentence? 🎧

7   Draw a diagram of the syllable structure of Korean and state which elements are obligatory and which are optional.

8   List examples of CV languages and CVC languages.

9   Draw syllable structures for the following words.

a. 선생님 /sʌnsɛŋnim/ 'teacher'

b. 방언 /paŋʌn/ 'dialect'

c. 감언이설 /kamʌnisʌl/ 'sweet talk'

10 What are the characteristics of the intonational phrase in Korean?

11 Listen carefully to the following sentences and state the mood of the sentence.   🎧

a. declarative, interrogative, propositive, imperative, exclamatory

b. declarative, interrogative, propositive, imperative, exclamatory

c. declarative, interrogative, propositive, imperative, exclamatory

d. declarative, interrogative, propositive, imperative, exclamatory

12 What are the most distinctive prosodic differences between English and Korean?

13 Are the following sequences of sounds possible syllable structures in Korean? If so, mark the syllable boundary for each word. If not, explain why?

a. [tɑlk]

b. [noin]

c. [spolk]

d. [pɑlɑm]

e. [soŋatɕi]

f. [nʌks]

g. [ʌlini]

h. [kisk]

i. [nos]

8 Phonological rules of Korean (I)

The Korean alphabet, or Hangeul, is a phonemic alphabet. In other words, each letter corresponds to one phoneme. However, unlike the roman alphabet, Hangeul is not written letter by letter (e.g. ㅎ ㅏ ㄴ ㄱ ㅡ ㄹ for Hangeul), but in syllables. That is, two or three letters which form one syllable are written together as one orthographic unit. In this book, we have displayed Hangeul with the corresponding IPA transcription alongside. However, knowing how each letter sounds is not enough when learning how to pronounce Korean texts. When the basic units of Hangeul orthography, which each correspond to one syllable, are put together to form a morpheme or a unit bigger than a word, phonological rules will affect their pronunciation wherever they are applicable. For example, the words in (1) would not usually be pronounced syllable-by-syllable, unless perhaps they were being dictated to another person. For instance, the words in (1) show Nasalisation of the /k/ in the first syllable.

(1)   국물 /kuk + mul/ → [kuŋmul] 'soup-liquid'
      속내 /sok + nɛ/ → [soŋnɛ] 'intention'

This means that without knowing the Nasalisation rule in Korean, it is hard to pronounce the words in (1) properly. Native speakers apply phonological rules such as Nasalisation automatically, as such rules are innate in native speakers' knowledge of their mother tongue. Sometimes, Korean speakers can even be heard to pronounce *good morning* as [kun moniŋ] rather than [gʊd mɔːrnɪŋ]. This occurs when Korean native speakers use the Nasalisation rule of Korean phonology in their pronunciation of English words.

Native speakers acquire the phonological rules of their language without much effort, but learners of a second language need to study them one by one to be able to speak the language fluently. Therefore, anyone who wants to speak Korean fluently must be aware of the constraints placed on pronunciation and general phonological rules.

In this book, phonological rules are divided into two types: (i) rules that can be applied without knowledge of the word's morphological information; and (ii) rules that can be applied in consideration of the word's morphological information. The first type of rule is automatically applied to every sound sequence in Korean, but to apply the rules of the second type, one needs to know how a word is formed. In this chapter, we will concentrate on the first type of phonological rule. The second type is to be discussed in Chapter 9.

The first type of phonological rule can be further classified into (i) rules related to syllable structure constraints; and (ii) rules related to surface phonetic constraints. Rules relating to syllable structure constraints will be discussed in 8.1, and rules relating to surface phonetic constraints will be discussed in 8.2.

DID YOU KNOW...?

Leg or moon? Liaison in Korean

Normally, phonemic letter systems like the English alphabet are written from left to right, horizontally, and one letter at a time. When the Korean word for 'leg', [tɑli], is written in a like manner in Hangeul, it becomes ㄷㅏㄹㅣ. However, Hangeul is not written with each letter acting as an individual unit, as in ㄷㅏㄹㅣ. Instead, the sounds are divided into syllable units, and each syllable is written as one group. The example of [tɑli] can be divided into two syllables – [tɑ] and [li] – and when it is written in syllable units, it becomes 다리, not ㄷㅏㄹㅣ.

In addition to writing in groups of syllables, Hangeul utilises a system of demarcating morphemes. This kind of orthography usually preserves each morpheme's original form rather than reflecting the phonological changes it undergoes in a given context. Thus when the Korean word, 달 'moon', is combined with the subject particle -이, it sounds like [tɑli], but is nonetheless written as 달이 (noun + subject particle), rather than 다리. Although the ㅇ of the subject particle, 이, [i], is written down in this case, it is an empty letter that has no phonetic value attached to it. Thus, the ㅇ used here acts merely to point out the initial position of a syllable.

Liaison refers to the phenomenon by which a word written as 달이 is realised phonetically as [tɑ.li]. Although Liaison is not a phonemic rule, it is a necessary and central principle in reading Hangeul where the text must be read as a continuous linking of morphemes. In the case of 달 + 이, the grouping of CVC + V in writing becomes [CV.CV] in pronunciation. As a result, 다리 'leg' and 달 + 이 ('moon' + subject particle) are written differently, but pronounced the same.

Then have these rules for writing existed from the time when Hangeul was first invented? Hangeul was created in 1443 under the name, 훈민정음 *Hunminjeongeum*, and from that time it has always been written in groups of syllables, not in units of letters. This principle is outlined in 훈민정음 해례 (訓民正音 解例) *Hunminjeongeum Haerye* 'Explanation and Examples of *Hunminjeongeum*', which was published in 1446. Although Hangeul is a phonemic system of writing, it was designed to be written top to bottom, and right to left. Moreover, each letter was supposed to be arranged into units of syllables to fit in the space of a square. As can be seen in the picture, the reason why the committee behind 훈민정음 *Hunminjeongeum* chose this method of writing was because of the powerful influence of Chinese characters.

Thus the principle of grouping existed from the very inception of Hangeul. However, when Hangeul was first created, the groupings were not based on morphemes but on pronunciation; in other words, syllables were marked not in units of morphemes, but in units of sound. In texts of this time, 달이 was still written as 다리.

8.1 Phonological rules related to syllable structure constraints

As discussed in Chapter 7, syllables in Korean must have a vowel as their medial sound, and may optionally have consonants as their initial and/or final sounds. There are two important constraints in Korean syllable structures. The first is that syllable-final consonants should be pronounced as unreleased sounds after central closure. The second is that only one consonant may appear in the initial and final positions of a syllable. These two constraints result in the following phonological rules that we shall now discuss: Neutralisation (8.1.1) and Consonant-cluster Simplification (8.1.2).

8.1.1 Neutralisation

낯도 두껍다 /(natɕʰ + -to) (tuk˺ʌp- + -ta)/ → [nat˺o | tuk˺ʌpt˺a] in Korean is an idiomatic expression, meaning 'thick-skinned'. However, when this phrase is heard, this can also refer to thickness of 낫 /nas/, meaning a sickle. In Korean, consonants in syllable-final position should never be released after complete central closure. All 'released' sounds should be replaced with unreleased sounds pronounced in a similar place of articulation. This rule is called Neutralisation, because the lax/tense/aspirated contrast existing in Korean consonants is neutralised in syllable-final position. In addition, the fricative/affricate contrast is neutralised and syllable-final fricatives and affricates are all pronounced the same, as /t/. This is the cause of the ambiguity between /natɕʰ/ 낯 'face' and /nas/ 낫 'sickle'. Consider (2) and (3). Coda consonants in (2) and (3) are pronounced the same.

(2) 각 /kak/ → [kak] 'angle'
     부엌 /puʌkʰ/ → [puʌk] 'kitchen'
     깎- /k˺ak˺-/ → [k˺ak] 'to carve'

(3) 낫 /nas/ → [nat] 'sickle'
     낳- /nah-/ → [nat] 'to bear'
     낮 /natɕ/ → [nat] 'daytime'
     낯 /natɕʰ/ → [nat] 'face'

The examples in (2) show the three-way distinction in stop sounds (e.g. /k, kʰ, k˺/) being neutralised. The examples in (3) show fricatives or affricates being neutralised into the alveolar sound /t/. Because all syllable-final consonants need to be unreleased and pronounced with complete central closure, fricatives and affricates, by definition released sounds cannot appear in syllable-final position. They need to be replaced by unreleased sounds. All fricatives

Table 8.1 Pronunciation of syllable-final consonants 🎧

	Stop (plosive)	Fricative	Affricate	Nasal	Liquid	Syllable-final phonetic realisation	Example
Bilabial	/p/ ㅂ /pʰ/ ㅍ					/p/ ㅂ	밥 [pap] 'rice' 앞 [ap] 'front'
				/m/ ㅁ		/m/ ㅁ	밤 [pam] 'chestnut'
Alveolar	/t/ ㄷ /tʰ/ ㅌ	/s/ ㅅ /s*/ ㅆ				ㄷ /t/	닫- [tat] 'to close' 솥 [sot] 'pot' 낫 [nat] 'sickle' 있- [it] 'to be'
				/n/ ㄴ		/n/ ㄴ	간 [kan] 'liver'
Alveolo-palatal			/tɕ/ ㅈ /tɕʰ/ ㅊ			/t/ ㄷ	낮 [nat] 'daytime' 낯 [nat] 'sickle'
					/l/ ㄹ	/l/ ㄹ	칼 [kal] 'knife'
Velar	/k/ ㄱ /kʰ/ ㅋ /k*/ ㄲ					/k/ ㄱ	각 [kak] 'angle' 부엌 [puʌk] 'kitchen' 깎- [k*ak] 'to carve'[a]
				/ŋ/ ㅇ		/ŋ/ ㅇ	강 [kaŋ] 'river'
Glottal		/h/ ㅎ				/t/ ㄷ	낳- [nat] 'to bear'

[a] It is noticeable that there are no Korean words whose roots end with /p*/, /t*/ or /tɕ*/.

(s, s*, h) and affricates (tɕ, tɕ*, tɕʰ) in syllable-final position are therefore replaced by the lax stop /t/, which is pronounced in the alveolar position, relatively close to where these fricatives and affricates are produced. This lax stop is then ultimately produced as an unreleased sound, [t̚].

In sum, due to Neutralisation, /s/, /s*/, /h/, /tɕ/, /tɕʰ/ all become the lax stop /t/, and then as this lax stop is unreleased, the sound is realised as [t]. As a result of Neutralisation, the only distinctive sounds in syllable-final position are the following seven sounds: /k, n, t, l, m, p, ŋ /.[1] Table 8.1 shows the patterns of Neutralisation.

Syllable-final consonants however can be pronounced differently if grammatical morphemes starting with vowels are attached to each of the words above. Consider (4) and (5).

🎧 (4) In syllable-final position

    a. noun

       각 /kak/ → [kak̚] 'angle'

       밥 /pap/ → [pap̚] 'rice'

b. verb
박- /pɑk/ → [pɑt˺] 'to nail'
닫- /tat-/ → [tat˺] 'to close'

(5) Followed by grammatical morphemes, starting with a vowel
   a. noun
      각이 /kɑk + -i/ → [kɑki] 'angle (subject particle)'
      밥이 /pɑp + -i/ → [pɑpi] 'rice (subject particle)'
   b. verb
      박아 /pɑk- + -ɑ/ → [pɑkɑ] 'to drive (connective)'
      닫아 /tat- + -ɑ/ → [tatɑ] 'to close (connective)'

For instance, in /kɑk/ 각 'angle' in example (4), the last consonant should be pronounced as [k], where the body of the tongue presses against the velum. Likewise, the last sound of /tat-/ 닫- 'to close' should be pronounced as [t˺], with the end of the tongue touching the alveolar ridge. The second /p/ in /pɑp/ 밥 should also be pronounced as [p˺], with the upper and lower lips touching. However, in (5), syllable-final lax stops are all moved to the initial position of the next syllable. Hence, constraints upon syllable-final consonants are no longer applicable.

8.1.2 Consonant-cluster simplification

There are no consonant clusters in Korean. Although orthography allows consonant clusters in the syllable-final position of a letter, as in /talk/ 닭 'chicken' and /salm/ 삶 'life', only one of the sounds in the consonant cluster will actually be pronounced. Consonant-clusters did exist in fifteenth-century Korean in both syllable-initial and syllable-final position, but they are no longer found in contemporary Korean.[2] Consider the following.

(6)   삶 /salm/ → [sam] 'life'
      흙 /hɯlk/ → [hɯk] 'mud'

In (6), /salm/ 삶 is pronounced [sam], not [sal]. Likewise, /hɯlk/ 흙 is pronounced [hɯk], not [hɯl]. The second sound in the cluster is however realised when it is followed by a grammatical particle starting with a vowel, as shown in (7).

(7)   삶이 /salm + -i/ → [salmi] 'life (subject particle)'
      흙이 /hɯlk + -i/ → [hɯlki] 'mud (subject particle)'

Table 8.2 Pronunciation of consonant clusters in syllable-final position

Consonant cluster	Phonetic realisation	In syllable-final position	Followed by grammatical morphemes, starting with a vowel
/ks/ ㄳ	[k]	몫 /moks/ → [mok] 'portion'	몫이다 /moks + -i- + -ta/ → [moks*ita]
/ntɕ/ ㄵ	[n]	앉다 /antɕ- + -ta/ → [ant*a] 'to sit'	앉아 /antɕ- + -a/ → [antɕa]
/nh/ ㄶ	[n]	않네 /anh- + -nε/ → [annε] 'negating verb'	않아 /anh- + -a/ → [ana]
/lp/ ㄼ	[l]	넓다 /nʌlp- + -ta/ → [nʌlt*a] 'to be broad'	넓어 /nʌlp- + -ʌ/ → [nʌlpʌ]
	[p]	밟다 /palp- + -ta/ → [papt*a] 'to step on'	밟아 /palp- + -a/ → [palpa]
/ls/ ㄽ	[l]	외곬 /we- + kols/ → [wɛkol] 'single track'	외곬이다 /we- + kols + -i- + -ta/ → [wɛkols*ita]
/ltʰ/ ㄾ	[l]	핥다 /haltʰ- + -ta/ → [halt*a] 'to lick'	핥아 /haltʰ- + -a/ → [haltʰa]
/ps/ ㅄ	[p]	값 /kaps/ → [kap] 'price'	값이 /kaps + -i/ → [kaps*i]
/lk/ ㄺ	[k]	흙 /huɪlk/ → [huɪk] 'mud'	흙이 /huɪlk + -i/ → [huɪlki]
	[l]	맑게 /malk- + -kε/ → [malk*ε] 'clearly'	맑아 /malk- + -a/ → [malka]
/lm/ ㄻ	[m]	삶 /salm/ → [sam] 'life'	삶이 /salm + -i/ → [salmi]
/lpʰ/ ㄿ	[p]	읊다 /uɪlpʰ- + -ta/ → [uɪpt*a] 'to recite'	읊어 /uɪlpʰ- + -ʌ/ → [uɪlpʰʌ]
/lh/ ㅀ	[l]	뚫는 /t*ulh- + -nuɪn/ → [t*ulluɪn] 'to bore (adnominal)'	뚫어 /t*ulh- + -ʌ/ → [t*ulʌ]

Table 8.2 shows how consonant clusters are phonetically realised in speech. At this point one might ask whether there is any rule which guides the selection of the 'one' sound to be pronounced in consonant clusters. As we can see in Table 8.2, it is not always the first sound in a sequence that is chosen to be pronounced.

There are some rules, however, to which we shall now turn our attention. Consonant clusters can be divided into two types according to the phonetic characteristics of the consonants such as manner of articulation and place of articulation as in (8).

(8) a. Sounds with [+sonorant] features will be chosen

/ls/ → [l]: 외곬 /wɛ- + kols/ → [wɛkol] 'intently'

/ltʰ/ → [l]: 핥는 /haltʰ- + -nɯn / → halnɯn → [hallɯn] 'to lick (adnominal)'

/ntɕ/ → [n]: 앉다 /antɕ- + -ta/ → antɕt*a → [ant*a] 'to sit (down)'

/lh/ → [l]: 뚫는 /t*ulh- + -nɯn/ → t*ulnɯn → [t*ullɯn] 'to punch (adnominal)'

/nh/ → [n]: 많네 /manh- + -nɛ/ → [mannɛ] 'to be plentiful'

b. Sounds with [−coronal] features will be chosen

/lm/ → [m]: 삶네 /salm- + -nɛ/ → [samnɛ] 'to boil'

/lk/ → [k]: 흙 /hɯlk/ → [hɯk] 'mud'

/ks/ → [k]: 넋 /nʌks/ → [nʌk] 'soul'

/ps/ → [p]: 값 /kaps/ → [kap] 'price'

Let us consider the examples in (8) carefully. First of all, we see that consonants with [+sonorant] or [−coronal] features are almost always chosen. This is why in (8a), only sounds with [+sonorant] are chosen. However, in (8b), where the sounds are either both sonorants or both obstruents, non-coronals are chosen.

However, this does not explain all cases. In fact, the pronunciation of sequences such as /lk/ ㄺ and /lp/ ㄼ are very interesting since these are combinations of a sound with [+sonorant, +coronal] features (/l/) and a sound with [−sonorant, −coronal] features (/p, k/). We have shown that within a consonant cluster, a sound with [−sonorant] or [+coronal] features is avoided. However, in a sequence of /lk/ and /lp/, each consonant has either a [−sonorant] or [+coronal] feature. How, then, can the 'one' sound be chosen? It is not easy to prioritise between the two constraints that (i) [−sonorant] should be avoided and (ii) [+coronal] should be avoided.

(9) a. /lk/ → [l]:

닭게 /malk- + -kɛ/ → malkk*ɛ → [malk*ɛ] 'to be clean (conjunctive)'

닭다 /malk- + -ta/ → malkt*a → [makt*a] 'to be clean'

b. /lp/ → [l]:

넓다 /nʌlp- + -ta/ → nʌlpt*a → [nʌlt*a] 'to be wide'

넓고 /nʌlp- +- ko/ → nʌlpk*o → [nʌlk*o] 'to be wide (connective)'

Further investigations are necessary in order to choose the 'one sound' in such cases. According to K.-W. Nam and J.-H. Oh (2009), in sequences of /lk/ and /lp/, the coronal consonant /l/ is often preferred over its counterparts when the following verbal endings are /-ko/ –고 or /-tɕi/–지. This shows a

Table 8.3   Dialectal differences in consonant cluster realisation 🎧

	+Sonorant >> −Sonorant	−Coronal >> +Coronal	Hierarchy is not clear
Seoul			
읽다 /ilk- + -ta/			[ikt*a]
읽거나 /ilk- + -kʌna/			[ilk*ʌna]
읽네 /ilk- + -nɛ/			iknɛ → [iŋnɛ]
읽는다 /ilk- + -nɯn- + -ta/			iknɯnta → [iŋnɯnta]
Gyeongsang			
읽다 /ilk- + -ta/	[ilt*a]		
읽거나 /ilk- + -kʌna/	[ilk*ʌna]		
읽네 /ilk- + -nɛ/	ilnɛ → [illɛ]		
읽는다 /ilk- + -nɯn- + -ta/	ilnɯnta → [illɯnta]		
Jeolla			
읽다 /ilk- + -ta/		[ikt*a]	
읽거나 /ilk- + -kʌna/		ikk*ʌna → [ik*ʌna]	
읽네 /ilk- + -nɛ/		iknɛ → [iŋnɛ]	
읽는다 /ilk- + -nɯn- + -ta/		iknɯnta → [iŋnɯnta]	

growing tendency to choose a consonant with [+sonorant] feature in 리 /lk/ and 래 /lp/ clusters.

Interestingly, some variation is observed between dialects due to the differing hierarchy between the constraints. For example, in the *Gyeongsang* dialect, the [+sonorant] constraint takes priority over the [−coronal] constraint. On the other hand, in the *Jeolla* dialect, the [−coronal] constraint takes priority over the [+sonorant] constraint. This is why the pronunciations of /ilk- + -ta/ 읽다, /ilk- + -kʌna/ 읽거나, /ilk- + -nɛ/ 읽네, /ilk- + -nɯn- + -ta/ 읽는다 differ in those regions. Consider Table 8.3, which shows dialectal differences in the pronunciation of consonant clusters.

DID YOU KNOW...?

The simplification of consonant clusters is like playing musical chairs

Let's compare the phenomenon of Consonant Cluster Simplification with playing musical chairs. Musical chairs is a game where there is always one chair fewer than the number of people playing, and where the players have to go around the chairs in a circle until the music comes to an end. When the music stops, everyone must try to find a seat, and whoever does not get a seat is out of the game. The game continues until there is only one chair left, and whoever gets that seat is the winner of the game.

Then what characterises the people who are eliminated early on? They are probably less agile or weaker than the rest. Those who have either of these traits would lose out to the person who does not. But if two people were playing musical chairs, and one person were slow and the other one weak, who would be the first to be eliminated? Of course, it would depend on which factor contributes more to losing. If lack of agility mattered more, then the 'slow' person would lose to the 'weak' player; and if physical strength mattered more, the 'weak' person would lose to the 'slow' player. But what if such a clear hierarchy did not exist? This is indeed the case in Seoul Korean. Since there is no clear hierarchy in Seoul Korean, sometimes the consonant with the [−coronal] feature is chosen and sometimes the consonant with the [+sonorant] is chosen.

8.2   Phonological rules via surface phonetic constraints

In this section, we will discuss the phonological rules related to phonetic constraints in Korean. These rules are applicable in any corresponding phonetic environment, regardless of morphological information of the sound sequence. Unlike some rules that we shall discuss in Chapter 9, rules relating to surface phonetic constraints are applied to pure-Korean, Sino-Korean and loan words.

As we shall discuss, certain sound sequences are not available in Korean at all, whereas certain sounds and sound sequences are frequently observed. Hence, even if Korean speakers do not clearly hear what is spoken, when they hear a certain sound sequence, even from a distance, they will recognise it as Korean. Likewise, all native speakers will be able to do the same for their own languages. In this section, we will discuss phonological rules which are caused largely by surface phonetic constraints. In other words, the rules discussed in this section are applied automatically, regardless of morphological information in a given phonetic environment. The rules to be discussed include:

Post-obstruent Tensification (8.2.1)
Obstruent Nasalisation (8.2.2)
Liquid Nasalisation (8.2.3)
Lateralisation (8.2.4)
Non-coronalisation (Bilabialisation and Velarisation) (8.2.5)
Aspiration (8.2.6)

Similar-place Obstruent Deletion (8.2.7)
/j/ Deletion (8.2.8)
/h/ Deletion (8.2.9)

8.2.1   Post-obstruent Tensification

One of the popular winter dishes in Korean cuisine is /kuk + pap/ 국밥 'boiled rice served in soup'. You will hear Korean people pronouncing it with a tense [pˀ] as in [kukpˀap] rather than with a lax [p] as in [kukpap]. This is due to Post-obstruent Tensification in Korean phonology.

Post-obstruent Tensification refers to the process in which a lax obstruent becomes tensified when it is preceded by stops, such as /p, t, k/ for instance. Post-obstruent Tensification is the result of a surface phonetic constraint which forbids a sequence of an obstruent and a lax stop. Post-obstruent Tensification is an obligatory rule. Consider (10).

(10) a. /p, t, k/ + lax obstruent
밥도둑 /pap + totuk/ → [paptˀotuk] 'delicious side dish'
닫고 /tat- + -ko/ → [tatkˀo] 'to close (connective)'
먹다 /mʌk- + -ta/ → [mʌktˀa] 'to eat'

b. /pʰ, tʰ, kʰ/ (→ replaced by /p, t, k/) + lax obstruent
옆집 /jʌpʰ + tɕip/ → jʌptɕip → [jʌptɕˀip] 'next door'
밭고랑 /patʰ + kolaŋ/ → patkolaŋ → [patkˀolaŋ] 'furrow'
부엌방 /puʌkʰ + paŋ/ → puʌkpaŋ → [puʌkpˀaŋ] 'scullery'

c. /pˀ, tˀ, kˀ/ (→ replaced by /p, t, k/) + lax obstruent
깎다 /kˀak- + -ta/ → kˀakta → [kˀaktˀa] 'to carve'
(Note that in Korean, no verbal stem ends with pˀ or tˀ.)

d. /s, sˀ, tɕ, tɕʰ/ (→ replaced by /t/) + lax obstruent
옷방 /os + paŋ/ → otpaŋ → [otpˀaŋ] 'dress room'
있고 /isˀ- + -ko/ → itko → [itkˀo] 'to be (connective)'
잊고 /itɕ- + -ko/ → itko → [itkˀo] 'to forget (connective)'
꽃가루 /kˀotɕʰ + kalu/ → kˀotkalu → [kˀotkˀalu] 'pollen'

DID YOU KNOW...?

Finding the underlying form through playing word chains

'Word chain', also known as 'grab on behind' and 'last and first', is a word game in which one person says a word, and the next person has to say a new word starting with the last syllable of the previous word. If the next person cannot come up with a new word that starts with that particular syllable, he or she loses the game. If A and B were to play, for example, and had the chain A: [puŋ.ʌ] 붕어 'carp' → B: [ʌ.pu.pɑ] 어부바 'piggybag' → A: [pa.nɑ.nɑ] 바나나 'banana' → B: [nɑ.pi] 나비 'butterfly' → A: [pi.nɯl] 비늘 'scales' going, A would win if B were unable to think of a new word starting with 늘 [nɯl].

Even when 4- to 6-year-olds play word chains, one can see that they have an awareness of base forms and the rules for Tensification. For example, if the word /os + kam/ 옷감 [otkʰɑm] 'cloth' were given, the child might then answer, [kɑmtɕa] 감자 'potatoes' recovering the base form, /kɑm/ 감, prior to Tensification, even though he would actually hear [kʰɑm] in [otkʰɑm] 'cloth'. This shows that even young children understand the principle of Tensification and can recover the appropriate base form before finding the new word that they want.

8.2.2 Obstruent Nasalisation

밥 먹었니 /(pɑp) (mʌk- + -ʌsʰ- + -ni)/ → [pɑmmʌkʌnni] is a common greeting in Korean, meaning, 'Did you have a meal?' However, this can also mean, 'Did you eat chestnuts?' This is because the /pɑp/ 밥 in /(pɑp) (mʌk- + -ʌsʰ- + -ni)/ 밥 먹었니 is nasalised into [pɑm] before /(mʌk- + -ʌsʰ- + -ni)/ 먹었니, which starts with a sonorant sound. Nasalisation refers to the process by which an obstruent is nasalised when it is followed by a sonorant such as /m, n, l/.[3] Nasalisation is the result of a surface phonetic constraint which forbids a sequence consisting of an obstruent and a sonorant. An obstruent sound followed by a sonorant is assimilated into a nasal that is articulated in the same place of articulation.

Consider (11). Hence, /p/ is assimilated into /m/ in (11a), since both are bilabial sounds; /t/ is assimilated into /n/ in (11b), as both are alveolar sounds; and /k/ is assimilated into /ŋ/ in (11c), since both are velar sounds. The examples in (11d) show cases where two phonological rules are applied: (i) Obstruent Nasalisation and (ii) Liquid Nasalisation.[4] Firstly, syllable-final /p, k/ in /ap/ 압 and /ak/ 악 are nasalised as /m, ŋ/ in /am/ and /aŋ/ and then the following /l/ in /ljʌk/ is nasalised into /n/ in /njʌk/.

(11) a. /p/ + /m, n/ → [m] + [m, n]

　　　밥맛 /pɑp + mɑs/ → pɑpmɑt → [pɑmmɑt] 'taste of rice'
　　　겹눈 /kjʌp + nun/ → [kjʌmnun] 'compound eyes'

　　b. /t/ + /n/ → [n] + [n]

　　　닫는 /tɑt- + -nɯn/ → [tɑnnɯn] 'to close (adnominal)'

c. /k/ + /m, n/ → [ŋ] + [m, n]

각막 /kɑk- + -mɑk/ → [kɑŋmɑk] 'cornea'

먹는 /mʌk- + -nun/ → [mʌŋnun] 'to eat (adnominal)'

d. /p, k/ + /l/ → m, ŋ + l (Nasalisation of /p, k/) → [m, ŋ] + [n]
(Nasalisation of /l/)

압력 /ap- + -ljʌk/ → amljʌk → [amnjʌk] 'pressure'

악력 /ak- + -ljʌk/ → aŋljʌk → [aŋnjʌk] 'grip'

Consider the further examples given in (12). Firstly, in (12a–c), aspirated stops are replaced by lax stops due to Neutralisation. Then, they are further nasalised. In (12d), tense stops are replaced by lax stops and then nasalised. In (12e), fricatives and affricates are neutralised into /t/ and then /t/ is further nasalised into /n/.

(12) Neutralisation and Nasalisation

a. /pʰ/ → p → [m]

앞마당 /apʰ + matɑŋ/ → apmatɑŋ → [ammatɑŋ] 'front yard'

잎눈 /ipʰ + nun/→ ipnun → [imnun] 'leaf bud'

b. /tʰ/ → t → [n]

곁눈 /kjʌtʰ + nun/ → kjʌtnun → [kjʌnnun] 'a side glance'

겉모습 /kʌtʰ + mosɯp/ → kʌtmosɯp → [kʌnmosɯp] 'appearance'

c. /kʰ/ → k → [ŋ]

부엌문 /puʌkʰ + mun/ → puʌkmun → [puʌŋmun] 'a kitchen door'

d. /k*/ → k → [ŋ]

깎는 /k*ak*- + -nɯn/ → k*aknɯn → [k*aŋnɯn] 'to peel (adnominal)'

e. /s, s*, h, tɕ, tɕʰ/ → t → [n]

옷맵시 /os + mɛpsi/ → otmɛpsi → [onmɛps*i] 'style of clothes'

있는 /is*- + -nɯn/ → itnɯn → [innɯn] 'to be (adnominal)'

놓는 /noh- + -nɯn/ → notnɯn → [nonnɯn] 'to lay (adnominal)'

낮말 /natɕ + mal/ → natmal → [nanmal] 'words spoken in the daytime'

꽃말 /k*otɕʰ + mal/ → k*otmal → [k*onmal] 'the language of flowers'

8.2.3 Liquid Nasalisation

When a sequence of a non-alveolar nasal and a liquid occurs in Korean, that is, two kinds of sonorant appear in a row, the liquid becomes a nasal. The nasalisation of liquids is the result of a surface phonetic constraint in Korean, which forbids a sequence of a non-alveolar nasal plus a liquid /l/. Hence, [m–l] and [ŋ–l] sequences are replaced by [m–n] and [ŋ–n] sequences respectively, as shown in (13).

🎧 (13) a. /m/ + /l/ → [m] + [n]

금리 /kɯm- + -li/ → [kɯmni] 'interest rate'

담론 /tɑm- + -lon/ → [tɑmnon] 'discussion'

b. /ŋ/ + /l/ → [ŋ] + [n]

공리 /koŋ- + -li/ → [koŋni] 'public interest'

등록 /tɯŋ- + -lok/ → [tɯŋnok] 'registration'

One might ask what happens in the case of the dental nasal /n/ plus liquid /l/. Just as in the case of non-dental nasals plus liquid /l/, a sequence consisting of /n/ and /l/ cannot be realised due to a surface phonetic constraint. However, as we shall see in Chapter 9, unlike the examples in (13), /n/ and /l/ can be assimilated into either a sequence of nasals, /n/ and /n/, or a sequence of liquids, /l/ and /l/. Since the phonetic realisation of the sequence of /n/ and /l/ depends on how the word is formed rather than purely on phonetic environment, we will discuss this in Chapter 9.

DID YOU KNOW...?

Who is [hɛmnit]?

The nasalisation of liquid sounds is so ingrained in Korean that it is even applied to loan words, and affects the pronunciation of foreign words. Because of this principle, *Hamlet* cannot but be pronounced as [hɛmnit] in Korean. Korean speakers are restrained by the nasalisation principle even when they speak English, and cannot pronounce English words in the way they ought to be pronounced. Native Korean speakers who are learning English, unless they are particularly attuned to their own pronunciation, would pronounce *Hamlet* not as [hæmlɪt], but as [hɛmnit].

Such changes in Korean occur even when there is a phonological phrase boundary, such as in /(kokoŋ) (lokʰɛt)/ [kokoŋ| nokʰɛt] 고공 로켓 'altitude rocket'. When Korean speakers are only saying the one word, /lokʰɛt/, they would pronounce it as [lokʰɛt], but when /lokʰɛt/ is pronounced within the phrase of /(kokoŋ) (lokʰɛt)/, regardless of whether a phonological phrase boundary exists or not, it is pronounced as [kokoŋnokʰɛt] or [kokoŋ| nokʰɛt], with [nokʰɛt] in both cases.

8.2.4 Lateralisation

Not only do liquids become nasalised as we have discussed in 8.2.3, but nasals also become lateralised when the two sounds co-occur, as shown in (14). Again, this rule is the consequence of a surface phonetic constraint in Korean, which forbids liquid–nasal sequences, /l/–/n/.

(14) a. Sino-Korean words with /l/–/n/ sequence
실내 (室內) /sil- + -nɛ/ → [sillɛ] 'interior'
질녀 (姪女) /tɕil- + -njʌ/ → [tɕilljʌ] 'a niece'

b. Pure-Korean words with /l/–/n/ sequence
겨울날 /kjʌul + nal/ → [kjʌullal] 'winter days'
과일나무 /kwail + namu/ → [kwaillamu] 'fruit trees'

8.2.5 Non-coronalisation (Bilabialisation and Velarisation)

In this section, we will discuss two types of phonological processes that turn coronal sounds into peripheral (= non-coronal) sounds. Simply speaking, sounds that are articulated in the default (i.e. coronal) position are either assimilated into the front position or into the back position, depending on the sounds that follow them. The first type of assimilation includes Bilabialisation and the second type includes Velarisation. Bilabialisation can be defined as an alveolar sound becoming a bilabial sound when followed by a bilabial sound. In a similar way, Velarisation is defined as an alveolar or bilabial sound becoming velar when followed by a velar sound. Examples are given in (15). We can see that the two options are equally applicable in most cases. This is because both processes are known to be optional rather than obligatory. Non-coronalisation is more frequently observed in spontaneous, informal speech, in particular, more in fast speech than in slow speech.

(15) a. /n/ → [m]
신문 /sin- + -mun/ → [sinmun ~ simmun] 'newspaper'
신발 /sin + pal/ → [sinpal ~ simpal] 'shoes'

b. /n / → [ŋ]
한강 /han- + kaŋ/ → [hankaŋ ~ haŋkaŋ] 'the *Han* river'
간격 /kan- + -kjʌk/ → [kankjʌk ~ kaŋkjʌk] 'interval'

c. /m/ → [ŋ]
감기 /kamki/ → [kamki ~ kaŋki] 'cold'
임금님 /imkɯm + -nim/ → [imkɯmnim ~ iŋkɯmnim] 'king'

DID YOU KNOW...?

Why is there no change in [kɑmnɑmu] 감나무 'persimmon tree'?

In a chain of 'an alveolar sound and a bilabial/velar sound' (in other words, [−coronal] sounds,) such as /sin- + -mun/ 신문 'newspaper', Hangeul /han + kɯl/, or in a chain of 'a bilabial and a velar sound' such as in /kɑmki/ 감기 'cold', Non-coronalisation occurs. However, in a chain of 'a bilabial and an alveolar sound', such as in /kɑm + nɑmu/ 감나무 'persimmon tree' no change occurs. We can make two observations from this.

First, Bilabialisation is a process in which the following sound influences the preceding sound. Thus, when a bilabial sound is placed in front of an alveolar sound, such as in /kɑm + nɑmu/ 감나무 no change occurs. Secondly, patterns of influence, which are based on place of articulation, differ depending on the category of the consonant. Although the bilabial sound /m/ influences the alveolar /n/ in /sin- + -mun/ 신문 [sinmun ~ simmun] 'newspaper', this is not the case if the consonants are reversed. So /kɑm + nɑmu/ 감나무 can never be pronounced as [kɑnnɑmu].

In addition, since /kamki/ 감기 'cold' is pronounced as [kaŋki] but /kaŋ + mul/ 강물 'river water' is not pronounced as [kammul], we can see that although velar sounds can influence bilabials, the opposite does not hold true; bilabial sounds cannot influence velars. Therefore, even within a fixed place of articulation, there is a hierarchy of sounds that determines how sounds influence one another. Here, we have observed that the hierarchy, "velar > bilabial > alveolar", exists among places of articulation.

8.2.6 Aspiration

In Korean, when /h/ and a lax obstruent appear together in the same sequence, they are contracted. As a result, the lax obstruent becomes aspirated. Examples are shown in (16). Shown in (16a) are examples where /h/ precedes lax obstruents, and (16b) shows examples where /h/ follows lax obstruents.

(16) a. /h/ + /k, t, tɕ/ → [kʰ, tʰ, tɕʰ]
          놓고 /noh- + -ko/ → [nokʰo] 'to put (connective)'
          놓다 /noh- + -ta/ → [notʰa] 'to put (declarative)'
          놓지 /noh- + -tɕʰi / → [notɕʰi] 'to put (connective)'
      b. /k, t, p/ + /h/ → [kʰ, tʰ, pʰ]
          독학 /tok- + -hak/ → [tokʰak] 'self-study'

만형 /mɑt- + hjʌŋ/ → [mɑtʰjʌŋ] 'the eldest brother'
곱하기 /kop + -hɑ- + -ki/ → [kopʰɑki] 'multiplication'

The examples in (17) show the two steps of the phonological processes Neutralisation and Aspiration, occurring consecutively.

🎧 (17) 이웃하다 /ius + -hɑ- + -tɑ/ → iuthɑtɑ → [iutʰɑtɑ] 'to be close to each other'
꽃향기 /kˀotɕʰ + hjɑŋki/ → kˀothjɑŋki → [kˀotʰjɑŋki] 'the scent of a flower'

8.2.7 Similar-place Obstruent Deletion

In Korean, when a sequence contains two consecutive consonants that are pronounced in similar positions, one of them is deleted for ease of pronunciation. In natural speech, the first consonant in the sequence of obstruents is deleted. Consider (18).[5]

🎧 (18) a. In a bilabial sequence of /p/ and /pʰ/, the first consonant, /p/ is deleted.
집필 /tɕip- + -pʰil/ → [tɕipʰil] 'writing'
밥풀 /pɑp + pʰul/ → [pɑpʰul] 'rice paste'

    b. In a velar sequence of /k/ and /kʰ/, the first consonant, /k/ is deleted
식칼 /sik + kʰɑl/ → [sikʰɑl] 'kitchen knife'
킥킥 /kʰik + kʰik/ → [kʰi kʰik] 'giggle'

    c. In an alveolar sequence as below, the first consonant is deleted.
낫도 /nɑs + -to/ → nɑtto → nɑttˀo → [nɑtˀo] 'sickle-even'
낮도 /nɑtɕ + -to/ → nɑtto → nɑttˀo → [nɑtˀo] 'daytime-even'
낯도 /nɑtɕʰ+ -to/ → nɑtto → nɑttˀo → [nɑtˀo] 'face-even'
옷장 /os + tɕɑŋ/ → ottɕɑŋ → ottɕˀɑŋ → [otɕˀɑŋ] 'closet'
낯처럼 /nɑtɕ + -tɕʰʌlʌm/ → nɑttɕʰʌlʌm → [nɑtɕʰʌlʌm] 'like daytime'
옷솔 /os + sol/ → otsol → otsˀol → [osˀol] 'clothes brush'

FURTHER STUDY

Pronouncing 젖소 and 옷솔: dictionary transcription vs. real pronunciation

How are /tɕʌtɕ + so/ 젖소 'cow' and /os + sol/ 옷솔 'clothes brush' pronounced?

The Korean dictionary stipulates that the pronunciation of 젖소 is [tɕʌtsˀo] and the pronunciation of 옷솔 is [otsˀol]. However, these are unlikely to be how the words are actually pronounced, because obstructive sounds in similar articulation positions are not eliminated. When Korean speakers say these words naturally, they pronounce them as [tɕʌ.sˀo] and [o.sˀol] respectively by eliminating the stop sounds. It is hard to conceive of [tɕʌt.sˀo] or [ot.sˀol] as natural pronunciations of the words. The figure shows a spectrogram of a standard Korean speaker's pronunciation of /os + sol/ 옷솔. As this shows, the fricative region (marked by the bold square in the picture) can only be observed between vowels in the way that /os + sol/ 옷솔 is actually pronounced. If it were pronounced as [otsˀol], a stop region (marked by a white space on the spectrogram) ought to be detected prior to the fricative region, but this does not happen in natural speech. Essentially, the actual pronunciation of /os + sol/ 옷솔 is [osˀol].

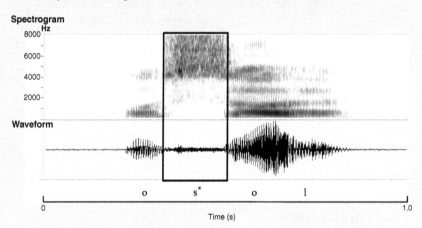

8.2.8 /j/ Deletion

In Korean, [tɕ, tɕˀ, tɕʰ] cannot appear with a [j] sound. Therefore, no words in Korean have any of the following sequences: [tɕjʌ, tɕˀjʌ, tɕʰjʌ] or [tɕjo, tɕˀjo, tɕʰjo], etc. Hence, when verbs whose stems have /tɕ, tɕˀ, tɕʰ/ and an /i/ vowel such as /tɕi- + -tɑ/ 지다 'to lose', /tɕˀi- + -tɑ/ 찌다 'to steam' or /tɕʰi- + -tɑ/ 치다 'to hit' are inflected with a verbal ending starting with –어/-ʌ/, they are pronounced with an /ʌ/ vowel instead of an /jʌ/ vowel as in (19), as [j] is deleted.

(19) 지어서 /tɕi- +-ʌsʌ/ → tɕjʌsʌ → [tɕʌsʌ] 'to lose (connective)'
     찌어서 /tɕˀi- + -ʌsʌ/ → tɕˀjʌsʌ → [tɕˀʌsʌ] 'to steam (connective)'
     치어서 /tɕʰi- + -ʌsʌ/ → tɕʰjʌsʌ → [tɕʰʌsʌ] 'to hit (connective)'

However, [j] is not deleted in all cases, as shown in (20), where the preceding consonants are not /tɕ, tɕ*, tɕʰ/.

🎧 (20) 구기어서 /kuki- + -ʌsʌ/ → [kukjʌsʌ] 'to wrinkle (connective)'
꾸미어서 /k*umi- + -ʌsʌ/ → [k*umjʌsʌ] 'to decorate (connective)'

8.2.9 /h/ Deletion

In natural speech in Korean, an /h/ appearing between voiced sounds is avoided. This is more frequently observed in spontaneous, informal speech, in particular, more in fast speech than in slow speech. Examples are given in (21).

🎧 (21) a. /h/ between vowels
외할머니 /wɛ- + halmʌni/ → [wɛhalmʌni ~ wɛalmʌni] 'grandmother'
대학 /tɛ- + -hak/ → [tɛhak ~ tɛak] 'university'

b. /h/ between a vowel and a sonorant consonant
영향 /jʌŋ- + -hjaŋ/ → [jʌŋhjaŋ ~ jʌŋjaŋ] 'influence'
문화 /mun- + -hwa/ → [munhwa ~ munwa] 'culture'
실현 /sil- + -hjʌn/ → [silhjʌn ~ siljʌn] 'realisation'

FURTHER STUDY

Writing perfect Korean

Writing in Korean is not easy because the way people pronounce words and the way they write them down are not the same. Dictation training is one of the key features of Korean language education at school. However, even if one is thoroughly trained in dictation, it is still not easy to write Korean without mistakes. Take the example of 곡물을 바치다 /(kokmul + -ɯl) (patɕʰi- + -ta)/ [koŋmulɯl | patɕʰita] 'to offer grain'. This sounds exactly the same as 공물을 바치다 /(koŋmul + -ɯl/) (patɕʰi- + -ta)/ [koŋmulɯl | patɕʰita] 'to offer an official gift'. There are many examples like this. For instance, 아끼다 /ak*i- + -ta/ [ak*ita] 'to save' sounds exactly the same as 악기다 /ak-+ -ki + -ta/ [ak*ita] '(it is a) musical instrument'. Likewise, 금리 /kɯm- + -li/ [kɯmni] 'interest' sounds exactly the same as 금니 /kɯm + ni/ [kɯmni] 'gold teeth' due to Nasalisation. The only way to determine the correct orthography from two identical sound sequences is to determine the correct meaning for the given context.

8.3 Summary

In this chapter, we have seen phonological rules that are particularly motivated by syllable structure constraints and surface phonetic constraints. Rules affected by syllable structure constraints include Neutralisation and Consonant-cluster Simplification. Rules affected by surface phonetic constraints include (i) Post-obstruent Tensification; (ii) Obstruent Nasalisation; (iii) Liquid Nasalisation (iv) Lateralisation; (v) Non-coronalisation (Bilabialisation and Velarisation); (vi) Aspiration; (vii) Similar-place Obstruent Deletion; (viii) /j/ Deletion; and (ix) /h/ Deletion. Table 8.4 shows a summary of the phonological rules discussed in this chapter.

Table 8.4 Phonological rules of Korean (I)

Rule	Core example: underlying form	Core example: pronunciation
Neutralisation	부엌 /puʌkʰ/	[puʌk] 'kitchen'
Consonant-cluster simplification	삶 /salm/	[sam] 'life'
Post-obstruent tensification	먹다 /mʌk- + -ta/	[mʌktˀa] 'to eat'
	옆집 /jʌpʰ + tɕip/ → jʌptɕip	[jʌptɕˀip] 'next door'
Obstruent nasalisation	밥맛 /pap + mas/ → papmat	[pammat] 'taste of rice'
	겹눈 /kjʌp + nun/	[kjʌmnun] 'compound eyes'
Liquid nasalisation	금리 /kɯm- + -li/	[kɯmni] 'interest rate'
Lateralisation	겨울날 /kjʌul + nal/	[kjʌullal] 'winter days'
Non-coronalisation (bilabialisation and velarisation)	신문 /sin- + -mun/	[sinmun ~ simmun] 'newspaper'
	한강 /han- + kaŋ/	[hankaŋ ~ haŋkaŋ] 'the *Han* river'
	감기 /kamki/	[kamki ~ kaŋki] 'cold'
Aspiration	놓다 /noh- + -ta/	[notʰa] 'to put'
	독학 /tok- + -hak/	[tokʰak] 'self-study'
Similar-place obstruent deletion	집필 /tɕip- + -pʰil/	[tɕipʰil] 'writing'
	옷장 /os + tɕaŋ/ → ottɕaŋ → ottɕˀaŋ	[otɕˀaŋ] 'closet'
/j/ deletion	지어서 /tɕi- +-ʌsʌ/ → tɕjʌsʌ	[tɕʌsʌ] 'to carry (connective)'
/h/ deletion	대학 /tɛ- + -hak/	[tɛhak ~ tɛak] 'university'
	영향 /jʌŋ- + -hjaŋ/	[jʌŋhjaŋ ~ jʌŋjaŋ] 'influence'

EXERCISES

1   Explain why /pɑt-/ 받- 'to accept' and /pɑtʰ/ 밭 'field' are pronounced the same.

2   Explain why the /tʰ/ in /pɑtʰ/ 밭 and /pɑtʰ + -ɛ/ 밭에 'field (prepositional particle)' or /pɑtʰ + -ɯl/ 밭을 'field (object particle)' are pronounced differently.

3   Explain why a consonant cluster cannot occur in syllable-final position.

4   Is it natural to pronounce /os/ 옷 'clothes' as [os] and /otɕʰ/ 옻 'sap of the lacquer tree' as [otɕʰ] in Korean? If not, explain why.

5   Please pronounce the following and explain the processes of phonetic realisation for these words.
    a. /ɑntɕ- + -ko/ 앉고 'to sit down (connective)'
    b. /mɑnh- + -so/ 많소 'to be plentiful (declarative)'
    c. /sɑlm- + -tɑ/ 삶다 'to boil (declarative)'
    d. /nʌlp- + -ko/ 넓고 'to be wide (connective)'
    e. /ɯlpʰ- + -nɛ/ 읊네 'to recite (exclamative)'

6   Explain why /s/ in 색 /sɛk/ 'colour' is tensified in (a) but not in (b).
    a. 녹색 /nok + sɛk/ 'green'
    b. 노란색 /norɑn + sɛk / 'yellow'

7   Illustrate the phonological processes by which /puʌkʰ + -to/ 부엌도 'kitchen (additional meaning particle)' is pronounced as [puʌkˀo], using relevant phonological rules.

8   Illustrate the phonological processes by which /kuk + mul/ 국물 'soup-liquid' is pronounced as [kuŋmul] using relevant phonological rules.

9   Illustrate the phonological processes by which /koŋ- + -li/ 공리 'public interest' is pronounced as [koŋni] using relevant phonological rules.

10 Illustrate the phonological processes by which /kjʌul + nɑl/ 겨울날 'winter days' is pronounced as [kjʌullɑl] using relevant phonological rules.

11 Why is /tɕip- + -pʰil/ 집필 'writing' pronounced as [tɕipʰil] instead of [tɕippʰil]?

12 Why is /h/ in the following words very often not pronounced?
    a. /mun- + -hwɑ/ 문화 'culture'
    b. /tɛ- + -hɑk/ 대학 'university'
    c. /wɛ- + hɑlapʌtɕi/ 외할아버지 'maternal grandfather'
    d. /ju- + -hjʌŋ/ 유형 'type'

9 Phonological rules of Korean (II)

9.1 Background

In Chapter 8, we discussed phonological rules related mainly to surface phonetic constraints and syllable structure constraints. The phonological rules discussed in Chapter 8 are applied to a sequence of sounds regardless of morphological information. For instance, a /k/–/m/ sequence in Korean automatically changes into a /ŋ/–/m/ sequence regardless of the morphological structure or origin of a word. This is the case for all the following types of word. In this chapter, we will use + for morpheme boundary, # for word boundary and - to indicate bound morpheme.

🎧 (1)   a. Morphological structure
Compounding: 국물 /kuk # mul/ → [kuŋmul] 'soup liquid'
Derivation: 첫날 /tɕʰʌs- # nal/ → tɕʰʌtnal → [tɕʰʌnnal] 'first day'
   b. Word origin
Pure Korean words: 국물 /kuk # mul/ → [kuŋmul] 'soup liquid'
Sino-Korean words: 곡물 (穀物) /kok- + -mul/ → [koŋmul] 'grain'

However, not all phonological rules can be applied in this way. Indeed, knowing how and by what types of morpheme a word is formed is crucial in understanding Korean phonology. For instance, Tensification is affected by the underlying morphological information of the word. The nature of the morpheme boundary in a given type of a word also influences the application of Tensification. Hence, although orthographically the pairs of words in Table 9.1 each look the same, only in the former is there Tensification, not in the latter.

This shows that the way in which a word is formed determines the pronunciation of that word. In this chapter, as above, we will discuss the phonological rules for which morphological information plays a crucial part in their application. Before going further, we will briefly re-cap grammatical terms,

Table 9.1 Tense vs. lax contrast for words with the same orthography

Words	Second syllable onset consonant being tensified	Second syllable onset consonant not being tensified (remains as lax consonant)
잠자리	Morphological boundary: 잠자리 /tɕam # tɕali/ [tɕamtɕ*ali] 'bed'	No morphological boundary: 잠자리 /tɕamtɕali/ [tɕamtɕali] 'dragonfly'
발병	Within a compound: 발병 /pal # pjʌŋ/ [palp*jʌŋ] 'sore feet'	Within a simple word: 발병 (發病) /pal- + -pjʌŋ/ [palpjʌŋ] 'to become sick'
신고	Pure Korean verbal inflection: 신고 /sin- + -ko/ [sink*o] 'to put on (connective)'	Sino-Korean stem: 신고 (申告) /sin- + -ko/ [sinko] 'declare'

since understanding how and from which elements a word is formed is crucial in understanding its phonological realisation. The examples in (2) and (3) show how a morpheme, the smallest meaning-bearing unit, can be further classified. Morphemes can be divided into either free or bound morphemes and into lexical or grammatical morphemes. Below we provide examples of each type.

(2)   a. Free morpheme (i.e. can be used independently)
눈 /nun/ 'eye'
사람 /salam/ 'person'
잠자리 /tɕamtɕali/ 'dragonfly'

   b. Bound morpheme (i.e. can't be used independently)
Pure Korean prefix: 첫- /tɕʰʌs/ 'first' as in 첫사랑 /tɕʰʌs- # salaŋ/ 'first love'
Pure Korean suffix: -끼리 /-k*ili/ 'together' as in 친구끼리 /tɕʰinku # -k*ili/ 'together with friends'
Sino-Korean prefix: 초 (超)- /tɕʰo-/ 'extremely' as in 초호화 /tɕʰo- # hohwa/ 'Extremely luxurious'
Sino-Korean suffix: -식 (式) /-sik/ 'style' as in 영국식 /jʌŋkuk # -sik/ 'English style'
Inflectional suffixes: -시- /-si-/ 'subject honorification', -었- /-ʌs*-/ 'past tense', -다 /-ta/ 'declarative'

(3)   a. Lexical morpheme (i.e. has lexical meaning)
눈 /nun/ 'eye'
사람 /salam/ 'person'
잠자리 /tɕamtɕali/ 'dragonfly'
하- /ha-/ 'to do'
먹- /mʌk-/ 'to eat'

   b. Grammatical morpheme (i.e. has only grammatical function)
      (i)   particles: -이 /-i/ 'subject particle', -을 /-ɯl/, 'object particle',
            도 /-to/ 'too, also'
      (ii) derivational suffixes: -이 /-i/ 'causative suffix', -히 /-hi/
            'passive suffix'
      (iii) inflectional suffixes: -시-/-si-/ 'subject honorification', -었
            /-ʌs*-/ 'past tense', -다 /-ta/ 'declarative'

In the following, in 9.2, we will discuss the phonological rules applied where one lexical morpheme meets another and in 9.3, we will discuss rules that are applied where a lexical morpheme meets a grammatical morpheme.

9.2 Rules where two lexical morphemes meet

In this section, we will discuss phonological rules that are applied at the boundary between two lexical morphemes. Lexical morphemes coincide with free morphemes in most cases but not all the time. As noted above, Sino-Korean vocabulary constitutes a major part of Korean vocabulary. The phonological rules to be discussed here are mainly observed between Sino-Korean lexical morphemes. In particular, we will focus on the Lateralisation and Nasalisation of Sino-Korean words (9.2.1), the Tensification of Sino-Korean words (9.2.2), /t/ Insertion (9.2.3) and /n/ Insertion (9.2.4).

9.2.1 Lateralisation and Nasalisation of Sino-Korean words

Why is the /nl/ sequence sometimes pronounced [ll] and at other times [nn]?

When /n/ and /l/ appear in a row, /n/ is assimilated into /l/ when a morpheme boundary occurs between the two sounds.[1] This rule is not, however, applicable when a word boundary occurs between the two sounds. In such cases, assimilation occurs in the opposite direction, with /l/ becoming /n/. Consider (4).

(4)   a. /n/ becomes /l/ when there is a morpheme boundary between the
          sounds
          권력 (勸力) /kwʌn- + -ljʌk/ → [kwʌlljʌk] 'power'
          논리 (論理) /non- + -li/ → [nolli] 'logic'
      b. /l/ becomes /n/ when there is a word boundary between the sounds
          판단력 (判斷力) /(pʰan- + -tan) # -ljʌk/ → [pʰantannjʌk] 'decision'
          음운론 (音韻論) /(ɯm- + -un) # -lon/ → [ɯmunnon] 'phonology'

Table 9.2 shows examples of Lateralisation and Nasalisation.

Table 9.2 Phonetic realisation of /nl/: Lateralisation vs. Nasalisation 🎧

Words	/nl/ → [ll] (i.e. Lateralisation)	/nl/ → [nn] (i.e. Nasalisation)
음운론 (音韻論) /(ɯm- + -un) # -lon/ 'phonology'	N/A	[ɯmunnon]
공권력 (公權力) /(koŋ- + -kwʌn) # -ljʌk/ 'governmental authority'	N/A	[koŋk*wʌnnjʌk]
동원령 (動員令) /(toŋ- + -won) # -ljʌŋ/ 'mobilisation order'	N/A	[toŋwonnjʌŋ]
광한루 (廣寒樓) /kwaŋ- + -han- + -lu/ 'a tower in Namweon'	[kwaŋhallu]	N/A
난로 (煖爐) /nan- + -lo/ 'a heater'	[nallo]	N/A

DID YOU KNOW...?

Knowing word structure is important in pronouncing a word!

Sometimes whether the /nl/ sequence should be lateralised [ll] or nasalised [nn] is ambiguous. Moreover, morphological information plays an important role in deciding the appropriate phonetic realisation, as shown in the example below. In (a), if one means a particular noodle eaten in the *Silla* 신라 period in Korean history (668–935 AD), then the word structure is /(sin- + -la) # mjʌn/ and /sin- + -la/ forms one word together. As a result, Lateralisation will be applicable and the pronunciation of the word will be [sillamjʌn]. On the other hand, if one means a particular instant noodle (ramen) brand, 'Sin-ramen' 신 (辛)라면, then the word structure is /sin- # (lamjʌn)/ and /sin/ and /la/ do not form one word together. As a result, Nasalisation will be applicable and the pronunciation of the word will be [sinnamjʌn].

🎧 a. 신라면 (新羅# 麵) /(sin- + -la) # mjʌn/ → [sillamjʌn]
   (Lateralisation applicable, Nasalisation **not** applicable)

 b. 신라면 (辛# 라면) /sin- # lamjʌn/ → [sinnamjʌn]
   (Lateralisation **not** applicable, Nasalisation applicable)

9.2.2 Tensification of Sino-Korean words

Why is /kjʌl + tɑn/ 결단 (決斷) pronounced [kjʌltˀɑn]?

A sequence consisting of an /l/ and a lax consonant with [+coronal] features such as /t, s, tɕ/ may not appear in a Sino-Korean word. Instead, those lax consonants are pronounced as /tˀ, sˀ, tɕˀ/. However, when /l/ is followed by [−coronal] lax consonants in a Sino-Korean word, this rule is not applicable. Consider (5).

(5) Tensification of Sino-Korean words
   a. /l/ followed by coronal lax consonant: Tensification applicable
      결단 (決斷) /kjʌl- + -tɑn/ [kjʌltˀɑn] 'decision'
      결선 (決選) /kjʌl- + -sʌn/ [kjʌlsˀʌn] 'final (competition)'
      발전 (發展) /pɑl- + -tɕʌn/ [pɑltɕˀʌn] 'improvement'
   b. /l/ followed by non-coronal lax consonant /k/ or /p/: Tensification non-applicable
      결과 (結果) /kjʌl- + -kwɑ/ [kjʌlkwɑ] 'result'
      발견 (發見) /pɑl- + -kjʌn/ [pɑlkjʌn] 'finding'
      결박 (結縛) /kjʌl- + -pɑk/ [kjʌlpɑk] 'strap'

In (5a), /t, s, tɕ/ become /tˀ, sˀ, tɕˀ/ according to the rule. However, in (5b), the rule is not applied. In addition, this rule is applied to Sino-Korean words only.

9.2.3 /t/ Insertion

Why is the same /pi/ 비 pronounced differently in /pom # pi/ 봄비 and /nun # pi/ 눈비?

In Chapter 8, we saw that lax consonants are tensified when followed by another obstruent consonant due to the surface phonetic constraint which forbids a sequence of obstruents. This rule (Post-obstruent Tensification) is automatically applied regardless of how the word is formed.

However, if we turn our attention to the pronunciation of /pom # pi/ [pompˀi] 봄비 'spring rain' and /nun # pi/ [nunpi] 눈비 'snow and rain', the Tensification rule appears to be less predictable except in the cases of obstruent–obstruent sequences. The same /pi/ 비 is tensified in /pom # pi/ 봄비 'spring rain' but not in /nun # pi/ 눈비 'snow and rain'.

Why is this the case? Is there any way of making a prediction as to whether Tensification should be applied? Some argue that Tensification via /t/ Insertion can be predicted, in that it occurs when a subordinate relation holds between sub-compounds instead of a coordinate relation. In /pom # pi/ 봄비 'spring rain', /pom/ 봄 'spring' modifies /pi/ 비 'rain'. Hence, a subordinate relation holds in the compound. As the result of this, /pi/ 비 'rain' is tensified. On the other hand, in /nun # pi/ 눈비 'snow and rain', a coordinate, parallel relation exists between /nun/ 눈 'snow' and /pi/ 비 'rain'. Hence, /pi/ 비 'rain' is not tensified.

(6)   a. /t/ Insertion occurs in subordinated compound words.

         봄비 /pom # pi/ → pom # t # pi (/t/ Insertion) → pom t pʰi
         (Post-obstruent Tensification) pom t pʰi (Consonant-cluster
         Simplification) → [pompʰi] 'spring rain'
         상다리 /saŋ # tali/ → saŋ # t # tali (/t/ Insertion) → saŋ t tʰali
         (Post-obstruent Tensification) → saŋ tʰali (Consonant-cluster
         Simplification) → [saŋtʰali] 'table legs'
         산새 /san # sɛ/ → san # t # sɛ (/t/ Insertion) → san t sʰɛ
         (Post-obstruent Tensification) → sansʰɛ (Consonant-cluster
         Simplification) → [sansʰɛ] 'mountain bird'

       b. /t/ Insertion does not occur in coordinated compound words.
         눈비 /nun # pi/ → [nunpi] 'snow and rain'
         봄가을 /pom # kaɯl/ → [pomkaɯl] 'spring and fall'
         손발 /son # pal/ → [sonpal] 'hands and feet'

In this book, we argue that the pronunciation of /pom # pi/ 봄비 becoming [pompʰi] cannot be simply explained by Tensification, but must be explained as Tensification via /t/ Insertion. This is due to examples such as /wi # os/ [witot] 윗옷 'top clothes' or /alɛ # maɯl/ [alɛnmaɯl] 아랫마을 'next village', where Tensification itself cannot be applicable, since the word-initial sound for the second sub-compound starts with a vowel or a nasal consonant instead of a lax consonant. In order to allow for examples such as /wi # os/ 'top clothes' becoming [witot] and /alɛ # maɯl/ 'next village' becoming [alɛnmaɯl], we argue that /pom # pi/ becoming [pompʰi] is not merely the result of Tensification, but of Tensification via /t/ Insertion. (7) shows the phonological processes resulting in the surface form of these two words.

(7)   Phonological processes for /wi # os/ 윗옷 and /alɛ # maɯl/ 아랫마을
        윗옷 /wi # os/ → wi # t # os → witot (Neutralisation) → [witot] 'top
        cloth' 아랫마을 /alɛ # maɯl/ → alɛ # t # maɯl (/t/ Insertion) →
        alɛnmaɯl (Obstruent Nasalisation) → [alɛnmaɯl] 'next village'

However, counter-examples can easily be found. For instance, /koki/ 고기 is pronounced differently in /mul # koki/ 물고기 'fish' and /pul # koki/ 불고기 'marinated beef': it is tensed in [mulkʰoki] but not in [pulkoki]. More examples

Table 9.3 Tensification via /t/ Insertion variation among subordinated compounds 🎧

	/t/ Insertion applicable	/t/ Insertion not applicable
Compounds where the preceding word is the same	불빛 /pul # pitɕʰ/ → pul # t # pitɕʰ → [pulpʼit] 'light'	불볕 /pul # pjʌtʰ/ → [pulpjʌt] 'burning sun'
	돌덩어리 /tol # tʌŋʌli/ → tol # t# tʌŋʌli → [toltʼʌŋʌli] 'rock'	돌기둥 /tol # kituŋ/ → [tolkituŋ] 'stone pillar'
	쌀가게 /sʼal # kakɛ/ → sʼal # t # kakɛ → [sʼalkʼakɛ] 'rice shop'	쌀밥 /sʼal # pap/ → [sʼalpap] 'boiled rice'
	꿈결 /kʼum # kjʌl/ → kʼum # t # kjʌl → [kʼumkʼjʌl] 'a dreamy state'	꿈자리 /kʼum # tɕali/ → [kʼumtɕali] 'a dream'
	콩가루 /kʰoŋ # kalu/ → kʰoŋ # t # kalu → [kʰoŋ kʼalu] 'bean flour'	콩기름 /kʰoŋ # kiluɯm/ → [kʰoŋkiluɯm] 'soybean oil'
Compounds where the following word is the same	강바닥 /kaŋ # patak/ → kaŋ # t # patak → [kaŋpʼatak] 'river bed'	골바닥 /kol # patak/ → [kolpatak] 'the lowest part of the valley'
	그믐달 /kuɯmɯm # tal/ → kuɯmɯm # t # tal → [kuɯmɯmtʼal] 'dark moon'	반달 /pan # tal/ → [pantal] 'half moon'
	물새 /mul # sɛ/ → mul # t # sɛ → [mulsʼɛ] 'water bird'	파랑새 /pʰalaŋ # sɛ/ → [pʰalaŋ sɛ] 'bluebird'
	겨울잠 /kjʌul # tɕam/ → kjʌul # t # tɕam → [kjʌultɕʼam] 'hibernation'	두벌잠 /tupʌl # tɕam/ → [tupʌltɕam] 'the second sleep that one falls into after the first sleep'
	말장난 /mal # tɕaŋnan/ → mal # t # tɕaŋnan → [mal tɕʼaŋnan] 'pun'	불장난 /pul # tɕaŋnan/ → [pultɕaŋnan] 'play with fire'

like this one can be found in Table 9.3. Table 9.3 shows cases where the Tensification rule resulting from /t/ Insertion is applied as well as the cases where the rule is not applicable.

Table 9.4 Pronunciation of days of the week showing /n/ Insertion in *Gyeongsang* dialect

Words	Seoul	*Gyeongsang*
월요일 /wʌl # joil/ 'Monday'	[wʌljoil]	wʌl # n # joil → [wʌlljoil] (further Lateralisation)
목요일 /mok # joil/ 'Thursday'	[mokjoil]	mok # n # joil → [moŋnjoil] (further Nasalisation)
금요일 /kɯm # joil/ 'Friday'	[kɯmjoil]	kɯm # n # joil → [kɯmnjoil]

9.2.4 /n/ Insertion

/n/ Insertion can happen when the preceding word ends with a consonant and the following word starts with /i/ or /j/. Therefore, even though two words may be formed in a similar way, if their phonological environments differ, /n/ Insertion may occur in one word but not in the other. (8) shows examples of /n/ Insertion in compounding and derivation.

(8) a. /n/ Insertion in compounding

솜이불 /som # ipul/ → som # n # ipul → [somnipul] 'a cotton-wool duvet.'

들일 /tɯl # il/ → tɯl # n # il → tɯlnil → [tɯllil] 'farm work' (further Lateralisation)

북유럽 /puk # julʌp/ → [pukjulʌp] ~ [puŋnjulʌp] 'Northern Europe'

색연필 /sɛk # jʌnpʰil/ → [sɛkjʌnpʰil] ~ [sɛŋnjʌnpʰil] 'coloured pencil'

b. /n/ Insertion in derivation

늦여름 /nɯtɕ- # jʌlɯm/ → nɯtɕ-n # jʌlɯm → nɯtnjʌlɯm → [nɯnnjʌlɯm] 'late summer'

한여름 /han- # jʌlɯm/ → han- n # jʌlɯm → [hannjʌlɯm] 'midsummer'

겹이불 /kjʌp- # ipul/ → kjʌp- n # ipul → kjʌpnipul → [kjʌmnipul] 'layered blanket'

막일 /mak- # il/ → mak- n # il → maknil → [maŋnil] 'physical labour' (further Nasalisation)

The /n/ Insertion rule varies from dialect to dialect. In North Korean dialects, /n/ Insertion is not as frequently observed. For instance, in North Korean, /po- + -l # il/ 볼일 'something to do' is pronounced as [polil], instead of [pollil] as in the South. On the other hand, /n/ Insertion is widespread in the *Gyeongsang* dialect. So, for instance, in the examples in Table 9.4, referring to days of the week, Seoul Korean speakers will pronounce each word without /n/ Insertion, but *Gyeongsang* dialect speakers will pronounce them with /n/ inserted.

9.3 Rules between lexical morphemes and grammatical morphemes

Some phonological phenomena are observed between lexical and grammatical morphemes. These include Palatalisation (9.3.1); Verbal Suffix Tensification (9.3.2); Glide Formation in Verbal Inflection (9.3.3); /h/ Deletion in Verbal Inflection (9.3.4); /ɯ/ Deletion in Verbal Inflection (9.3.5); /ɑ/ or /ʌ/ Deletion in Verbal Inflection (9.3.6).

9.3.1 Palatalisation

Why is /katʰ + i/ 같이 never pronounced as [katʰi] but as [katɕʰi]?

When a lexical morpheme ending with /t, tʰ/ is followed by a grammatical morpheme beginning with /i/, /t, tʰ/ is palatalised into /tɕ, tɕʰ/.

(9) a. Noun + subject particle
밭이 /patʰ + -i/ → [patɕʰi] 'field (subject particle)'
b. Noun + copula
밭이다 /patʰ + -i- + -ta/ → [patɕʰita] 'field (copula)'
c. Noun + conjunctive
밭이랑 /patʰ + -ilaŋ/ → [patɕʰilaŋ] 'field (conjunctive)'
d. Adverbial suffix
같이 /katʰ- + -i/ → [katɕʰi] 'together'
굳이 /kut- + -i/ → [kutɕi] 'willingly'
e. Nominalising suffix
미닫이 /mitat- + -i/ → [mitatɕi] 'sliding door'
f. Causative suffix
붙이다 /putʰ- + -i- + -ta/ → [putɕʰita] 'to stick'

However, 밭이랑 can be pronounced not only as [patɕʰilaŋ] but also as [pannilaŋ]. Consider (10). In (10a), /patʰ + -ilaŋ/ 밭이랑 is pronounced [patɕʰilaŋ]. That is, /t/ is palatalised. But in (10b), /patʰ # ilaŋ/ 밭이랑 is pronounced [pannilaŋ], with /n/ Insertion.

(10) a. Palatalisation
밭이랑 /patʰ + -ilaŋ/ → [patɕʰirang] 'field (conjunctive particle)'
(이랑 /-ilaŋ/ is a grammatical morpheme meaning 'and')

b. Neutralisation and /n/ Insertion

밭이랑 /patʰ # ilaŋ/ → patʰ # n # ilaŋ (/n/ Insertion)
→ patnilaŋ (Neutralisation) → [pɑnnilɑŋ]
(Obstruent Nasalisation)
(이랑 /ilaŋ/ is a lexical morpheme meaning 'furrow')

Why is this the case? This is because Palatalisation occurs between a lexical morpheme and a grammatical morpheme. In (10a), /-ilaŋ/ 이랑 is used as a conjunctive particle, that is, a grammatical morpheme. Therefore, Palatalisation is applied and the pronunciation becomes [patɕʰilaŋ]. On the other hand, in (10b), /ilaŋ/ 이랑 is used as a lexical morpheme. Hence, Palatalisation is not applicable and the pronunciation becomes [pɑnnilɑŋ] as a result of applying /n/ Insertion and subsequent Neutralisation and Obstruent Nasalisation.

9.3.2 Verbal suffix Tensification: after a nasal-ending stem

When a lax consonant, such as /k, t, s, tɕ/, is preceded by a verbal stem ending with a nasal /n, m/, the lax consonant is tensed and pronounced as /k*, t*, s*, tɕ*/. This Tensification rule is applicable only in verbal inflections between the stem of a verb and verbal suffix. Consider the following.

(11) Verbal stem + suffix

a. 안- /an-/ 'to hug'
/an- + -ko/ → [ank*o] 'to hug (connective)'
/an- + -ta/ → [ant*a] 'to hug (declarative)'
/an- + -so/ → [ans*o] 'to hug (declarative)'
/an- + -tɕa/ → [antɕ*a] 'to hug (propositive)'

b. 감- /kam-/ 'to coil'
/kam- + -ko/ → [kamk*o] 'to coil (connective)'
/kam- + -ta/ → [kamt*a] 'to coil (declarative)'
/kam- + -so/ → [kams*o] 'to coil (declarative)'
/kam- + -tɕa/ → [kamtɕ*a] 'to coil (propositive)'

c. 삶- /salm/ 'to boil'
/salm- + -ko/ → salmk*o → [samk*o] 'to boil (connective)'
/salm- + -ta/ → salmt*a → [samt*a] 'to boil (declarative)'
/salm- + -so/ → salms*o → [sams*o] 'to boil (declarative)'
/salm- + -tɕa/ → salmtɕ*a → [samtɕ*a] 'to boil (propositive)'

FURTHER STUDY

In addition to the Tensification discussed above, another type of
Tensification occurs between a grammatical morpheme and a lexical
morpheme. When a noun starting with a lax consonant follows the
adnominal ending /-ɯl/ or /-l/ –을/-ㄹ, the lax consonant is tensified.
When the following lexical morpheme is a dependent morpheme (noun),
Tensification is obligatory. However, when the following lexical morpheme
is an independent morpheme, Tensification occurs only when the two
words form one phonological phrase.

a. Adnominal ending plus dependent nouns (forming one
    phonological word)
    갈곳 /kɑ- + -l # -kos/ → [kɑlk*ot] 'the place to go'
    놀데 /nol- + -l # -tɛ/ → [nolt*ɛ] 'the place to play'
b. Adnominal ending plus independent nouns (forming one
    phonological phrase)
    갈사람 /kɑ- +- l # sɑlɑm/ → [kɑls*ɑlɑm] 'someone to go'
    놀장소 /nol- + -l # tɕɑŋso/ → [nolt͡ɕ*ɑŋso] 'the place to play'
c. Adnominal ending plus independent nouns (not forming one
    phonological phrase)
    가버릴사람에게 /kɑ- + pʌli- + -l # sɑlɑm + -ɛkɛ/ → [kɑpʌlil |
    sɑlɑmɛkɛ]
    'to someone to go'
    먹고놀장소에서 /mʌk- + -ko #nol- + -l # tɕɑŋso + -ɛsʌ/ →
    [mʌk*onol | tɕɑŋsoɛsʌ] 'at the place to eat and play'

9.3.3 Glide Formation in verbal inflection

When a verbal stem ending with a consonant and /i/ sequence is inflected with
a suffix beginning with /ʌ/, /i/ often becomes a glide. This is because vowel–
vowel sequences are avoided in Korean. /j/ Glide Formation is more frequently
observed when the verbal stem in question has more than two syllables.

(12) a. Words with one syllable verbal stem: /i/ Glide Formation is optional.
          기어서 /ki- + -ʌsʌ/ ~ [kiʌsʌ] ~ [kjʌsʌ] 'to crawl (connective)'
      b. Words with more than two syllable verbal stem: /j/ Glide Formation
          is more frequently observed.

새기어서 /sɛki- + -ʌsʌ/ → [sɛkjʌsʌ] 'to carve (connective)'
가리키어서 /kɑlikʰi- + -ʌsʌ/ → [kɑlikʰjʌsʌ] 'to point (connective)'

In addition, when the stem of a verb ends with a vowel, /w/ Glide Formation occurs. Consider (13).

(13) a. Verbal stem ending with a vowel: /w/ Glide Formation is obligatory.
와서 /o- + -ɑsʌ/ → [wɑsʌ] 'to come (connective)'
배워서 /pɛu- + -ʌsʌ/ → [pɛwʌsʌ] 'to learn (connective)'
   b. Verbal stem ending with a CV sequence: /w/ Glide Formation is optional.
가두어서 /kɑtu- + -ʌsʌ/ → [kɑtuʌsʌ] ~ [kɑtwʌsʌ] 'to imprison (connective)'
미루어서 /milu- + -ʌsʌ/ → [miluʌsʌ] ~ [milwʌsʌ] 'to imprison (connective)'

9.3.4 /h/ Deletion in verbal inflection

When /h/ occurs at the end of a verbal stem, it is deleted automatically if followed by verbal endings starting with a vowel. The examples in (14) show how /h/ is dropped both when used alone, as in (14a), and also when it forms part of a cluster and is followed by a verbal ending which begins with a vowel, as in (14b).

(14) a. 좋아서 /tɕoh- + -ɑsʌ/ → [tɕoɑsʌ] 'to like (connective)'
   b. 싫어서 /silh- + -ʌsʌ/ → [silʌsʌ] 'to hate (connective)'

9.3.5 /ɯ/ Deletion in verbal inflection

As noted above, vowel–vowel sequences are avoided in Korean. Because of this, the /ɯ/ vowel is deleted when it appears at the end of a verbal stem and is followed by a verbal ending which begins with a vowel. This rule is only applied between a verbal stem and a verbal ending as in (15a), and not between a noun and a particle as in (15b). Consider the following.

(15) a. 꺼서 /k*ɯ- + -ʌsʌ/ → [k*ʌsʌ] 'to turn off (connective)'
   b. 카드에 /kʰɑtɯ + -ɛ/ → [kʰɑtɯɛ] 'card (prepositional)'
Verbs which display /ɯ/ Deletion are listed in (16).

(16) 끄- /k*ɯ-/ 'to turn off'
   뜨- /t*ɯ-/ 'to float'
   쓰- /s*ɯ-/ 'to write'

크- /kʰɯ-/ 'to be big'
트- /tʰɯ-/ 'to sprout'

9.3.6 /ɑ/ or /ʌ/ Deletion in verbal inflection

When a verbal stem ending with /ɑ/ or /ʌ/ is followed by a verbal ending starting with the same vowel /ɑ/ or /ʌ/, one of them is deleted.

(17) a. /ɑ/ Deletion: when the verbal stem ends with /ɑ/, this rule is
         obligatory.
         가서 /kɑ- + -ʌsʌ/ → [kɑsʌ] 'to go (connective)'
      b. /ʌ/ Deletion: when the verbal stem ends with /ʌ/, this rule is
         obligatory.
         서서 /sʌ- + -ʌsʌ/ → [sʌsʌ] 'to stand (connective)'
      c. /ʌ/ Deletion: when the verbal stem ends with /ɛ/, this rule is
         optional.
         베어서 /pɛ- + -ʌsʌ / → [pɛʌsʌ] ~ [pɛsʌ] 'to cut (connective)'
         개어서 /kɛ- + -ʌsʌ / → [kɛʌsʌ] ~ [kɛsʌ] 'to fold up (connective)'
         되어서 /twɛ- + -ʌsʌ/ → [twɛʌsʌ] → [twɛsʌ] 'to become
         (connective)'

9.4 Rules relating to the word-initial liquid or nasal in Sino-Korean words

Two specific phonological rules are applicable to word-initial liquid or nasal
/n/ in Sino-Korean words. That is, the word-initial liquid sound /l/ is changed
into nasal /n/. Word-initial nasal /n/ is deleted before /i/ or /j/. These two processes occur sequentially.

9.4.1 /l/ into /n/ in Sino-Korean words

In Pure Korean /l/ cannot appear in word-initial position. However,
Sino-Korean words can start with /l/. Sino-Korean words that start with /l/ are
nasalised into, or substituted by /n/, which is pronounced in the same place of
articulation. Consider Table 9.5.

9.4.2 /n / Deletion in Sino-Korean words

Another rule stipulates that /n/ cannot appear in word-initial position when
the following sounds start with /i/ or /j/. In such cases, /n/ is deleted automatically. Consider the words in Table 9.6.

Table 9.5 Pronunciation of word-initial and medial /l/ ⌒

Underlying form	Word-initial /l/ → /n/	Non-word-initial /l/
락 (樂) /lɑk/ 'joy'	낙원 (樂園) [nɑkwʌn] 'paradise'	쾌락 (快樂) [kʰwɛlɑk] 'delight'
래 (來) /lɛ/ 'to come'	내일 (來日) [nɛil] 'tomorrow'	미래 (未來) [milɛ] 'future'
로 (勞) /lo/ 'troublesome'	노동 (勞動) [notoŋ] 'labour'	피로 (疲勞) [pʰilo] 'fatigue'

Table 9.6 Pronunciation of word-initial and medial /n/ ⌒

Underlying form	Word-initial /n/ deletion	Non-word-initial /n/
녀 (女) /njʌ/ 'woman'	여자 (女子) [jʌtɕɑ] 'woman'	마녀 (魔女) [mɑnjʌ] 'witch'
년 (年) /njʌn/ 'year'	연세 (年歲) [jʌnsɛ] 'age'	매년 (每年) [mɛnjʌn] 'annually'
닉 (匿) /nik/ 'to hide'	익명 (匿名) [iŋmjʌŋ] 'anonymous'	은닉 (隱匿) [unnik] 'being hidden'

Table 9.7 Three types of application of the rules governing word-initial /l/ and /n/

(i) l → n	(ii) n → ø	(iii) l → n → ø
락원 (樂園) → 낙원 /lɑk- + -wʌn/ → [nɑkwʌn] 'paradise'	녀자 (女子) → 여자/njʌ- + -tɕɑ]/ → [jʌtɕɑ] 'woman'	리유 (理由) → 니유 → 이유/li- + -ju/ → niju → [iju] 'reason'
일 (來日) → 내일/lɛ- + -il/ → [nɛil] 'tomorrow' 로동 (勞動) → 노동 /lo- + -toŋ/ → [notoŋ] 'labour'	년세 (年歲) → 연세/njʌn- + -sɛ/ → [jʌnsɛ]'age' 닉명 (匿名) → 익명 /nik- + -mjʌŋ/ → [ikmjʌŋ] 'unanimous'	려객 (旅客) → 녀객 → 여객/ljʌ- + -kɛk/ → njʌkɛk → [jʌkɛk] 'passenger' 량심 (良心) → 냥심 → 양심 /ljɑŋ- + -sim/ → njɑŋsim → [jɑŋsim] 'conscience'

Word-initial /l/ is first nasalised into /n/, which is then deleted, as in the case of /li- + -ju/ 이유 (理由) 'reason'. Consider (18).

(18) a. First step: application of /l/ becoming nasalised into /n/
이유 (理由) /li- + -ju/ 'reason' → niju
  b. Second step: /n/ Deletion
niju → [iju]

More examples along with three types of application of the rules governing the word-initial /l/ or /n/ are provided in Table 9.7.

Table 9.8 Sino-Korean vocabularies with word-initial /l/ or /n/: South vs. North

l → n South	No change in the North	n → ø South	No change in the North	l → n → ø South	No change in the North
낙원 (樂園) /lak- + -wʌn/ → [nakwʌn]	락원 (樂園) /lak- + -wʌn/ → [lakwʌn]	여자 (女子) /njʌ- + -tɕa]/ → [jʌtɕa]	녀자 (女子) /njʌ- + -tɕa]/ → [njʌtɕa]	이유 (理由) /li- + -ju/ → niju → [iju]	리유 (理由) /li- + -ju/ → [liju]
내일 (來日) /lɛ- + -il/ → [nɛil]	래일 (來日) /lɛ- + -il/ → [lɛil]	연세 (年歲) /njʌn- + -sɛ/ → [jʌnsɛ]	년세 (年歲) /njʌn- + -sɛ/ → [njʌnsɛ]	여객 (旅客) /ljʌ- + -kɛk/ → njʌkɛk → [jʌkɛk]	려객 (旅客) /ljʌ- + -kɛk/ → [ljʌkɛk]
노동 (勞動) /lo- + -toŋ/ → [notoŋ]	로동 (勞動) /lo- + -toŋ/ → [lotoŋ]	익명 (匿名) /nik- + -mjʌŋ/ → [ikmjʌŋ]	닉명 (匿名) /nik- + -mjʌŋ/ → [nikmjʌŋ]	양심 (良心) /ljaŋ- + -sim/ → njaŋsim → [jaŋsim]	량심 (良心) /ljaŋ- + -sim/ → [jaŋsim]

Examples in Table 9.8 show differences in Sino-Korean vocabulary in North and South Korea due to different application of the rules for word-initial /l/ and /n/.

FURTHER STUDY

Word-initial /l/ and /n/ North vs. South

After their division, for a while North and South Korea both used the same orthographic system, which was called Standard Korean Orthography in 1933, until the North published their own Cultured Korean Orthography in 1966, which was revised in 1987 and 2000. In the South, a partially revised edition of the Standard Korean Orthography was published in 1988. As a result, the North and South now have many disparities in the number of basic letters (South 24, North 40), the ordering of the letters in the dictionary and the rules for pronunciation and writing. Among these differences, a particularly prominent one is the way that each writes and pronounces the Sino-Korean word, 樂園. In the South, it is pronounced as [nakwʌn] and written as 낙원, whilst in the North, it is pronounced as [lakwʌn] and written as 락원.

At the moment, the North and the South are compiling a Unified Korean Language Dictionary (Information about this dictionary can be found at www.gyeoremal.or.kr:8080/navigator?act=index). In order to compile a unified dictionary, it is necessary to have a unified set of orthographical

Table 9.9 Phonological rules of Korean (II)

Rule	Morphological information	Lexical origin	Core example: underlying form	Core example: pronunciation
Lateralisation	Morpheme boundary between /l/ and /n/	Sino-Korean	권력 /kwʌn- + -ljʌk/	[kwʌlljʌk]
Nasalisation	Word boundary between /l/ and /n/	Sino-Korean	결단력 /(kjʌl- + -tɑn) # -ljʌk/	[kjʌltˀɑnnjʌk]
Tensification	Within a lexical and functional morpheme	Sino-Korean	결단 /kjʌl- + -tɑn/	[kjʌltˀɑn]
/t/ Insertion	Compound word		봄비 /pom # pi/	[pompˀi]
/n/ Insertion	Derivative or compound word		솜이불 /som # ipul/	[somnipul]
Palatalisation	Between lexical morpheme and grammatical morpheme		같이 /katʰ- + -i/	[katɕʰi]
Verbal suffix Tensification	Verbal stem + ending		안고 /an- + -ko/	[ankˀo]
Glide Formation in verbal inflection	Verbal stem + ending		남기 + 어서 /namki- + -ʌsʌ/ 배우+어서 /pɛu- + -ʌsʌ/	[namkjʌsʌ] [pɛwʌsʌ]
/h/ Deletion in verbal inflection	Verbal stem + ending		좋+아서 /tɕoh- + -asʌ/	[tɕoasʌ]
/ɯ/ Deletion in verbal inflection	Verbal stem + ending		끄+어서 /kˀɯ- + -ʌsʌ/	[kˀʌsʌ]
/a, ʌ/ Deletion in verbal inflection	Verbal stem + ending		가+아서 /ka- + -asʌ/ 서+어서 /sʌ + ʌsʌ/	[kasʌ] [sʌsʌ]
/l/ into /n/ in Sino-Korean	Word-initial position	Sino-Korean	낙원 /lak- + -wʌn/	[nakwʌn]
/n/ deletion in Sino-Korean	Word-initial position	Sino-Korean	여자 /njʌ- + -tɕa/	[jʌtɕa]
/l/ → /n/ → ø in Sino-Korean	Word-initial position	Sino-Korean	이유 /li- + -ju/	[iju]

rules as well; one of the greatest challenges in the unification of spelling necessary for this dictionary is the question of how to write Sino-Korean words such as 樂園. Because neither country is willing to change their position, it seems more likely that both spellings – '낙원' and '락원' – will be accepted, rather than one being chosen over the other.

9.5 Summary

In this chapter, we have seen phonological rules that require morphological information. We have classified these rules based on the morphological characteristics of combined morphemes as follows: (i) lexical morpheme and lexical morpheme; and (ii) lexical and grammatical morpheme. In Table 9.9 we present a summary of each rule with its core example.

EXERCISES

1   State whether the letter-initial consonants in underlined letters should undergo Tensification or not and explain why.
   a. 갈증 (渴症) /kal- + -<u>tɕ</u>ɯŋ/ 'thirst'
   b. 달성 (達成) /tal- + -<u>s</u>ʌŋ/ 'achievement'
   c. 발달 (發達) /pal- + -<u>t</u>al/ 'development'
   d. 고갈 (枯渴)되다 /(ko- + -kal) # -<u>t</u>wɛ- + -ta/ 'to be exhausted'
   e. 발견 (發見) /pal- + -<u>kj</u>ʌn/ 'discover'
   f. 침몰 (沈沒)도 /(tɕʰim- + -mol) + -<u>t</u>o/ 'even sinking'

2   Pronounce the following words, write down the Standard Korean Pronunciation for each and explain why it is pronounced like this.
   a. (生産量) /(sɛŋ- + -san) + -ljaŋ/ 'output'
   b. (分量) /pun- + -ljaŋ/ 'amount'
   c. (園林) /wʌn- + -lim/ 'garden'
   d. (自然林) /(tɕa- + -jʌn) + -lim/ 'natural forest'

3   Illustrate the phonological processes by which /pom # pi/ 봄비 'spring rain' is pronounced [pompʼi] using relevant phonological rules.

4   Illustrate the phonological processes by which /han- # jʌlɯm/ 한여름 is pronounced [han njʌlɯm] using relevant phonological rules.

5   Pronounce the following words and explain the relevant phonological rules.
   a. 같이 /katʰ- + -i/ 'together with'
   b. 붙이다 /putʰ- + -i- + -ta/ 'to stick'
   c. 굳이 /kut- + -i/ 'willingly'

6 Discuss the dialectal differences between North and South regarding the pronunciation of word-initial liquids.

7 Please write down the pronunciation of each inflected verbal form given below and state which phonological rule should be applied. If more than one phonological rule should be applied, list them in order.

Note: 긋- /kɯs-/ 'to draw' and 낫- /nɑs-/ 'to recover' in Korean are /s/ (ㅅ) irregular verbs. That is, in these verbs, /s/ is deleted in verbal inflection when a vowel-initial ending follows the stem.

Stem	Ending	Pronunciation	Phonological rule
낳- /nɑh-/ 'to bear'	-아서 /-ɑsʌ/ 'connective'	[ ]	
낳- /nɑh-/ 'to bear'	-고 /-ko/ 'connective'	[ ]	
나- /nɑ-/ 'to grow'	-아서 /-ɑsʌ/ 'connective'	[ ]	
나- /nɑ-/ 'to grow'	-고 /-ko/ 'connective'	[ ]	
낫- /nɑ-/ 'to recover'	-아서 /-ɑsʌ/ 'connective'	[ ]	
낫- /nɑ-/ 'to recover'	-고 /-ko/ 'connective'	[ ]	
크- /kʰɯ-/ 'to be big'	-어서 /-ɑsʌ/ 'connective'	[ ]	
크- /kʰɯ-/ 'to be big'	-고 /-ko/ 'connective'	[ ]	
긋- /kɯ-/ 'to draw'	-어서 /-ɑsʌ/ 'connective'	[ ]	
긋- /kɯs-/ 'to draw'	-고 /-ko/ 'connective'	[ ]	

10 Loanword phonology

Loanwords are words which, although foreign in origin, have become like native words and are frequently used. In Korean, Sino-Korean words undoubtedly form the major part of Korean vocabulary. In the history of the Korean language, Sino-Korean words started to be included from as early as the second to third century and since then they have formed a major part of Korean vocabulary. According to the *Standard Korean Language Dictionary*, around 57 per cent of Korean vocabulary consists of Sino-Korean loanwords.

During the twentieth century, loanwords, particularly those of English origin, rapidly increased in number in line with the Westernisation of the country. In this chapter, therefore, we will focus on phonological aspects of English loanwords.

Since the Korean alphabet is a phonetic alphabet, on the whole, it is suitable for realising a variety of sounds in English. Nevertheless, in naturalising English loanwords into Korean, there are some unavoidable limitations. First, the sound inventories of the two languages are different. In addition, the phonologies of the two languages, including syllable structure, are not the same. For instance, film is spelled 필름 and pronounced with a [pʰ] in [pʰillɯm]. This happens simply because [f] doesn't exist in Korean, so the sound [pʰ] which is pronounced in a similar position to [f], is substituted for it.

Inevitably, once loanwords are nativised, they follow the phonology of the target language, unless they are already used so frequently that their pronunciation is set in stone. For instance, the French word *renaissance* is pronounced as 're-Nay-sonce' by British English speakers but also as 'Ren-a-sonce' just as it is pronounced in France.

In the following, we will discuss origin and orthography of loanwords (10.1) and how different sound inventories (10.2, 10.3) and different syllable structures (10.4) influence the Korean pronunciation of English loanwords. In 10.5

there are examples of how phonological rules in Korean are applied to English loanwords and we provide a summary in 10.6.

10.1 Origin and orthography of loanwords

There are different ways for foreign words to be nativised. In the following, we will discuss briefly how loanwords are adopted, spelled and pronounced.

Often, loanwords are adopted when there are no native words to express a particular meaning. These days, Korean has many IT-related loanwords – most of which do not have any corresponding Korean words. On the other hand, when loanwords have corresponding words in the native language, their adoption could cause further meaning division. For instance, these days in Korean the word 치킨 /tɕʰikʰin/ 'chicken' does not mean chicken in general, but refers only to fried or seasoned chicken that is often delivered to one's home. Hence, when cooking chicken at home, Koreans will use the native Korean word 닭튀김 /talk + tʰwikim/ 'fried chicken' instead of the loanword 치킨 /tɕʰikʰin/ 'chicken'. Moreover, if you are ordering fried chicken from a restaurant, you will hear the word 치킨 instead of 닭튀김 'chicken'.

Consider the examples below. Loanwords which do not have Korean counterparts are given in (1a) and those which do have Korean counterparts, but with a difference in meaning between the Korean words and English loanwords, are given in (1b). Generally speaking, the examples included here are sufficiently nativised that they may be found in the *Standard Korean Language Dictionary*.

🎧 (1) a. No equivalent words in Korean
컴퓨터 [kʰʌmpʰjutʰʌ] 'computer'
커피 [kʰʌpʰi] 'coffee'
라디오 [lɑtio] 'radio'
마우스 [mɑusˀɯ] 'mouse'
인터넷 [intʰʌnɛt] 'internet'
b. Semantic difference between Korean words and English loanwords
닭튀김 [taktʰwikim] 'fried chicken dish' vs. 치킨 [tɕʰīkʰin] 'home delivered fried chicken'
경기 [kjʌŋki] 'sports game' vs. 게임 [kˀɛim] 'computer game'
선 [sʌn] 'line' vs. 라인 [lɑin] 'personal connections'

At the beginning of the twentieth century, English words were adopted via Japan, but gradually, more and more English words have been adopted directly, rather than via Japan. Examples are given in (2) of some English loanwords that were adopted via Japan, along with versions of the same words adopted directly from English into Standard Korean.

🎧 (2) English loan words vs. English loan words via Japan.
배터리 [pɛtʰʌli] 'battery' vs. 빠떼리 [p*at*ɛli]
샐러드 [s*ɛllʌtɯ] 'salad' vs. 사라다 [salata]
머플러 [mʌpʰɯllʌ] 'muffler' vs. 마후라 [mahula]
프라이팬 [pʰɯlɑipʰɛn] 'frypan' vs. 후라이팬 [hulɑipʰɛn]

The way in which loanwords are adopted, including Sino-Korean words, is one of the major differences between North and South Korean dialects. As shown in Chapter 1, the North often chose to translate both Sino-Korean and English words into Pure Korean. Moreover, many loanwords used in the North are of Russian origin due to the influence of the Soviet Union after the Korean War. Consider the following.

🎧 (3) South Korean loanwords vs. North Korean loanwords.
케이블 [kʰɛipɯl] 'cable' vs. 까벨 [k*apɛl]
캠페인 [kʰɛmpʰɛin] 'campaign' vs. 깜빠니아 [k*amp*ania]
트럭 [tʰɯlʌk] 'truck' vs. 뜨락또르 [t*ɯlɑkt*olɯ]

In this chapter, we will discuss in particular how directly adopted English loanwords are spelled and pronounced. Loanwords in Korean were initially spelled according to how they sounded in their original language using only the twenty-four basic letters of Hangeul. Nevertheless, some discrepancies can be seen between the spelling and pronunciation of those loanwords. One of the major problems lies in the prohibition of the tense consonants /k*, t*, p*, s*, tɕ*/. Interestingly, although the original English words do not contain tense consonants, when they are nativised into Korean, they tend to be tensified. However, Korean orthography prohibits the use of these consonants in the written forms of the loanwords, as the letters representing the tense sounds are not included among the basic letters. Hence, the English word banana is spelled as 바나나, but is pronounced more like [p*anana] than [panana]. For those cases, we will provide additional explanation as we go along.

10.2 Consonant correspondence between English and Korean

As shown in Table 10.1, Korean has a limited range of fricative sounds when compared to English. On the other hand, Korean stop consonants possess three subdivisions, that is, the lax–tense–aspirated contrast between stop consonants (i.e. k, k*, kʰ – t, t*, tʰ – p, p*, pʰ) and affricates (i.e. tɕ, tɕ*, tɕʰ). One thing to note

Table 10.1 Consonant correspondence charts of English and Korean 🎧

		English consonants	Korean consonants	Examples
Stop	Voiceless	p t k	pʰ tʰ kʰ	paint: 페인트 [pʰɛintʰɯ]
	Voiced	b d g	p/p* t/t* k/k*	ballad: 발라드 [palatɯ]; banana: 바나나 [p*anana]
Fricative	Voiceless	f	pʰ	foul: 파울 [pʰaul]
		θ	s/s*/tʰ	thrill: 스릴 [sɯlil]; health: 헬스 [hɛls*ɯ]; marathon: 마라톤 [malatʰon]
		s	s/s*	sports: 스포츠 [sɯpʰotɕʰɯ];
		ʃ	s/s*+j	mask: 마스크 [mas*ɯkʰɯ] shower: 샤워 [sjawʌ]
		h	h	hall: 홀 [hol]
	Voiced	v	p	virus: 바이러스 [pailʌs*ɯ]
		ð	t	rhythm: 리듬 [litɯm]
		z	tɕ	zipper: 지퍼 [tɕipʰʌ]
		ʒ	tɕ	massage: 마사지 [mas*atɕi]
Affricate	Voiceless	tʃ	tɕʰ	cheese: 치즈 [tɕʰitɕɯ]
	Voiced	dʒ	tɕ	jelly: 젤리 [tɕɛlli]
Nasal		m n ŋ	m n ŋ	mouse: 마우스 [maus*ɯ]
Approximant		r	l	radio: 라디오 [latio]
Lateral approximant		l	l	league: 리그 [likɯ]
Glide		j w	j w	yacht: 요트 [jotʰɯ] quiz: 퀴즈 [kʰwitɕɯ]

is that, as discussed in Chapter 5, glides such as /w/ and /j/ are considered consonants in English, but vowels in Korean. How each of the English consonants in loanwords is realised in Korean is demonstrated in Table 10.1.

10.2.1 Correspondence between /p, t, k/ in English and /pʰ, tʰ, kʰ/ in Korean

The voiceless stops /p, t, k/ in English correspond to /pʰ, tʰ, kʰ/ in Korean, regardless of the position in which they occur. Consider the following.

🎧 (4) a. Word-initial
      paint: 페인트 [pʰɛintʰɯ]
      tennis: 테니스 [tʰɛnis*ɯ]
      key: 키 [kʰi]

b. Elsewhere
  rope: 로프 [lopʰɯ]
  note: 노트 [notʰɯ]
  knock: 노크 [nokʰɯ]

10.2.2 Correspondence between /b/, /d/, /g/ in English and /p, p*/, /t, t*/, /k, k*/ in Korean

The voiced stops /b, d, g/ in English correspond to the lax stops /p, t, k/ in Korean. But, in certain circumstances, they can be tensified and pronounced as [p*, t*, k*]. However, as mentioned above, Korean orthography does not allow the spelling of loanwords to reflect their Tensification. In other words, gown is spelled 가운 instead of 까운, even though it is pronounced [k*aun].

🎧 (5) /b, d, g/ correspond to lax stop /p, t, k/
  a. Word-initial
    ballad: 발라드 [pallɑtɯ]
    date: 데이트 [tɛitʰɯ]
    guide: 가이드 [kɑitɯ]
  b. Elsewhere
    ribbon: 리본 [lipon]
    model: 모델 [motɛl]
    league: 리그 [likɯ]

🎧 (6) Word-initial /b, d, g/ in English can be tensed particularly in spontaneous speech
  banana: 바나나 [p*anana ~ panana]
  dance: 댄스 [t*ɛns*ɯ ~ tɛns*ɯ]
  gown: 가운 [k*aun ~ kaun]

10.2.3 Correspondence between /f/, /s/, /θ/, /ʃ/ in English and /pʰ/, /s, s*/, /s, s*/, /s + j, s* + j/ in Korean

The voiceless fricatives /f/, /s/, /θ/, /ʃ/ in English correspond to /pʰ/, /s, s*/, /s, s*/, /s + j, s* + j/ respectively in Korean. Let's first look at /f/. Consider (7). Regardless of its position, /f/ corresponds to /pʰ/ in Korean.

🎧 (7) /f/ corresponds to /pʰ/
  foul: 파울 [pʰaul]
  foundation: 파운데이션 [pʰauntɛisjʌn]
  coffee: 커피 [kʌpʰi]
  muffler: 머플러 [mʌpʰɯllʌ]

The case of /s/ is a little complicated. English /s/ corresponds to [s] or [s*].
Consider the following.

🎧 (8) Pronunciation of /s/
      a. /s/ in word-initial cluster in English: /s/ in English corresponds to /s/
        in Korean[1]
        sports: 스포츠 [sɯpʰotɕʰɯ]
        style: 스타일 [sɯtʰail]
        screen: 스크린 [sɯkʰɯlin]
      b. /s/ after a vowel in English: /s/ in English corresponds to /s*/ in
        Korean
        Christmas: 크리스마스 [kʰɯlis*ɯmas*ɯ]
        boss: 보스 [pos*ɯ]
        mask: 마스크 [mas*ɯkʰɯ]
      c. /s/ before a vowel in English: /s/ in English corresponds to /s/ or /s*/
        in Korean
        cider: 사이다 [saita]
        syrup: 시럽 [silʌp]
        Cinderella: 신데렐라 [sintɛlella]
        soprano: 소프라노 [s*opʰɯlano]
        sofa: 소파 [s*opʰa]
        solo: 솔로 [s*ollo]

English /θ/ usually corresponds to /s/ or /s*/ in Korean. However, in certain
circumstances, /θ/ is spelled with ㅌ and is pronounced /tʰ/.

🎧 (9) thrill: 스릴 [sɯlil]
       health: 헬스 [hɛls*ɯ]
       marathon: 마라톤 [malatʰon]

The sound /ʃ/, usually spelled in English as 'sh' or 'ti', is spelled and pronounced /s, s*/ plus a diphthong such as /ja/, /jo/, /jʌ/ or /ju/ in Korean.

🎧 (10) shower: 샤워 [sjawʌ]
        shock: 쇼크 [s*jokʰɯ]
        lotion: 로션 [losjʌn]

10.2.4 Correspondence between /v/, /z/, /ʒ/ and /ð/ in English and /p/, /tɕ/, /tɕ/, /t/ in Korean

The voiced fricatives /v/, /z/, /ʒ/, and /ð/ in English correspond to /p/, /tɕ/,
/tɕ/, /t/ in Korean respectively. None of these consonants exists in Korean and

therefore they are replaced by approximate consonants pronounced in a similar position.

🎧 (11) /v/ corresponds to /p/
   virus: 바이러스 [pɑilʌs*ɯ]
   oven: 오븐 [opɯn]

🎧 (12) /z/ and /ʒ/ correspond to /tɕ/
   zero: 제로 [tɕɛlo]
   zipper: 지퍼 [tɕipʰʌ]
   beige: 베이지 [pɛitɕi]
   massage: 마사지 [mɑs*ɑtɕi]

🎧 (13) /ð/ corresponds to /t/ in Korean.
   rhythm: 리듬 [litɯm]

10.2.5 Correspondence between /tʃ/ and /dʒ/ in English and /tɕʰ/ and /tɕ/ in Korean

The affricates /tʃ/ and /dʒ/ in English correspond to /tɕʰ/ and /tɕ/ in Korean.

🎧 (14) a. /tʃ/ corresponds to /tɕʰ/
   cheese: 치즈 [tɕʰitɕɯ]
   chicken: 치킨 [tɕʰikʰin]
   chocolate: 초콜릿 / tɕʰokʰollis/ → [tɕʰokʰollit]

   b. /dʒ/ corresponds to /tɕ/
   juice: 주스 [tɕus*ɯ]
   jogging: 조깅 [tɕokiŋ]
   jelly: 젤리 [tɕɛlli]

10.2.6 Correspondence between /l/ and /r/ in English and /l/ in Korean

The English liquid sounds /l/ and /r/ correspond to /l/ in Korean. But, when /l/ occurs between vowels in word-medial position, often /l/ is doubled to /ll/ in Korean.

🎧 (15) a. /l/ corresponds to /l/
   league: 리그 [likɯ]
   bell: 벨 [pɛl]
   liter: 리터 [litʌ]

   b. /l/ → /ll/
   jelly: 젤리 [tɕɛlli]
   club: 클럽 [kʰɯllʌp]
   cola: 콜라 [kʰollɑ]

c. /r/ → /l/
radio: 라디오 [lɑtio]
Rome: 로마 [lomɑ]
orange: 오렌지 [olɛntɕi]

10.2.7   Correspondence between /j/ and /w/ in English and /j/ and /w/ in Korean

Glides in English, such as /j/ and /w/ correspond to /j/ and /w/ in Korean. Glides are regarded as consonants in English, but as vowels in Korean (see discussion in Chapter 5).

(16) a. /j/ corresponds to /j/
yacht: 요트 [jotʰɯ]
yoghurt: 요구르트 [jokuɰtʰɯ]

b. /w/ corresponds to /w/
twist: 트위스트 [tʰɯwisʼɯtʰɯ]
quiz: 퀴즈 [kʰwitɕɯ]

10.3   Vowel correspondence between English and Korean

Table 10.2 shows vowel correspondence between Korean and English with respect to frequently used English loanwords. The pronunciation for English words is based on RP.

The following characteristics can be drawn from Table 10.2.

(i) The English front-high vowels /ɪ/ and /i/ corresponds to /i/ in Korean. The distinction between tensed vowels and lax vowels disappears in Korean.

(ii) The distinction in English between /e/ and /æ/ is not present in Korean (though it may be maintained in Korean orthography). Instead the two are merged into /ɛ/ in Korean pronunciation.

(iii) The distinction in English between /ɑ/ and /ɒ/ is not present in Korean; the two invariably correspond to /ɑ/ in Korean.

(iv) The distinction between /u/ and /ʊ/ is not present. Both correspond to /u/ in Korean.

(v) The distinction between /ʌ/ and /ɜ/ is not present. Both correspond to /ʌ/ in Korean.

In addition, some diphthongs in English correspond to two syllables in Korean, because no Korean words contain off-glides such as /ej/. Examples can be seen in (17).

Table 10.2 Vowel correspondence examples between English and Korean 𝆕

English vowels	English words	Corresponding Korean vowel	Loanword examples
ɪ	hit [hɪt]	i	히트 [hitʰɯ]
e	dress [dres]	ɛ	드레스 [tɯlesʼɯ]
æ	manner [mænə]	ɛ	매너 [mɛnʌ]
ɒ	documentary [dɒkjumentəri]	ɑ	다큐멘터리 [tɑkʰjumentʰʌli]
ʌ	muffler [mʌflə]	ʌ	머플러 [mʌpʰɯllʌ]
ʊ	cushion [kʊʃn]	u	쿠션 [kʰusʼjʌn]
i:	league [li:g]	i	리그 [likɯ]
u:	boomerang [bu:məræŋ]	u	부메랑 [pumɛlaŋ]
ɑ:	card [kɑ:d]	ɑ	카드 [kʰɑtɯ]
ɔ:	fork [fɔ:k]	o	포크 [pʰokʰɯ]
ɜ:	burner [bɜ:nə]	ʌ	버너 [pʌnʌ]
eɪ	date [deɪt]	ɛi	데이트 [tɛitʰɯ]
aɪ	guide [gaɪd]	ɑi	가이드 [kɑitɯ]
ɔɪ	boiler [bɔɪlə]	oi	보일러 [poillʌ]
əʊ	boat [bəʊt]	o	보트 [potʰɯ]
aʊ	out [aʊt]	ɑu	아웃 [ɑut]
ɪə	earphone [ɪəfəʊn]	iʌ	이어폰 [iʌpʰon]
eə	hardware [hɑ:dweə]	ɛʌ	하드웨어 [hɑtɯwɛʌ]
ʊə	tour [tʊə]	uʌ	투어 [tʰuʌ]

𝆕 (17) cake: 케이크 [kʰɛikʰɯ]
date: 데이트 [tɛitʰɯ]

10.4 Syllable structure and loanword phonology

Syllable structure has been previously discussed in 7.3, where it was noted that a syllable is an abstract and psychological unit embedded in a native speaker's knowledge of their mother tongue. The general structural skeleton of a syllable is language-universal. Hence, a syllable nucleus forms the essential part of a syllable, an onset precedes the syllable nucleus, and a coda follows it. However, from language to language, the way in which syllables are structured is different. Even the same sound sequence will represent different syllable structures when heard by people who speak different languages. For instance, a word like *bus* would be regarded as a one-syllable word by a native English speaker, but native Korean speakers would regard it as having two syllables. Therefore, understanding the syllable structure of the target language is important in understanding loanword pronunciation. The syllable structure of Korean is shown in Figure 7.3.

All syllable nuclei in Korean have a vowel. A glide can precede that vowel, but this is optional. In addition, the following constraints are found in the syllable structure of Korean.

(18) Syllable structure restrictions
　　a. Syllable-initial position (= onset)
　　　　Neither /ŋ/ nor any other consonant cluster may occur.
　　b. Syllable-medial position (= nucleus)
　　　　Off-glides may not occur. Therefore, (C) V (G)(C) cannot appear as a syllable structure, and a sequence such as /aj/ cannot exist in Korean.
　　c. Syllable-final position (= coda)
　　　　(i)   Consonant clusters may not appear. Only one consonant may be realised in that position.
　　　　(ii) Consonants should not be released after central closure. Therefore, fricatives or affricates cannot appear in syllable-final position. As a result, only seven of the stop sounds which exist in Korean, namely /k, n, t, l, m, p, ŋ/ may occur, since they remain distinct even after central closure. These constraints influence the pronunciation of English loanwords.

First, since consonant clusters in syllable-initial position are not allowed in Korean phonology, a /ɯ/ vowel is inserted into the consonant cluster. Hence, all the following sound sequences in English are regarded as a sequence with two syllables in Korean.

(19) a. Words with an 'sk-' sequence
　　　　　skate: 스케이트 [sɯkʰɛitʰɯ]
　　b. Words with an 'st-' sequence
　　　　　star: 스타 [sɯtʰa]
　　c. Words with an 'sp-' sequence
　　　　　sports: 스포츠 [sɯpʰotɕʰɯ]

Off-glides may not occur in syllable-medial position. Therefore, off-glides are regarded as two syllables. Examples include:

(20) mike: 마이크 [maikʰɯ]
　　　nylon: 나일론 [naillon]

(a) First step: find a nucleus and build the bone structure of a syllable

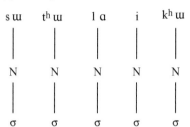

(b) Second step: link the onset by the onset-first principle

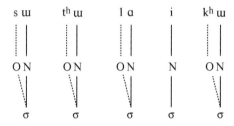

Figure 10.1   Syllabification of *strike* (O = onset, N = nucleus)

Consonant clusters may not appear in syllable-final position, just as in syllable-initial position. Moreover, in syllable-final position, consonants should not be released after central closure. Therefore, fricatives and affricates cannot occur in syllable-final position, since they are released sounds. English loanwords which end with released consonant have an additional /ɯ/ vowel added in order to make it onset. This is one of the major causes of discrepancy in the number of syllables between English and Korean. Example words are shown in (21). Numbers in parentheses are the number of syllables.

(21) bus (1) vs. 버스 [pʼʌsʼɯ] (2)
     sports (1) vs. 스포츠 [sɯpʰotɕʰɯ] (3)
     strike (1) vs. 스트라이크 [sɯtʰɯlɑikʰɯ] (5)

This is why an English word like *strike*, which is a one-syllable word in English, is regarded as a five-syllable word in Korean. In Figure 10.1 we show how *strike* is syllabified by native Korean speakers.

Regarding the pronunciation of *strike*, some readers may have heard native speakers of Korean pronouncing it as [sɯ.tʰɯ.lɑ.ik] (i.e. a four-syllable word) instead of [sɯ.tʰɯ.lɑ.i.kʰɯ] (i.e. a five-syllable word). For instance, in a baseball game, you may have heard [sɯtʰɯlɑik] instead of [sɯtʰɯrɑikʰɯ]. Why is *strike* pronounced differently? This is because the word *strike* has an alternative way of syllabification. That is, the final consonant (i.e. /k/ in the case of *strike*) can be placed as the coda of the preceding syllable instead of creating an extra syllable by inserting a new /ɯ/ vowel.

🎧 (22) a. strike: 스트라이크 [sɯ.tʰɯ.la.i.kʰɯ] ~ 스트라익
      sɯ.tʰɯ.la.ik]
      cake: 케이크 [kɛ.i.kʰɯ] ~ 케익 [kɛ.ik]
   b. graph: 그래프 [kɯlɛpʰɯ] vs. 그랩 [kɯlɛp] (never
      pronounced as this)
      mark: 마크 [makʰɯ] vs. 막 [mak] (never pronounced as this)

In addition, of all the stop sounds present in Korean, only seven, /k, n, t, l, m, p, ŋ/, can appear in syllable-final position, since they remain distinct even after central closure. The same rule is applied to loanwords. We will discuss this further in the next section.

10.5 Application of Korean phonological rules

Once loanwords are nativised, they are subject to the same phonological rules as native words. In this section, we will discuss some examples to show how phonological rules that have been discussed in Chapters 8 and 9 can be also applied to loanwords.

10.5.1   Why is *out* pronounced as [aut] not [aus]?

This is due to Neutralisation (see 8.1.2) in syllable-final position. The evidence for this can be seen by adding a series of case particles to the word, as shown in (23). The underlying form for 아웃 is /aus/, but in syllable-final position, it is realised as [aut].

🎧 (23) a. 아웃이다 /aus +-i-+ -ta/ → [ausita] 'to foul off (in baseball)'
     b. 아웃 /aus/ → [aut] 'out'

10.5.2   Why is *rugby* pronounced as [lʌkpˀi]?

This is because two lax obstruent consonants cannot occur in a row in Korean. If the second obstruent is a lax consonant, it is tensified (see 8.2.1). This is why the /p/ in 럭비 /lʌkpi/ 'rugby' is tensified.

🎧 (24) 럭비 /lʌkpi/ → [lʌkpˀi] 'rugby'

10.5.3 Why is *Good morning* pronounced as [kun moniŋ]?

Korean speakers who do not pay close attention are not able to pronounce *Good morning* as English speakers do. Most Korean speakers will say this morning greeting as [kun moniŋ] rather than [gʊd mɔːrnɪŋ]. This is because Korean speakers automatically change obstruent–nasal sequences like 'd–m' to a nasal–nasal sequence like 'n–m', following Nasalisation rules in Korean phonology. As discussed in 8.2.2, an obstruent–sonorant sequence cannot appear in a row in Korean, unlike in English. Similar examples include:

🎧 (25) 북마크 /puk + makʰɯ/ → [puŋmakʰɯ] 'book mark'
   업로드 /ʌp + lotɯ/ → ʌmlotɯ → [ʌmnotɯ] 'upload'

10.5.4 Why is *Hamlet* pronounced as [hɛmnit]?

As discussed in 8.2.3, a sequence of a non-dental nasal and a liquid sound is assimilated into a nasal–nasal sequence. In the case of *Hamlet*, /l/ becomes a nasal /n/, showing Liquid Nasalisation. Similar examples include:

🎧 (26) 앙리 /aŋli/→[aŋni] 'Henry' (French name)

10.5.5 Why is *Finland* pronounced as [pʰillɑntɯ]?

In the case of 핀란드 /pʰinlantɯ/, the preceding nasal /n/ is assimilated into the liquid /l/, giving [pʰillɑntɯ]. Similar examples include:

🎧 (27) 헨리 /hɛnli/ → [hɛlli] 'Henry' (English name)

Sometimes, a sequence of a nasal and a liquid can be assimilated in both ways, i.e. the nasal can be assimilated into the liquid or the liquid can be assimilated into the nasal. For instance, *online* can be pronounced either as [ollɑin] or [onnɑin].

In addition, the following phonological rules are also applied to English loanwords:

🎧 (28) Bilabialisation and Velarisation
   inflation: 인플레이션 [inpʰɯllɛisjʌn] ~ [impʰɯllɛisjʌn]
   concrete: 콘크리트 [kʰonkʰɯlitʰɯ] ~ [kʰoŋkʰɯlitʰɯ]
   camcorder: 캠코더 [kʰɛmkʰotʌ] ~ [kʰɛŋkʰotʌ]

🎧 (29) Aspiration
   black hole: 블랙홀 /pɯllɛk+hol/→[pɯllɛkʰol]

🎧 (30) Similar-position Obstruent Deletion
background: 백그라운드 /pɛk+kɯlɑuntɯ/ →
pɛkkʰɯlɑuntɯ → [pɛkʰɯlɑuntɯ]
hot dog: 핫도그 /hɑstokɯ/ → hɑttokɯ → hɑttʰokɯ → [hɑtʰokɯ]

🎧 (31) /h/ Deletion
Bohemian: 보헤미안 /bohɛmiɑn/ → [bohɛmiɑn] ~ [boɛmiɑn]
manhole: 맨홀 /mɛnhol/ → [mɛnhol] ~ [mɛnol]

10.6 Summary

In this chapter, we have focused on English loanwords and discussed how English loanwords have been adapted in Korean in terms of spelling and pronunciation. First, we examined both consonant and vowel correspondence between Korean and English. In addition, we have shown that, once nativised, English loanwords follow the rules of Korean phonology, which are discussed in Chapters 8 and 9. Some English loanwords were adopted via Japan, particularly in the early twentieth century. However, since then, most loanwords have been imported directly. In principle, the original pronunciation of loanwords is respected, although nativisation of their pronunciation, in accordance with Korean phonology, is inevitable. In particular, discrepancies between the original English word and its nativised loanword in Korean are caused by differences in sound inventory as well as syllable structure between the two languages. For instance, Korean has fewer fricatives and liquids, hence, it is inevitable that English words containing fricatives and liquids will be pronounced differently in Korean. In terms of syllable structure, unlike in English, syllable-final consonants are not released in Korean after central closure. In addition, consonant clusters are not allowed in syllable-initial position in Korean. These rules cause extra /ɯ/ vowels to be inserted into English loanwords.

EXERCISES

1 State how many syllables the following English words have when used as loanwords in Korean and whether there is any difference in the number of syllables. If so, explain why.
desk, sports, milk, film, mouse
2 Compare the consonant inventories of English and Korean.
3 Compare the syllable structures of Korean and English with examples.

4   Why is *Finland* pronounced [pʰillɑntɯ] in Korean?
5   Why is *download* pronounced [tɑunnotɯ] in Korean?
6   Why is *concrete* pronounced [kʰoŋkʰɯlitʰɯ] in Korean?
7   Why is *manhole* pronounced [mɛnol] in Korean?
8   Why is *outside* pronounced [ɑusˀɑitɯ] in Korean?

Notes

2 Production of sounds

1 Although Korean stops and affricates have three phonation types, fricatives have only two. For more information see section 4.1.

3 Basic concepts of phonology

1 Of course, the view that a phoneme is a unit of sound which cannot be divided further has itself been modified with the the advent of feature theory. Feature theory assumes that phonemes can themselves be further divided into smaller units called phonological features (or distinctive features) which can be defended as linguistically significant properties of sounds. However, even after the advent of feature theory, the phoneme continues to be used as a linguistic unit. In feature theory, the phoneme is defined as a bundle of phonological features. For further discussion of phonological features, see 3.6.

2 Of course, when pronouncing the /p/ in *nip*, the lips can be opened after closure. However, we will leave this case out of the current discussion, and return to it in 3.3 when we discuss free variation.

3 Because writing in itself is abstract, these written phonetic forms are far more likely to be allophones than to be physical phonetic sounds.

4 That is why Korean people who eat 라이스 버거 are not actually eating a 'lice burger' but rather a 'rice burger'.

5 Prosodic units will be discussed in detail in Chapter 7. In this chapter, only a few basic terms relating to syllables will be briefly introduced.

6 A consonant that can form the nucleus of a syllable is called a "syllabic consonant". In English, whether or not a consonant is syllabic depends on the sonority of its surrounding segments.

7 For a more detailed look at the difference between the syllabic systems of English and Korean, see Chapter 7.

8 Here, an arrow → indicates what is changing to what, a forward slash / signifies the end of the change, and underlining denotes the place where the change occurs. For instance, k → ŋ/ _ m would mean that 'k' changes to 'ŋ' when it precedes 'm'.

9 In Korean an obstruent that precedes a nasal becomes a nasal itself, and this is called nasalisation. For a more detailed discussion of this phenomenon, see Chapter 8.

4 Consonants

1 "Liquids" is the name given to the letters of the alphabet notated as 'r' and 'l', which encompass sounds produced through various different manners of articulation, including approximants, taps and trills. In spite of the fact that these sounds are articulated in many different ways, they are either grouped together as "liquids" in many languages, or the category "liquids", under which these sounds are grouped, is used for convenience's sake in phonology, because they are realised as allophones of one phoneme. As will soon be seen, in Korean, the phoneme /l/ has two allophones; it may be realised either as a lateral approximant or a tap according to the phonological environment in which it is found.

2 As will be seen in more detail in 8.1.1, this is due to a restriction in the syllable structure of Korean, namely that syllable-final coda sounds must not be released. Because consonants in word-final position correspond to codas in the syllable structure, stop sounds in word-final position must be realised as unreleased stop sounds, in accordance with this principle. Because of this, distinctions in phonation type made on the basis of whether or not a sound is released become irrelevant.

3 All the spectrograms in this chapter show samples from the speech of the same speaker.

4 It is impossible to determine accurately the starting point of closure in a word-initial stop sound by analysing a sound signal. This is because the period of closure created by stoppage in the oral cavity and the period of silence prior to vocalisation cannot be distinguished using sound signal alone. However, since it is necessary to show the point of closure for convenience of explanation, the point at which closure occurs has been set arbitrarily. Therefore, (a), (b) and (c) on the diagram bear no relation to the true starting points of closure.

5 The time difference between the release of a stop sound and the point at which vibration begins in the vocal cords in order to produce the following vowel is known as Voice Onset Time, or VOT for short. The length of VOT is usually proportional to breathiness. The more breathiness a stop sound has, the longer it takes until the vocal folds begin to vibrate for the following vowel, because the vocal folds are separated further during closure. Breathiness is caused by turbulent air escaping through the glottis, which is narrowed as the vocal folds come together; hence it appears on the spectrogram as an irregular, blurry mark, and on the waveform as an aperiodic wave. In the example in Figure 4.1, the VOT for the lax, tense and aspirated sounds are 47 ms, 13 ms, and 76 ms respectively.

6 In the case of tense sounds, vibrations in the vocal folds begin almost at the same time as the release of the closure, because these sounds are articulated with the two vocal folds almost touching during closure (Kagaya 1974). Therefore, there is almost no aspiration. Despite the closeness of the vocal folds, they do not vibrate during the closure itself, because they are tensed.

7 Except in special cases, all phonetic notation here uses broad transcription. This will also be used in explaining phonological processes.

8 The closure period between vowel sounds is clearly visible on the spectrogram as a white space where sound energy suddenly drops between the vowels, and on the waveform as the amplitude suddenly drops and nearly approaches zero.

9 In the example in Figure 4.2, the closure duration for the lax, tense and aspirated stops are 80 ms, 148 ms and 134 ms respectively.

10 In the examples in Figure 4.2, the VOTs for the tense and aspirated sounds are 8 ms and 45 ms respectively. In word-medial position, VOT tends to be shorter, and this phenomenon is universal to all languages. Since lax sounds are realised as voiced sounds during the closure period, it is pointless to measure their VOT.

11 In Figure 4.2, the lengths of the vowels preceding the lax, tense and aspirated stops are 132 ms, 80 ms, and 72 ms respectively.

12 Because Korean syllable structure does not allow consonant clusters in the onset or coda positions, a maximum of two consonants may appear in between vowels. Lax sounds may only appear between vowels or between a sonorant consonant and a vowel, and a lax sound after an obstruent changes into a tense sound as it undergoes Post-obstruent Tensification, an essential phonological process in Korean. See 8.2.1 for more information.

13 In Korean, because stop consonants in word-final position are realised as unreleased stops, the length of their closure cannot be measured by sound signal alone. Nor can the length of the closure and the period of silence that follows it be distinguished using sound signal alone. Therefore, the end point of the closure period, indicated by (b) on Figure 4.4, has been determined arbitrarily, as in the case of the start points of word-initial stops.

14 가ㄱ다 / kakak/ is a Sino-Korean noun meaning 'street corner (街角)'. Although not a commonly used word, it is useful here for demonstrating the differences between lax stops in different positions within a word.

15 As explained above, aspirated consonants have all the properties of glottal fricatives. Because /h/ is a glottal fricative, it could of course be said to be an aspirated sound. For a more detailed discussion of phonological properties please refer to 4.4.

16 In Korean, fricatives are only articulated at alveolar and glottal places, in contrast to English, which has fricatives articulated in various places. English has nine voiced and unvoiced fricatives, /f, v, θ, ð, s, z, ʃ, ʒ, h/, with five different places of articulation; labiodental, dental, alveolar, palato-alveolar and glottal. Therefore, English fricatives are always a struggle for native Korean speakers learning English. For more information on this, please see the section entitled "Why are fricative sounds so difficult for Korean speakers?" on p. 75.

17 In order to show the differences in energy distribution, a noise frequency band has been drawn at around 3,700 Hz. As can be seen on the diagram, it is characteristic of alveolar fricatives that friction noise begins to be observed in the high frequency band above 3,700 Hz and that the highest energy levels are observed above 6,500 Hz. The energy distribution of similar friction noise is linked to the particular features of their place of articulation.

18 The reason why glottal fricatives display similar energy distribution to that of the formant structure of the vowel which follows them is linked to the fact that glottal fricatives do not have a unique place of articulation within the vocal tract. As word-initial glottal fricatives already assume the form of the vowel that follows them at the start of articulation, strong energy can be seen in the formant frequency band of the following vowel. For this reason, glottal fricatives have many allophones depending on the following vowel, as will be described later.

19 The period of aspiration can be identified on the spectrogram as the irregular noise energy observed in the formant area of the following vowel.

20 Looking closely at the spectrogram, it can be seen that lax alveolar fricatives in intervocalic position are not articulated with stronger aspiration. The basis for

this is that, unlike in word-initial position, little difference can be seen between the onset and offset of the fricative, and an F1 (first formant) transition can be seen at the onset of the following vowel. In the presence of aspiration, one would not expect to observe an F1 transition, and this feature is known as an F1 cutback. This can easily be observed when compared to a vowel following a word-initial lax alveolar fricative, as seen in Figure 4.6.

21 In Figure 4.9 the friction durations for the lax and tense sounds were 106 ms and 177 ms respectively.

22 In Figure 4.9, the duration of the vowels preceding the lax and tense sounds were 94 ms and 60 ms respectively.

23 Previous studies on the realisation of Korean fricatives in various phonetic environments have observed that, like other obstruents, lax fricatives between voiced sounds are also realised as voiced sounds (K.-H. Lee 2001).

24 In fact, the results of the experiments in Kagaya (1974) need to be interpreted differently. Looking carefully at the results of this research, we see a tendency for glottal width, which differs greatly between lax and tense types of all obstruents in word-initial position, to be almost the same. A similar tendency can be seen in alveolar fricatives. If this is taken to mean that Korean fricatives should be subclassified into aspirated and tense variants, then large differences in glottal width between /s/ and /s*/ in word-medial position should be observed, as they are in other obstruents.

25 Since the starting point of the closure period of affricates in word-initial position cannot be determined using sound signal alone, the starting point of closure has been set arbitrarily as for the stop sounds above. Therefore the starting points of (a), (b) and (c) on the diagram bear no relation to the true starting points of closure.

26 In Figure 4.11 the lengths of the closure periods for lax, tense and aspirated sounds were 47 ms, 130 ms, and 106 ms respectively. The respective lengths of friction, including aspiration, were 45 ms, 47 ms, and 89 ms, while the respective lengths of the preceding vowels were 127 ms, 87 ms and 81 ms.

27 In word-initial position such weak nasality seems to be related to the strong voicelessness exhibited by word-initial stop sounds in Korean. All Korean stop sounds are voiceless, and as this voicelessness is most pronounced in word-initial position, Korean speakers are unlikely to find it difficult to distinguish nasals from other stop sounds, even when their nasality is not emphasised in word-initial position.

28 According to Yoshinaga (2002), based on the results of measurements of airflow volume through the nasal cavity at the time of articulation of three syllables in Korean and Japanese, namely /a/, /ama/ and /ana/, Korean nasals do not have much effect on the vowels that precede and follow them, whereas Japanese nasals do.

29 When the coda consonant is anything other than /n/, /l/ turns into /n/. When the coda consonant is /n/, depending on the morphological environment, either /l/ will turn to /n/ as with other consonants, or the preceding consonant will turn into /l/. For a more detailed discussion see chapter 8.2.3.

30 Generally speaking if a word boundary cannot be placed between the /n/ and the /l/ they are realised as /ll/, and if the word boundary can be placed there then they will be realised as /nn/. In the two examples in (8b), none of the morphemes {nan} and {lo} or {kwan} and {ljo} can exist as words in their own right. Therefore the

word boundary cannot be placed between them, and as such /n/–/l/ will be realised as /ll/. On the other hand, in the examples in (8c), the suffixes {-lon} and {-ljʌk} have been added to the words 'pikwɑn' and 'hɯpin', made up of {pi} and {kwɑn} and {hɯp} and {in} respectively, to create new words. Therefore, a word boundary can be placed between /n/ and /l/, and they will be realised as /nn/. The realisation of /n/–/l/ as /ll/ as in the examples in (8b) is related to the phonological process known as Lateralisation, and realisation as /nn/ is related to another phonological process, known as Nasalisation of laterals. For more details see Chapter 9.

31 The most noticeable phonetic difference between taps and nasals is whether or not the nasal passage remains open. However, because stops, like taps, are usually articulated with the nasal passage blocked, one has to understand the phonetic features that distinguish not only nasals and taps but also nasals and stops, and stops and taps, to explain why taps turn nasals into taps or why taps turn into nasals.

32 If laterals are set as the underlying forms of liquids, then Korean alveolar nasals can be distinguished from liquids depending on whether or not they are lateral. Therefore, it is possible to explain why alveolar nasals become liquids when they earn the lateral feature, and why liquids become alveolar nasals when they lose the lateral feature, and so it is also possible to explain the reasons behind this phonological phenomenon. For more details see Chapter 9.

33 Coronal consonants refer to consonants which have [+coronal] features. See the next section for the [coronal] feature.

34 In this book the definition of the feature [tense] is different from that given in SPE. In SPE, tense and lax vowels are distinguished using the feature [tense], and Korean tense sounds are distinguished using the feature [glottal constriction], which is classified as one of the sonorant cavity features. This feature can also be termed [constricted glottis], as in Halle and Stevens (1971).

35 The feature defined as [aspirated] in this book is not present in SPE. SPE uses the feature [heightened subglottal pressure], which is classed as one of the sound source features for aspirated sounds. This feature may also be termed [spread glottis], as is found in Halle and Stevens (1971).

5 Vowels

1 English data in Figure 5.7 are from Wells (1962). In Wells (1962), 25 native speakers of RP English were asked to read 11 words twice, each word containing a monophthong inserted between /h/ and /d/. The value of F1 and F2 in Figure 5.7 is the average for 50 measured values.

2 For the definition of the neutral position, see (11) in Chapter 4.

6 Frequency trends of Korean sounds

1 Words that are not included in *Standard Korean Language Dictionary* are not considered to be part of Standard Korean vocabulary.

7 Prosody

1 The change in pitch realised at a sentential level is called *intonation*.
2 A "phonological phrase" is exactly the same as an "accentual phrase" according to S.-A. Jun (1993, 2000). However, the term "accentual phrase" could lead to misunderstanding, as it suggests that Korean is a type of pitch accent language. This book therefore does not use the term "accentual phrase" but has replaced it with "phonological phrase".
3 Counting syllables is relatively easy in Korean because one complete character in Korean corresponds to one syllable. For instance, 각 'angle' has one syllable and 학교 'school' has two syllables.
4 T = tone. It is interesting that no other dialects except Seoul Korean have a rising tone at the end of the phonological phrase.
5 The data on spontaneous speech were drawn from the SLILC that we discussed in Chapter 6, and the data of speech read aloud was extracted from Korea Telecom's speech synthesis database.
6 The difference between -ʌ/ɑ and -ʌ/ɑ + jo is that the latter is an ending for listener-honorification, unlike the -ʌ/ɑ ending.

8 Phonological rules of Korean (I)

1 See Chapter 4 also for discussions on phonetic characteristics of word-final stops.
2 In fifteenth-century Korean, a maximum of three consonants could appear in syllable-initial position as in [pstɑj] 때 'time' and two consonants in syllable-final position as in [olmko] 옮고 'to move (connective)'.
3 In Korean, there are four sonorant sounds, /m, n, ŋ, l/, but /ŋ/ cannot occur in syllable-initial (= onset) position.
4 See 8.2.3 for the discussion on Liquid Nasalisation.
5 H.-S. Park (2007) found that there is no phonetic or articulatory difference between the V–C–V sequences of /pɑ.kʰɑ/ and /pɑ.k*ɑ/ and the corresponding V–C–C–V sequences /pak.kʰɑ/ and /pak.k*ɑ/. Both /pɑ.kʰɑ/ and /pak.kʰɑ/ as well as /pɑ.k*ɑ/ and /pak.k*ɑ/ are pronounced the same as [pɑ.kʰɑ] and [pɑ.k*ɑ] respectively.

9 Phonological rules of Korean (II)

1 This phonological rule is only applicable to Sino-Korean or English loanwords, as the sequence described above does not appear in any Pure Korean word.

10 Loanword phonology

1 As we shall discuss again shortly, consonant clusters starting with 'sp-', 'st-' or 'sk-' in English are pronounced in Korean with the /ɯ/ vowel inserted between.

Bibliography

Works in Korean

Bae, J.-C. (1996). *An Introduction to Korean Phonology (Gugeoeumunrongaeseol)*. Seoul: Singumunhwasa.

(2003). *The Sounds of Korean (Hangugeoui Bareum)*. Seoul: Sangyeongmunhwasa.

(2008). *Systematize the Theory of Korean Phonology (Gugeo Eumunnoui Chegyehwa)*. Seoul: Hangungmunhwasa.

Cha, J.-E., Jung, M.-S., and Shin, J.-Y. (2003). "A phonetic and phonological study on /h/-realization between sonorant sounds (Gongmyeongeum saiui /ㅎ/ui silhyeone daehan eumseong, eumunnonjeok gochal)", *Eoneo*, 28(4): 765–84.

Choi, H.-W. (2002). *A Survey on the Pronunciation of Standard Korean (Pyojuneo Baleum Siltae Josa)*. Seoul: Gungnipgueowon.

Choi, M.-O. (1989). "The history of study on umlaut of Korean (Gueo umlautui yeongusajeok gochal)", *Jusigyeonghakbo*, 3: 7–39.

(2004). *Korean Phonology (Gugeoemunnon)*. Seoul: Taehaksa.

Heo, U. (1965). *Korean Phonology* (new edn.) *(Gueoeumunhak* (gaekosinpan)*)*. Seoul: Jeongeumsa.

Jang, H.-J. and Shin, J.-Y. (2006). "An acoustic study on the generational difference of the monophthongs in the Daegu dialect (Daegu bangeon danmoeumui sedae gan chaie daehan eumhyang eumseonghakjeok yeongu)", *Malsori*, 57: 15–31.

Jang, H.-J. and Shin, J.-Y. (2007). "Gender difference of standard language orientation throughout the monophthongs by Daegu dialect speakers in their twenties (Daegu bangeon 20dae hwajaui danmoeum silhyeon yangsange natanan pyojuneo jihyangseongui seongbyeoljeok chai)", *Hangugeohak*, 36: 289–314.

Kang, B.-M. and Kim, H.-K. (2009). *Frequency of Korean Words (Hangukeo sayong bindo)*. Seoul: Hansinmunhwasa.

Kang, O.-M. (2003). *Korean Phonology (Hangukeo Eumunnon)*. Seoul: Taehaksa.

Kim, M.-R. (1992). *Korean Phonology (Gugeoeumunnon)*. Seoul: Hansinmunhwasa.

Kim, R.-J. (2005). "Morphological representation of one-syllable Sino-Korean base (Ilumjeol hanjaeo eogiui hyeongtaeronjeok jaehaeseok)" *Eomunronjip*, 52: 97–120.

Kim, Y.-S. (1981). *A Study on Korean Sounds* (2nd edn.) *(Urimal Soriui Yeongu* (gochinpan)*)*. Seoul: Gwahakssa.

Ko, Y.-K. and Koo, B.-K. (2008). *Grammar of Korean (Urimal Munbeopnon)*. Seoul: Jipmundang.

Lee, H.-Y. (1996). *Korean Phonetics (Gueoeumseonghak)*. Seoul: Taehaksa.

Lee, K.-H. (2001). "A Study on Korean Fricatives (Gugeo Machaleum Yeongu)". PhD dissertation: Korea University.

Lee, K.-M. (1998). *An Introduction to the History of Korean* (new edn.) (*Gueosagaeseol* (sinjeongpan)). Seoul: Taehaksa.

Lee, K.-M., Kim, C.-W., and Lee, S.-O. (2000). *Korean Phonology* (new edn.) (*Gueoeumunnon* (Jeungbopan)). Seoul: Hagyeonsa.

Lee, S.-N. (1960). "A study on the accent of contemporary Korean (Hyeondae Seoulmalui accentui gochal)", in *Anthology of Korean Linguistics (Isungnyeonggugeohakseonjip (eumunpyeon III))*. Seoul: Mineumsa, pp. 11–69.

Moon, S.-J. (1997). "An acoustical study of Korean 's' (Gueo 's' eumgae taehan eumhyanghakjeok yeongu)", *Malsori*, 33–4: 11–22.

Munhwagwankwangbu (2004) *Regulation of Korean* (23rd edn.) (*Gugeo Eomun Gujeongjip* (23pan))*. Seoul: Daehankyogwaseojusikoesa.

Nam, K.-W. and Oh, J.-H. (2009). "The analysis of the reasons and aspects of pronunciation of '러/랴' ('러', '랴' ui bareum silhyeon yangsanggwa wonin bunseok)". *Hangugeohak*, 42: 123–53.

Park, B.-C. (1989). *A History of the Korean Language (Gugeobaldalsa)*. Seoul: Seyeongsa.

Park, H.-S. (2007). "Temporal structure of Korean bisyllabic words, with special reference to the types of obstruents in intervocalic positions. (Hangugeo 2eumjeol daneoui sigan gujo -moeum gan jangaeeum nyuhyeonge ttareun chaireul jungsimeuro-)". *Eoneohak*, 49: 349–83.

Shi, C.-K. (1993). *Principles of Korean Word Formation (Gueoui Daneohyeongseong Weolli)*. Seoul: Hangungmunhwasa.

Shin, J.-Y. (1999a). "A diachronic study on the Korean diphthong /ㅢ/ (Ijungmoeum /ㅢ/ui tongsijeok yeongu)", *Minjongmunhwa*, 32: 473–97.

——— (1999b). "Prosodic units and tensification in Korean (Hangueoui unyul danwiwa gyeongeumhwa hyeonsang)", *Hangugeohak*, 10: 27–45.

——— (2000a). *Understanding Speech Sounds: For the Basis of Phonetics and Phonology (Malsoriui ihae)*. Seoul: Hangungmunhwasa.

——— (2000b). "Phonological implications of the realization of Korean plain obstruents: focusing on plain stops (Gueo Pyeongeumui eumseongjeok silhyeone daehan eumunnonjeok haeseok)", *Hangeul*, 250: 5–41.

——— (2008). "Phoneme and syllable frequencies of Korean based on the analysis of spontaneous speech data (Seongin jayu balhwa jaryo bunseogeul batangeuro han hangueoui eumso mit eumjeol gwallyeon bindo)", *Eoneocheonggakjangaeyeongu*, 13(2): 193–215.

——— (2009). "Frequency related information and syllable structure constraints on Sino-Korean (Hanguk hanjaeumui bimdo gwallyeon Jeongbo mit eumjeol gujo jeyak)", *Masoriwaeumseonggwahak*, 2: 129–40.

——— (2010). "Phoneme and syllable frequencies based on the analysis of the entries of a Korean dictionary (Hangueo sajeon pojeeo bareumui eumso mit eumjeol bindo)", *Eoneocheonggakjangaeyeongu*, 15(1): 94–106.

Shin, J.-Y. and Cha, J.-E. (2003). *The Sound Pattern of Korean (Urimal Soriui Chejye)*. Seoul: Hangungmunhwasa.

Shin, J.-Y., Kim, M.-J., and Kim, K.-H. (2000) "The phonetic realization of the accentual phrase and resyllabification in Korean (Hangueo gangseguui eumseonggeok silhyeon yangsanggwa jaeeumjeolhwa)", *Eoneo*, 25(3): 383–403.

Yoshinaga, Y. (2002). "A phonetic comparative study on nasals in Korean and Japanese: Through the acquisition of nasals in syllable-final positions by Japanese speakers of Korean (Hangueowa Ilbneoui Jaeum ap bieume gwanhan eumseonghakjeok bigyo yeongu)". MA thesis: Seoul National University.

Works in English

Abberton, E. (1972). "Some laryngographic data for Korean stops", *Journal of the International Phonetic Association*, 2(2): 67–78.

Abramson, A. S. and Lisker, L. (1972). "Voice timing in Korean Stops", *Proceedings of the Seventh International Congress of Phonetic Science*, 439–46.

Ashby, M. and Maidment, J. (2005). *Introducing Phonetic Science*. Cambridge University Press.

Borden, G. J., Harris, K. S., and Raphael, L. J. (1994). *Speech Science Primer* (3rd edn.). Baltimore: Williams & Wilkins.

Catford, J. C. (1977). *Fundamental Problems in Phonetics*. Bloomington: Indiana University Press.

(1988). *A Practical Introduction to Phonetics*. Oxford University Press.

Cho, M. H. and Shin, S. L. (1997). "A Comparison between [h] in English and Korean", *Korean Journal of Linguistics*, 24(4): 653–73.

Cho, Y.-M. Y. (1990). "Syntax and phrasing in Korean", in *The Phonology–Syntax Connection*, ed. S. Inkelas and D. Zec. University of Chicago Press, pp. 47–62.

Chomsky, N. and Halle, M. (1968). *The Sound Pattern of English*. New York: Harper and Row.

Clark, J. and Yallop, C. (1990). *An Introduction to Phonetics and Phonology*. Oxford: Blackwell.

Connell, B. and Arvaniti, A. (1995). *Phonology and Phonetic Evidence* (Papers in Laboratory Phonology IV). Cambridge University Press.

Crystal, D. (1995). *The Cambridge Encyclopedia of the English Language*. Cambridge University Press.

Cutler, A. and Ladd, D. R. (1983). *Prosody: Models and Measurements*. Berlin: Springer.

Dart, S. N. (1987). "An aerodynamic study of Korean stop consonants: measurements and modeling", *Journal of the Acoustical Society of America*, 81(1): 138–47.

Denes, P. B. and Pinson, E. N. (1993). *The Speech Chain: The Physics and Biology of Spoken Language* (2nd edn.). New York: W. H. Freeman and Company.

Fox, A. (2000). *Prosodic Features and Prosodic Structure: The Phonology of Suprasegmentals*. New York: Oxford University Press.

Fry, D. B. (1947). "The frequency of occurrence of speech sounds in Southern English", *Archives Néerlandaises de Phonétique Expérimentale*, 20.

Halle, M. and Stevens, K. (1971). "A note on laryngeal features", *Quarterly Progress Report MIT Research Laboratory of Electronics*, 101: 198–213.

Han, M. S. and Weitzman, R. S. (1970). "Acoustic features of Korean /P, T, K/, /p, t, k/ and /ph, th, kh/", *Phonetica*, 22: 112–28.

Hardcastle, W. J. (1973). "Some observations on the tense–lax distinction in initial stops in Korean", *Journal of Phonetics*, 1(3): 263–72.

Hirose, H., Lee, C. Y., and Ushijima, T. (1974). "Laryngeal control in Korean stop production", *Journal of Phonetics*, 2(2): 145–52.

Hong, K., Niimi, S., and Hirose, H. (1991). "Laryngeal adjustments for the Korean stops, affricates and fricatives: an electromyographic study", *Annual Bulletin Research Institute of Logopedics and Phoniatrics*, 25: 17–31.

International Phonetic Association (1999). *Handbook of the International Phonetic Association: A Guide to the Use of the International Phonetic Alphabet.* Cambridge University Press.

Iverson, G. K. (1983). "Korean *s*", *Journal of Phonetics*, 11: 191–200.

Jakobson, R., Fant, G., and Halle, M. (1952). *Preliminaries to Speech Analysis.* Cambridge, MA: MIT Press.

Jun, S.-A. (1993). "The Phonetics and Phonology of Korean Prosody". PhD dissertation: Ohio State University.

(1995). "Asymmetrical effects on the laryngeal gesture in Korean", in Connell and Arvaniti (eds.), pp. 235–53.

(1998). "The accentual phrases in the Korean prosodic hierarchy", *Phonology*, 15(2): 189–226.

(2000). "K-ToBI (Korean ToBI) labelling conventions: Version 3", *Speech Sciences*, 7: 143–69. [Version 3.1 is published in *UCLA Working Papers in Phonetics*, 99: 149–73. www.linguistics.ucla.edu/people/jun/sun-ah.htm]

Kagaya, R. (1974). "A fiberscopic and acoustic study of the Korean stops, affricates, and fricatives", *Journal of Phonetics*, 2: 161–80.

Kenstowicz, M. (1994). *Phonology in Generative Grammar.* Oxford: Blackwell.

Kim, C.-W. (1965). "On the autonomy of the tensity feature in stop classification", *Word*, 21: 339–59.

(1970). "A theory of aspiration", *Phonetica*, 21: 107–16.

Kim-Renaud, Y.-K. (1974). "Korean Consonantal Phonology". PhD dissertation: University of Hawaii.

Ladefoged, P. (2001). *Vowels and Consonants.* Oxford: Blackwell.

(2006). *A Course in Phonetics* (5th edn.). Boston, MA: Thomson Wadsworth.

Ladefoged, P. and Maddieson, I. (1996). *The Sounds of the World's Languages.* Oxford: Blackwell.

Lass, R. (1984). *Phonology: An Introduction to Basic Concepts.* Cambridge University Press.

Laver, J. (1994). *Principles of Phonetics.* Cambridge University Press.

Lisker, L. and Abramson, A. S. (1964). "A cross-language study of voicing in initial stops: acoustical measurements", *Word*, 20: 384–422.

Odden, D. (2005). *Introducing Phonology.* Cambridge University Press.

Pullman, G. K. and Ladusaw, W. A. (1986). *Phonetic Symbol Guide.* University of Chicago Press.

Roca, I. and Johnson, W. (1999). *A Course in Phonology.* Oxford: Blackwell.

Selkirk, E. (1984). *Phonology and Syntax: The Relation between Sound and Structure.* Cambridge, MA: MIT Press.

Silva, D. J. (1992). "The Phonetics and Phonology of Stop Lenition in Korean". PhD dissertation: Cornell University.

Spencer, A. (1996). *Phonology.* Oxford: Blackwell.

Vovin, A. (2008). *Korea-Japonica: A Re-evaluation of a Common Genetic Origin.* Honolulu: University of Hawaii Press.

Wells, J. C. (1962). *A Study of the Formants of the Pure Vowels of British English.* MA thesis: University of London.

Yoon, Y. B. and Derwing, B. L. (2001). "A language without a rhyme: syllable structure experiments in Korean", *The Canadian Journal of Linguistics*, 46(3–4): 187–237.

Index

Printed in the USA
CPSIA information can be obtained
at www.ICGtesting.com
JSHW051738210823
46934JS00006B/84